NĀGEŚA AND THE MAHĀBHĀṢYA

Sri Garib Dass Oriental Series No. 110

NĀGEŚA AND THE MAHĀBHĀṢYA

Dr. (Mrs) MEENAMBAL NARAYAN

SRI SATGURU PUBLICATIONS
A Division of
INDIAN BOOKS CENTRE
Delhi. India

Published by:
Sri Satguru Publications
A Division of
Indian Books Centre
40/5, Shakti Nagar
DELHI-110007
India

First Edition. DELHI. 1991

ISBN - 81-7030-243-9

PRINTED IN INDIA

DEDICATED

TO THE LOTUS — FEET OF MY ELDER SISTERS

Smt. K. S. Rajalakshmy
Smt. K. S. Parvathy
and
Smt. K. S. Thankamany

To whom I owe everything I have achived in My Life.

Contents

FOREWORD

In the vast realm of Sanskrit grammar, Nāgeśa Bhaṭṭa is a name to reckon with, not only for the profusion of his writings but also for the clarity of his thinking, lucidity of his expression and independence of his outlook. For nearly four decades, from 1688 to 1727, this versatile scholar of Maharashtra, settled in Varanasi, strode like a Collassus, the fields of Vyākaraṇa, Alaṅkāra, Dharmaśāstra, Purāṇa and Yoga. His works, said to number a hundred, are often expository in nature and carry the plume-word-*Śekhara* or *-Uddyota*, Of the different disciplines that Nāgeśa handled, Vyākaraṇa easily occupies the prime place and some of his works like the *Paribhāṣenduśekhara, Laghumañjūṣā* and *Śabdenduśekhara* are widely popular and justly famous. His works in this field achieved such prominence that a student of Pāṇinian grammar had to have made a study of his works to attain a mastery of the subject.

From among Nāgeśa's works, his commentary *Uddyota* on the *Mahābhāṣya-pradīpa* of Kaiyaṭa is highly significant. Nāgeśa has thrown fresh light on the implications of a number of passages both from the *Mahābhāṣya* and the *Pradīpa*. His critical observations, expositions, refutations and supplementations are extremely valuable. An analytical and elucidative exposition of Nāgeśa's views on various topics has been a desideratum. And, it is gratifying that Dr. Meenambal has attempted to shoulder this task and tackle it successfully with regard to the first nine *āhnika-s* of the *Mahābhāṣya*, being the portion of the work which forms the subject of wide study in Colleges and Universities.

Naturally enough, elsewhere too in his original works and other commentaries, Nāgeśa has elucidated several grammatical concepts like *Jāti, Sphoṭa* etc. It is in place that the present monograph takes under its purview these also and presents them under appropriate captions.

A serious student of Sanskrit grammar and the grammatical philosophy would find substantial material relating to the subject in this monograph, -collected, classified and studied in an exemplary manner. Viewed from this point of view, the author and the book deserve much credit. And, it behoves the author to take up the further *āhnika*-s of the work and treat them too in a similar manner, a task for which she is best fitted.

Adyar Library & Research Centre,
Adyar, Madras, Oct. 15, 1990 **K.V. Sarma**

Preface

The *Mahābhāṣyapradīpoddyota* is a monumental work written by Nāgesabhaṭṭa, a prolific writer and genius in grammar. The work aims at a careful study of the ideas in Patañjali's *Mahābhāṣya* as well as its commentary *Mahābhāṣyapradīpa* of Kaiyaṭa from the explanatory and critical point of view. The method of its approach to the text of *Mahābhāṣya* and *Pradīpa* and the clarity of its presentation have given it a wider popularity than the other commentaries on the same, the *Pradīpoddyotana* of Annambhaṭṭa probably claiming the second position. Being more closely connected with the work of Patañjali who is generally accepted as the supreme authority in grammar, the *Uddyota* occupies a prominent position among his grammatical works.

The study of Uddyota was undertaken by me at the instance of late Dr. S. Venkitasubramonia Iyer who had been the Professor and Head of the Department of Sanskrit in the University of Kerala. He had always been a source of inspiration to me and I express my deep sense of gratitude for the interest he had evinced in the progress of the work.

I am thankful to the authorities of the University of Kerala for granting me the permission to publish my doctoral thesis. The name of the original thesis was NAGESA'S COMMENTARY ON THE MAHABHASYAPRADIPA OF KAIYATA (NAVAHNIKA) -A STUDY. The present book form is given a concise yet suggestive title "NAGESA AND THE MAHABHASYA".

I am indebted to Dr. K.V. Sarma D.Litt. Professor of Sanskrit, Adyar Library and Research Centre, Madras for the valuable suggestions I received from him. I express my sincere thanks to him for embellishing this book with his Foreword.

My obligation to Sri Satguru Publications, a division of Indian Books Centre, Delhi cannot be expressed by mere words. They have neatly executed the printing of the book in a record time.

Thiruvananthapuram
17th October 1990. **Dr. (Mrs.) Meenambal Narayan**

Preface

The *Mahābhāṣyapradīpodyota* is a monumental work written by Nāgeśabhaṭṭa, a prolific writer and genius in grammar. The work aims at a careful study of the ideas in Patañjali's *Mahābhāṣya* as well as its commentary *Mahābhāṣyapradīpa* of Kaiyaṭa from the explanatory and critical point of view. The method of its approach to the text of *Mahābhāṣya* and *Pradīpa* and the clarity of its presentation have given it a wider popularity than the other commentaries on the same. The *Uddyota* [illegible] claiming the second position being more closely connected with the work of Patañjali who is generally accepted as the supreme authority in grammar, the *Uddyota* occupies a prominent position among his grammatical works.

The study of Uddyota was undertaken by me at the instance of late Dr. S. Venkitasubramonia Iyer who had been the Professor and Head of the Department of Sanskrit in the University of Kerala. He had always been a source of inspiration to me and I express my deep sense of gratitude for the interest he had evinced in the progress of the work.

I am thankful to the authorities of the University of Kerala for granting me the permission to publish my doctoral thesis. The name of the original thesis was NĀGEŚA'S COMMENTARY ON THE MAHĀBHĀṢYAPRADĪPA OF KAIYAṬA (NAVĀHNIKA)—A STUDY. The present book-form is given a concise yet suggestive title, "NĀGEŚA AND THE MAHĀBHĀṢYA".

I am indebted to Dr. K.V. Sarma D.Litt. Professor of Sanskrit, Adyar Library and Research Centre, Madras for the valuable suggestions I received from him. I express my sincere thanks to him for embellishing this book with his Foreword.

My obligation to Sri Satguru Publications, a division of Indian Books Centre, Delhi cannot be expressed by mere words. They have neatly executed the printing of the book in a record time.

Thiruvananthapuram
17th October 1990 Dr. (Mrs.) Meenambal Narayan

ABBREVIATIONS

Aṣṭ	-	Aṣṭādhyāyi of Pāṇini
Bhar	-	Bharthṛhari
Bṛ. Śab. Śekh	-	Bṛhacchabdenduśekhara of Nāgeśabhaṭṭa
conj	-	Conjugation
Gr.	-	Grammar
Kāt	-	Kātyāyana
Kṭ	-	Kaiyaṭa
Lagh. Manj	-	Vaiyākaraṇasiddhāntalaghumañjūṣā of Nāgeśabhaṭṭa
Lagh. Śab. Śekh	-	Laghuśabdenduśekhara of Nāgeśabhaṭṭa
Manj	-	Vaiyākaraṇasiddhāntamañjūṣā of Nāgeśbhaṭṭa
Mbh	-	Mahābhāṣya of Patañjali
NBh	-	Nāgeśabhaṭṭa
Pat	-	Patañjali
Par. Lagh. Manj.	-	Vaiyākaraṇasiddhāntaparmala-ghumañjūṣā of Nāgeśabhaṭṭa
Par.Śekh	-	Paribhāṣenduśekhara of Nāgeśabhaṭṭa
Prdp	-	Mahābhāṣyapradīpa of Kaiyaṭa
Udy	-	Mahābhāṣyapradīpodyota of Nāgeśabhaṭṭa
Vāk	-	Vākyapadīya of Bharṭhṛhari

NOTE - The page Nos. of *Mbh, Prdp, Udy,* and *Chāyā* referred to in the footnotes, correspond to those in the *Mahābhāṣya* with the commentaries *Pradīpa, Uddyota* and *Chāyā*, published by Motilal Banarsidas, Delhi, 1967.

Introduction

Vyākaraṇa, the most prominent of the six Vedāṅgas has been studied with great zeal in ancient India. In no other country has the Science of grammar been carried to such a perfection as in India. Different systems of Sanskrit grammar has arisen in India, of which the Pāṇinian is the most outstanding and the more important among the others are the Cāndra, the Sakaṭāyana, the Hemachandra, the Kātantra, the Sārasvata the Mugdhabodha, the Jaumāra and the Saupadma. Of these, the school of Pāṇini (c. 600 B.C.) has always enjoyed greater popularity because of its accuracy and thoroughness. Pāṇini has discussed his entire subject in a manner which is very simple in outline, could we once grasp it, but which has proved very complex in execution. His effort to economise expression without being misunderstood is obvious in the work.

The next great grammarian in the school of Pāṇini is Kātyāyana, the Vārttikakāra (c. 500 to 350 B.C.) His work is meant to correct, modify and supplement the rules of Pāṇini where they had become practically or totally inapplicable. Patañjali (c. 150 B.C.) is the author of *Mahābhāṣya*, a work on the sūtras of Pāṇini and the Vārttikas, the majority of which are of Kātyāyana. The chief aim of Patañjali in writing the *Mahābhāṣya* was to vindicate Pāṇini wherever possible against the criticisms of Kātyāyana and in this he has achieved remarkable success. The style of his work is unparelled in the whole of Sanskrit Literature. Pāṇini, Kātyāyana and Patañjali are traditionally known as the *'Munitraya'* who gave the law to the Science of grammar.

The *Mahābhāṣya* of Patañjali is divided into 8 adhyāyas of four pādas each corresponding to the *Aṣṭādhyāyī* and the commentary on each pāda is divided into āhnikas, the number of which varies from pāda to pāda. It has been commented upon by Kaiyaṭa (1100 A.D.) and the work is known as the *Mahābhāṣyapradīpa*. Nāgeśabhaṭṭa of the 18th century, an illustrious grammarian and a prolifie writer, commented on the Mahābhāṣyapradīpa of Kaiyaṭa in *Uddyota* incidentally commenting on the *bhāṣya* also. *Mahābhāṣyapradīpoddyota* is thus a voluminous commentary on the whole text of *Mahābhāṣya* and *Mahābhāṣyapradīpa*. Although the whole of the *Uddyota* merits intensive study, it will take a whole lifetime. So here the text on the first nine āhnikas is taken up for close study and critical examination.

The study is divided into three parts. Part I 'General' aims at introducing the author and his work. Chapter I deals with the author's life, teachers, disciples, date and works and it points out his vast erudition. Chapter 2 is devoted to an account of the aim, scope and characteristics of *Mahābhāṣyapradīpoddyota* and of the *Mahābhīsya* and *Pradīpa*, on which it is a commentary.

Part II 'Analytical Examination' examines the *Uddyota* from four points of view, namely, elucidation of *Mahābhāṣya*, elucidation of *Pradīpa*, citations of the views of others and criticism of Kaiyata. In Chapter 3 which is on the elucidation of the text of *Mahābhāṣya* it is pointed out that Nāgeṣabhaṭṭa has given great attention to various passages in *Mahābhāṣya* to bring out their full significance and to clear the objections raised by others. The fourth Chapter, which is in elucidation of *Pradīpa*, expounds several expressions and observations in it on the basis of the statements in the *Uddyota*. It also examines the statements of Nāgeśabhaṭṭa supplementing the *Pradīpa*. The next chapter enumerates the views of other grammarians, cited by Nāgeśabhaṭṭa in the course of the work. His refutation of certain views among them are also pointed out. Chapter 6 and 7 are on the criticism of *Pradīpa* and *Mahābhāṣya* by Nāgeśabhaṭṭa. The difference of opinion entertained by Nāgeśabhaṭṭa in regard to the interpretation of the passages in the *Mahābhāṣya* are taken into consideration. The point of disagreement with Kaiyaṭa in respect of the interpretation of sūtras, explanation of certain expressions and the like are indicated in detail. The succeeding chapter is on Nāgeśabhaṭṭa's refutation of some of the views of Kaiyaṭa, in regard to the interpretation of sūtras, vārttikas, and bhāṣya passages and on the self- contradictory statements occasionally met with in Kaiyaṭa. An instance where Nāgaśabhaṭṭa has criticized Patañjali too is pointed out.

Part III 'Observations' includes Chapters 8 and 9. Chapter 8 is devoted to the exposition of the views of Nāgeśabhaṭṭa on certain important topics referred to in the course of the work, like *Sphoṭa, Śakti, Jātipakṣa* etc., the views being classified as conceptual, phonological and interpretational. Chapter 9 sums up in a critical background the assertions of Nāgeśabhaṭṭa in *Uddyota* and concludes with an evaluation of the work.

All through the thesis, an attempt has been made to show the various aspects of Nāgeśabhaṭṭa's commentary, and to establish that he is objective in his criticism, independent in his outlook, clear in elucidation and unsparing of opponents in establishing a *siddhānta* and also that his masterly mind has penetrated into the whole of *Mahābhāṣya* and *Pradīpa.*

Part One
General

Chapter 1

The Author and his Works

Next to the *Munitraya* and Bhartṛhari, Nāgeśabhaṭṭa is the most prominent luminary in the galary of Sanskrit grammarians. Though chronologically he comes last in the list of illustrious grammarians relating to different systems of Sanskrit Grammar, he is one of the most eminent scholars of whom Indian scholastic learning can be proud of.[1] His literary activity is of an encyclopaedic character and Vyākaraṇa is his special forte. He flourished towards the end of the seventeenth century A.D. and the first half of the eighteenth century A.D.

The study of Sanskrit grammar, especially Pāṇiniyan Grammar, has been prosecuted on two lines, viz. morphological and philosophical. The works of Nāgeśabhaṭṭa bear testimony to his supremacy in both these fields. The important predecessors of Nāgeśabhaṭṭa in the Pāṇiniyam system of grammar are Vāmana and Jayāditya of the 7th century A.D., the authors of *Kāśikāvṛtti*, Jinendrabuddhi of the 8th century A.D. the author of the commentary *Nyāsa* on *Kāśikā*, Kaiyaṭa of the 11th century A.D., the author of *Mahābhāṣyapradīpa, Puruṣottama* and *Śaraṇadeva* of the 12th century A.D., the authors of *Bhāṣāvṛtti* and *Durghaṭavṛtti* respectively, Haradatta of the 13th century A.D. the author of the commentary on *Kāśikā, Padamañjarī*, Nārāyaṇabhaṭṭa and Bhaṭṭojidīkṣita of the 17th century A.D. the authors of *Prakriyāsarvasva* and *Vaiyākaraṇasiddhāntakaumudī* respectively. But unlike his predecessors,, he has won greater recognition.

Life

The details of the life history of Nāgeśabhaṭṭa are not much in oblivion. Having flourished at a time which is chronologically very near to us, unlike that of Pāṇini, Kātyāyana and Patañjali, we are able to know more about him through traditional reports, although no historical records on the matter is available.

From his works and the numerous traditional accounts, something about his life can be drawn.

Nāgeśabhaṭṭa is also known as Nāgojibhaṭṭa, and is also referred to as Nāgoji and Nagojī.[2] He refers to himself as Nāgeśa in the introductory verse of his work *Paribhāṣenduśekhara;*

"natvā, sāmbam śivam brahma
nāgeśaḥ kurute sudhīḥ |"

The word Nāgeśa is given an interesting derivation by a commentator of this verse.[3] It is *"nāgaḥ Patañjaliḥ īśaḥ pravartako yasya".* Here *Nāga* denotes Patañjali who is spoken of as the guiding spirit of Nāgeśabhaṭṭa.[4] However this interpretation appears to be far-fetched. Nāgeśabhaṭṭa had the surnames 'Kāla' and 'Upādhyāya' as is clear from the colophones at the end of his works *Uddyota* and *Bṛhacchabdenduśekhara.*[5] The latter was originally a distinction conferred on him by the learned men of Kāsi and later on, it became a surname.

Nāgeśabhaṭṭa, was a Ṛg Vedi Deśastha Brahmin of Mahārāṣtra. He hailed from Tasagon in the Satara District.[6] He was the son of Śivabhaṭṭa and Satī and in almost all his works he has mentioned this fact. In the beginning of *Laghuśabdenduśekhara,* he says,

"śivabhaṭṭasuto dhīmān
satīdevyāstu garbhajaḥ"

He was patronised by Rāmasimha of the Bisena family, a local prince of Sṛṅgiverapura (now Singarour) a few miles north of Allahabad.[7] He glorifies him in his *Uddyota* and in many of his other works, in the following terms;

"yācakānām kalpatarorarikakṣahutāśanād
sṛngiverapurādhīśād rāmato labdhajīvikaḥ |"

Nāgeśabhaṭṭa's spiritual descent from illustrious teachers is noteworthy. He was a pupil of Haridīkṣita,[8] who was the son of Vīreṣvara, pupil of Ramāśrama[9] and the grandson of the great grammarian Bhaṭṭojidīkṣita. Haridīkṣita was his preceptor in the science of grammar. He studied Nyāya Śāstra from Rāmarāma. He refers to these two preceptors at the end of his work *Sphoṭavāda.*

adhītya phaṇibhāṣyābdhim sudhīndraharidīkṣitād
nyāyatantram rāmarāmād vādirakṣoghnarāmataḥ |

. . . .

dṛḍhastarkesya nābhyāsa iti cintyam na dhīyutaiḥ
dṛṣadopīha samtīrṇāḥ payodhau rāmayogataḥ /

In the introductory verse to *Udy,* Nāgeśabhaṭṭa refers to Haridīkṣita in glorifying terms:-

"haridīkṣitapādābjasevanāvāptasanmatiḥ"

Tradition says that he composed the grammatical work Śabdaratna, a commentary on *Prauḍhamanoramā* of Bhaṭṭojidīkṣita and ascribed it to his teacher Haridīkṣita in gratitude. But in *Laghuśabdaratna* Haridīkṣita refers to the Śabdaratna as his own work and to the *Śabdenduśekhara* as that of his pupil.[10]

Sitārāma Śāstri refers to the view of some scholars that Nāgeśabhaṭṭa had Jagannātha Paṇḍita, as his preceptor in poetics.[11] This view is based on the fact that Nāgeśabhaṭṭa composed the commentary, by name *Gurumarmaprakāśikā* on the famous work *Rasagaṅgādhara* of Jagannātha Pandita. The word *'guru'* in the name of the gloss is taken as referring to the teacher. Sītārāma Śāstri does not favour this view. He points out that the view of Jagannātha Paṇḍita expressed in his works like *Manoramākucamardinī* and *Rasagaṅgādhara* have been refuted by Nāgeśabhaṭṭa in his works *Śabdenduśekhara* and the commentary *Gurumarmaprakāśa* on *Rasagaṅgādhara*. Therefore Sītārāma Śāstri says that there is no probability of such truth in the assumption that Jagannātha Paṇḍita was the preceptor of Nāgeśabhaṭṭa. Certain scholars are of opinion that the word *'guru'* in the name of the commentary is to be understood as denoting the comprehensiveness of the commentary, just as the work *'guru'* seen in the name of his another work *'Gurumañjūṣā'* implies that he might have composed another commentary by name *Laghumarmaprakāśikā* on the same work.

Vaidyanātha Pāyaguṇḍe was the most renowned among the disciples of Nāgeśabhaṭṭa. Bālāśrama, the son of Vaidhyanātha Pāyaguṇḍe, also was the disciple of Nāgeśabhaṭṭa. Pāyaguṇḍe had an intelligent student Mannudeva also named Manyudeva who composed a commentary by name *Mannudevī* on the *Par. Śekh* and an original work by name *Laghuśabdenduśekharadūṣaṇoddhāra*. Aufrecht says that Nāgeśabhaṭṭa was the preceptor of Gaṅgārāma the great-grandfather of Maṇirāma (1804 A.D.) who wrote the works *Kādambaryarthasāra* and Bhāmatīvilāsaṭīkā.[12] Pandit Sadashiva Sharma Śāstri names three as the disciples of Nāgeśabhaṭṭa.[13] They are Vaidyanātha Pāyaguṇḍe, Nārāyaṇadeva and Gurubhārīmiśra.

A known historical fact about the life-history of Nāgeśabhaṭṭa is that he observed *kṣetrasanyāsa*. There is a tradition, current at Jaipur and mentioned by Pandit Durgaprasād Śāstri, the learned editor of the Kāvyamāla series, in his introduction to *Rasagaṅgādhara*, which refers to an invitation for a horse sacrifice received in 1714 A.D. by Nāgeśabhaṭṭa from Savai Jeysimha, ruler of Jaipur (1688 to 1728 A.D.) an invitation which Nāgeśabhaṭṭa courteously declined on the ground that he had taken *kṣetrasanyāsa* and could not therefore leave Benares to attend the ceremony.

Date

Unlike in the case of the most celebrities in Sanskrit literature, sufficient data are available to fix the date of Nāgeśabhaṭṭa fairly accurately. Nāgeśabhaṭṭa's spiritual descent from illustrious predecessors helps us roughly to determine his time. Nāgeśabhaṭṭa was a pupil of Bhaṭṭojidīkṣita's grandson. Bhaṭṭojīdikṣita was a pupil of the Mīmāmsaka Śaṅkarabhaṭṭa and of Śeṣakṛṣṇa and almost a contemporary of Jagannātha Paṇḍita. He flourished in the first half of the seventeenth century and his date is accepted to be about 1630 A.D. as Jagannātha Paṇḍita himself was the pupil of the son of this Śeṣakṛṣṇa. This is also confirmed by the fact that a pupil of Bhaṭṭojidīkṣita, by name Nīlakaṇṭha Śukla wrote a work in Saṁvat 1693.[14] Nāgeśbhaṭṭa being the disciple of Bhaṭṭojidīkṣita's grandson, must have therefore flourished towards the end of the seventeenth century and the first half of the eighteenth century.[15]

P.K. Gode points out that in his work *Āśaucanirnaya*, Nāgeśabhaṭṭa mentions Nirṇayasindhu (A.D. 1612).[16] In his *Sāpiṇḍyapradīpa* Nāgeśabhaṭṭa mentions Saṅkarabhaṭṭa (between A.D. 1560 and 1600) Anantadeva (between A.D. 1645 and 1675) and Nandapaṇḍita (between A.D. 1595 and 1630). Therefore, Gode opines that Nāgeśabhaṭṭa must be later than A.D. 1670. He adds that the Ujjain Manuscript of Nāgeśabhaṭṭa's *Vaiyākaraṇasiddhāntamañjūṣā* is dated A.D. 1708. In his *Vaiyākaraṇasiddhāntamañjūṣā* Nāgeśabhaṭṭa mentions *Udy* which in its turn mentions *Manj*. This cross reference proves that both these works were being composed simultaneously sometime before A.D. 1708 which is the date of the Ujjain Manuscript of *Manj.* These voluminuous works are the products of Nāgeśabhaṭṭa's mature intellect and scholarship. Gode points out that presuming that Nāgeśabhaṭṭa was about 30 years at the time of their composition sometime before A.D. 1708, the date of a copy of one of these works, it may be easily inferred that Nāgeśabhaṭṭa was born, say, between A.D. 1670 and 1680. This reference is in harmony with his reference to Anantadeva (A.D. 1645 to 1675).

Yudhiṣhṭira Mīmāmsaka points out that Nāgeśabhaṭṭa has written a commentary on the *Rasamañjarī* of *Bhānudatta.*[17] A manuscript of this commentary is available at the Indian Office Library at London and the time of its writing is Saṁvat 1769 i.e, A.D. 1713. Balaśramā, son of Vaidyanātha Pāyaguṇḍe and disciple of Nāgeśabhaṭṭa, has, with the help of Mannudeva composed a work by name *Dharmaśāstrasaṅgraha* at the request of Henry Theodor Colebroke. Colebroke lived in India during the period 1783-1815. Therefore Yudhiṣthira Mīmāmsaka concludes that Nāgeśabhaṭṭa must have flourished during the period from 1673 to 1753 A.D. This view is confirmed by the tradition current at Jaipur, about the invitation for horse sacrifice received in 1714 A.D. by Nāgeśabhaṭṭa, referred to earlier.[18]

Sītārāma Śāstri points out that in 1657 A.D. (i.e. Vikrama era 1714) the assembly of learned men well-versed in all śāstras arrived at a decision, in Benares, settling on an age-long controversy that among the Maharashtra Brahmins, those titled "Devarukhe' were eligible for matrimonial alliance with the other Brahmins.[19] Among the 72 learned men who signed the judgement letter in the capacity as judges of the controversial problem, there is one Rāmārāma who is the preceptor of Nāgeśabhaṭṭa. Sītārāma Śāstri says that this judgement letter has been published by Sadāśivapimpuṭakara in a work by name *Citalebhaṭṭaprakaranam.* On the basis of this judgement letter and taking into consideration the fact that Nāgeśabhaṭṭa refers to Rāmarāma as his preceptor in Nyāya, one can assume the existence of Nāgeśabhaṭṭa in Vikrama Era 1731 which corresponds to 1674 A.D. and this too confirms the date pointed out previously.[20]

Mahamahopādhyāya Haraprasād Śāstri says that Nāgeśabhaṭṭa died in 1775.[21] P.V. Kane argues that this appears rather improbable.[22] If one of his works was copied in 1713 A.D. he could hardly have lived upto 1775 A.D. unless he was about 100 years old at that time. Sītārāma Śāstri says that the author of *Jñānakośa* had remarked that Nāgeśabhaṭṭa died in the age of 62, though he does not cite any proof thereof. This is quite contradictory to the previous assumption that Nāgeśabhaṭṭa was long- lived. Though, we have thus no historical record as to when exactly Nāgeśabhaṭṭa passed away, yet on the basis of the vast number of the works produced by his master-mind, it seems quite reasonable to assume that Nāgeśabhaṭṭa was long-lived.

Works

Nāgeśabhaṭṭa, the epoch-making Vaiyākaraṇa of the eighteenth century is credited with the authorship of a number of works which bear testimony to his vast erudition and deep knowledge. Apart from Vyākaraṇa he wrote standard works on Yoga, Poetics, Dharmaśāstra, Mīmāmsa, Purāṇas and other Śāstras. Even though a correct knowledge of all the works of Nāgeśabhaṭṭa is not even now obtained, we yet find that those which are undoubtedly taken to be his, are themselves numerous.

46 works are assigned to Nāgeśabhaṭṭa by Aufrecht in *Catalogus Catalagorum* Vol. I.

1. Alamkārasudhā (Kuvalayānandaṭīkā)
2. Aṣṭādhyāyīpāṭha (Grammar)
3. Ācārenduśekhara
4. Āśaucanirṇaya
5. Iṣṭikālanirṇaya
6. Kātyāyanītantra
7. Kāvyapradīpoddyota
8. Gurumarmaprakāśikā (Rasagaṅgādharaṭīkā)
9. Candrikā (Devīmahātmyaṭīkā)
10. Caṇḍīstotraprayogavidhi
11. Tarkabhāṣāṭīkā Yuktimuktāvalī
12. Tātparyadīpikā

13. Tiṅantasaṅgraha (Gr.)
14. Tīrthenduśekhara
15. Tristhalīsetu
16. Dhātupāṭhavṛtti (Gr.)
17. *Neraṇivādārtha (Gr.)
18. Prabhākaracandratatvadīpikāṭīkā
19. Prayogasāra
20. Prāyaścittenduśekhara
21. Mahābhāṣyapradīpoddyota (Gr.)
22. Rasataraṅgiṇīṭīkā
23. Rasamañjarīprakāśa
24. Rāmāyaṇaṭīkā
25. Lakṣaṇaratnamālikā
26. Viṣamapadī (Śabdakaustubhavyākhyā) (Gr.)
27. Vedasūktabhāṣya
28. Vaiyākaraṇakārikā (Gr.)
29. Vaiyākaraṇabhūṣaṇa (Gr.)
30. Vaiyākaraṇasiddhāntamañjūṣā (Gr.)
31. Nyāsasūtrenduśekhara
32. Śabdaratna (Gr.)
33. Sabdānantasāgarasamuccaya (Gr.)
34. Ṣuptiṅantasāgarasamuccaya (Gr.)
35. Śabdenduśekhara (Gr.)
36. Samskāraratnamālā
37. Laghusāṅkhyas}utravṛtti
38. Sāpiṇḍimañjarī
39. Sāpiṇḍyadīpikā
40. Sphoṭavāda (Gr.)
41. Nāgojibhaṭṭīya (Gr.)
42. Prāyaścittenduśekharasārasaṅgraha
43. Padārthadīpikā
44. Paribhāṣenduśekhara (Gr.)
45. Pātañjalasūtravṛtti and
46. Pātañjalasūtravṛttibhāṣyacchāyāvyākhyā

In *Catalogus Catalagorum* Vol. II he adds two other works of Nāgeśabhaṭṭa Viz. I. *Udāharaṇapradīpa (Kāvyaprakāśaṭīkā)* and 2. *Hemavatī (Paribhāṣenduśekharaṭīkā)*.

S.K. Belvalkar remarks that Nīgeśabhaṭṭa, ascribed his work *Rāmāyaṇaṭīkā*, a commentary on *Adhyātmarāmāyaṇa* to his patron.[23] We have already referred to the tradition that Nāgeśabhaṭṭa ascribed the grammatical work Śabdaratna to his teacher Haridīkṣita.[24] Sītārāma Śāstri refers to 56 works of Nāgeśabhaṭṭa. He mentions about the two versions of *Śabdenduśekhara* viz. 1. *Bṛhacchabdenduśekhara* and 2. *Laghuśabdenduśekhara*, the three versions of *Vaiyākaraṇasiddhāntamañjūṣā* viz. 1. *Vaiyākaraṇasiddhāntagurumañjūṣā* 2. *Vaiyākaraṇasiddhāntalaghumañjūṣā* and 3. *Vaiyākaraṇasiddhāntaparamalaghumañjūṣā*, the two versions of *Kavyapradīpoddyota* viz. 1. *Gurukāvyapradīpoddyota* and *Laghukāvyapradīpoddyota*. The other works mentioned by him in addition to those referred to by Aufrecht are:-

1. Vṛttivāda
2. Dhātuvṛtti
3. Tithīnduśekhara
4. Caṇḍīpāṭhaṭīkā
5. Pratyākhyānasaṅgraha
6. Paramārthasāravivaraṇa
7. Vṛttisaṅgraha
8. Sudhālaharīṭīkā and
9. Kālenduśekhara

Sītārāma Śāstri however does not mention the works *Vaiyākaraṇabhūṣaṇa* and *Sāpiṇḍyadīpikā* noted by Aufrecht. P.V. Kane remarks that it is not unlikely that Nāgeśabhaṭṭa first composed his commentaries on the comparatively easy śāstra of poetics and that he then worked upon Dharmaśāstra and Vyākaraṇa. P.K. Gode examins the relative chronolgoy of the works of Nāgeśabhaṭṭa and substantiates the views of Kane that Nāgeśabhaṭṭa's literary activity was between 1700 A.D. and 1750 A.D. The most celebrated grammatical works of Nāgeśabhaṭṭa are *Śabdenduśekhara*, *Vaiyākaraṇasiddhānta-mañjūṣā*, *Sphoṭavāda* and *Paribhāṣenduśekhara* which had won for him high renown from all quarters.

REFERENCES

1. Vide J.F. Staal, *A Reader on Sanskrit Grammarians*, p.xxiv.
2. Vide Aufrecht, *Catalogus Catalagorum*, Vol.I.
3. The commentator is one Nārāyaṇaśāstri who has written a commentary by name *Nāgeśāśayanirṇaya* on the *Paribhāṣendusekhara.*
4. This is in keeping with Nāgeśabhaṭṭa's renown as a grammarian since Patañjali is considered Ādiśeṣa in human form.
5. Vide the colophons - "iti kālopanāmakaśivabhaṭṭasutasatīgarbhajanāgeśabhaṭṭakṛte bhāṣyapradīpoddyote prathamādhyāyasya prathame pāde divitīyamāhnikam" at the end of the second āhnika of *Udy* and "iti srīmadupādhyāyopanāmakaśivabhaṭṭasutsatīgarbhajanāgeśabhaṭṭakṛte sabdendusekharākhye siddhāntạkaumudīvyākhyāne uttarādham" at the end of *Bṛ Sab. Sekh.*
6. Vide the introduction to *Paribhāṣenduśekhara* edited by K.V. Abhyankar, Vol. I. p.34.
7. Sītārāmaśāstri in his introduction to Bṛhacchabdenduśekhara edited by himself says that Nāgeśabhaṭṭa obtained from the king, about hundred rupees per year, an amount which was quite necessary for his livelihood.
8. Vide P.V. Kane, *History of Dharmaśāstra*, Vol. I, Poona, 1930, pp.453-456.
9. According to S.K. Belvalkar, Rāmāśrama is another name of Bhaṭṭojidikṣita's son Vīresvara who also had the name Bhānujidikṣita. Yudhiṣthira Mīmāmsaka in his work *Samskṛt Vyākaraṇ Sāstr Kā Itihās*, says that Rāmāśrāma was the son of Bhaṭṭojidīkṣita and Haridīkṣita was the son of Rāmāśrāma. Aufrecht also refers to Rāmaśrāma as the son of Bhaṭṭojidīkṣita (*Catalogus Catalagorum*, Vol.I) But P.V. Kane says that Bhaṭṭojidīkṣita had two sons Vīreśvara and Bhānujidīkṣita and the latter was named Rāmāśrāma.
10. Vide the statement "vistarastu asmatkṛte śabdaratne madantevāsikṛtaśabdenduṣekhạrādvā draṣṭavyaḥ" at the end of the *Pūrvārdha* of *Lagh. Sab. Sekh* and also the second introductory verse to the *Bṛhacchabdenduśekhara*
    "gūḍhoktigrathitām pitāmahakṛtām vidvatpramodāspadām bhaktyādhītya manoramām nirupamādramāśramād sadguroḥ /
    tatvajñānavaśat pareṇa kalitān doṣān samunmīlayan vyācaṣṭe harireva tām phaṇimatānyalocya vaireśvariḥ //'

11. See introduction to *Bṛhacchabdenduśekhara* edited by Sītārāma Śāstri, Vol.I, Varnasi, 1960. p.52.
12. Vide *Catalogus Catalagorum* Vol.1.
13. Vide the introduction to *Prauḍhamanoramā* edited by Pandit Sadashiva Sharma Śāstri, the Chowkhamba Sanskrit Series Office, Benares, 1934, p.8.
14. Vide S.K. Belvalkar, *Systems of Sanskrit Grammar*, p.47.
15. Vide P.V. Kane, *History of Dharmaśāstra* Vol.I. pp.453-456.
16. Vide studies in *Indian Literary History*, Vol.III, pp.213-220.
17. Vide Yudhiṣṭhira Mīmāmsaka, *Saṃskṛt Vyakāraṇaśāstr Kā Itihās*, Vol.I. p.393.
18. Vide Supra p.6
19. Op.cit., Vol.I. p.57.
20. Vide Supra p.6
21. Vide *Indian Antiquary* Vol.41, p.12 - "The great supporter of Bhaṭṭoji Dīxit, however was Nāgoji Bhaṭṭ a pupil of Haridixit who commented upon all his works and the works of his school.

    He had a long life and lived more than hundred years and died in 1775 on the day when Hasting's life was in jeopardy on account of the Benares revolt".
22. Vide P.V. Kane, op.cit. p.456.
23. Vide *Systems of Sanskrit Grammar*, p.47.
24. Vide Supra p.3.

Chapter II

The Mahābhāṣya, Pradīpa, and Uddyota

Nāgeśabhaṭṭa's work, the *Mahābhāsyapradīpoddyota* is a supercommentary on Kaiyaṭa's gloss on the *Mahābhāsya* of Patañjali. To understand the true nature of *Uddyota*, a knowledge of the Mahābhāsya and the *Pradīpa* on it is also, therefore necessary.

The Mahābhāsya

Mahābhāsya or 'The Great Commentary' is the work of Patañjali who with Pāṇini and Kātyāyana constitutes the Trinity of Sanskrit Grammar. Pat's work deals with the *Aṣṭādhyāi* of Pāṇ and *Vārttikas* of *Kāt*. Since unlike the other *bhāsya* works *Pat's bhāsya* deals with vārttikas also in addition to speculating over the sūtras, there is a saying prevalent among Pandits:- *"Mahatvam asya bhāsyasya vārttikopari cintanād"*.

Nature and Contents

Among the commentaries on Asṭ none excels Pat's effort in the sureness of the critical touch and in the unimpeachability of the authority[1]. Written in a language which is rendered almost unique by the combination of simplicity and vigour and consisting mainly of dialogues which impart to it an obsorbing interest saving it from the dryness that usually characterises a sastraic commentary, the *Mahābhāsya* stands out from the rest of its kind, deserving richly the esteem in which it has always been held as the great commentary. An important feature of the work is that it explains many rigid and recondite sastraic rules in terms of maxims derived from everyday life, which makes it higher and wider than a sastraic commentary and enables it to throw a flood of light on the religious social and other aspects of contemporary life. All these excellences entitle it to the first place in the Hindu Grammatical literature, as bringing out best their analytical acumen. Nbh adduces another reason to account for the greatness of *Mbh.* He points out that the distinctive feature of *Mbh* is that in this work, the author has given his own 'Istis' which add to the importance of the work.[2] Rightly goes the saying *"Mahābhāsyam vā paṭhanīyam mahārājyam vā Pālanīyam"*. Pat's genius overshadowed that of Kāt and attracted a greater measure of reverence from all the later commentators.

The contents of the *Mbh* are the discussions on the sūtras of Pāṇ and vārttikas of Kāt. Goldstucker, Keihorn and others consider that the *Mbh* is a commentary on Kat's vārttikas[3]. But the author of *Subdakalpadruma* maintains that it is a commentary on the sūtras of Pāṇ and vārttikas of Kāt.[4]. Of about 4000 sūtras found in the *Asṭ* about 1700 came to the purview of the *Mbh.* Of them 1200 have under them the vārttikas of one vārttikakāra, about 25 have under them the vārttikas of two or more vārttikakaras and about 425 have no varttikas but only bhāsya, i.e. about one fourth of the book form the interpretation of Pat on the sūtras. Among 1200 sūtras which have vārttikas, the varttikas under about 700 are simply explanatory. Pat begins with a lucid commentary on the vārttikas more than half of which is in the form of *Pūrvapaksavārttikas* and *siddhāntavārttikas.* Whenever he differs from the opinion of the vārttikakāra or vārttikakāras, he appends his view at the end. Pat almost always agrees with vārttikakaras wherever they deal with the change of words morphologically and semantically. He sometimes refutes the amendment of Kāt, through the instrument of *yoga vibhāga* introduced by Kāt himself. The use of a good many paribhāsās and nyāyas, some of which are his own, enables Pat not only to reject a large number of Kat's vārttikas but also to widen the scope of the *Asṭ* further. He gives his own iṣtis and makes very good use of the devices discovered by kāt. The spirit of independent thought combined with keen critical acumen and consummate scholarship pervades the whole of the Mbh.

The Mahābhāṣyapradīpa

The *Mahābhāsyapradīpa,* written by Kaiyaṭa of the 11th century A.D. is a voluminous commentary on the *Mbh* of Pat. As the name itself suggests, it correctly illuminates the ideas of the *Mbh* and among the commentaries on the *Mbh*, it occupies an unequalled place.

A Brief Survey

In the introductory verse of his work, Kaiyaṭa expresses his opinion about his own work. He says:-

"mahābhāṣyārṇavāvārapāriṇam vivṛtiplavam/
yathāgamam vidhāsyeham kaiyaṭo jaiyaṭātmajah//
bhāsyābdhiḥ kvātigambhīraḥ kvāham mandmatistataḥ/
chātrāṇām upahāstatvam yāsyāmi piśunātmanām//
tathāpi haribaddhena sāreṇa granthasetunā/
kramamāṇah śanaiḥ pāram tasya prāptāsmi paṅguvat//

Kaiyaṭa points out that his aim is to produce, according to the sāstras, an explanatory work which will act as a boat to cross over the ocean of the *Mbh*. Quite humbly, he remarks that he is possessed of an intellect which is slow in grasping, whereas the *Mbh* is an unfathomable ocean of knowledge. He may even be ridiculed in his attempt by narrow minded students. Even then, he has ventured to cross over that ocean moving slowly like a lame, crippled man to the other shore of that ocean by virtue of the sound bridge provided by Bhar, in the form of his best work. *Nbh* remarks that the expression *'śanaiḥ kramamāṇaḥ'* indicates that Kṭ's commentary is not too short and the simile expressed by the word *'paṅguvat'* implies that while commenting on the *Mbh* Kaiyaṭa has omitted nothing worthy of being commented upon and also that his work is not an elaborate one.[5]

While commenting on the *Mbh* Kaiyaṭa closely followed the views of Bhar. It is to the *Vākyapadiya* particularly to the *Prakīrṇakāṇda*, of Bhar, that Kaiyaṭa refers in his introductory verse. In the whole of his commentary, Kaiyaṭa has only once referred to the *Mahābhāsyadīpikā* of Bhar and he has never quoted *Mahābhāsyadīpikā* anywhere in his commentary.[6] We meet with more than a hundred quotations from *Vāk* in *Pradīpa*. The great scholarship of Kaiyaṭa is well exhibited in *Pradipa*. It is definitely a good asset to one who is intent on studying a profound text like the *Mbh*. Hence his commentary has got a great status in the system of Pāṇinīlyan Grammar. His commentary pervades the whole of the *Mbh.* He has elucidated the meaning of words, expressions and passages in the *Mbh* and has cited the different views held by scholars in regard to the meaning of particular passages in the *Mbh.* His approach to *Mbh* is that of an elucidatior and he does not seem an to make an attempt to criticise it.

Commentaries:

Owing to the greatness of *Pradīpa* among the commentaries on *Mbh,*[7] many a later commentator has resorted to commenting on *Pradāpa* instead of commenting upon the *Mbh.* The commentaries on *Mahābhāsyapradīpa,* which are available now number 15. They are *Mahābhāsyaprakāsa* of Cintāmaṇi of the 16th century A.d., a small work by name Vivaraṇa of Rāmachandra Sarasvathy of the 16th century A.D., the long commentary *Mahābhāsyapradīpavivaraṇa* of Isvarānanda Sarasvathy of the 16th century A.D., *Mahābhāsyapradīpoddyotana* of Nāganātha of the 17th century A.D., the commentary written by Mallaya Yajvā of the 17th century A.D., *Mahābhāsyapradīpoddyota* of Nāgesabhaṭṭa who flourished towards the end of the 17th century and the first half of the 18th century A.D., *Mahābhāsyapradīpoddyotana* of Annambhaṭṭa of the 18th century A.D., the commentary on *Pradīpa* written by Nārāyaṇa Sastri of the 18th century A.D., *Mahābhāsyapradipavyākhyā* of Rāmasevaka of 18th century A.D., *Mahābhāsyapradīpaprakāsikā* of Pravartakopādhyāya of unknown date, *Mahabhāsyapradīpasphūrti* of Ādenna of unknown date, *Mahābhāsyapradīpavivaraṇa* of Nārāyaṇa of unknown date, *Mahābhāsyapradīpasphūrti* of Sarvesvara Somayāji, *Mahābhāsyapradīpavyākhyā* of Harirāma and lastly the commentary by name *Pradāpavyākhyā* of unknown authorship and date, available at the Lalcand Library of the Dayānanda Anglo-Vedic College at Lahore. Of these, the *Mahābhāsyapradīpoddyota* of Nbh is the most popular one.

The Mahābhāṣyapradīpoddyota

NBh has named his gloss on *Mahābhāsyapradāpa* as *Uddyota.* This appears to be a favourite term of Nbh, since he has used this term to name another commentary namely *Kāvyapradīpoddyota* written by him.[8] The word 'Uddyota' derived from the root *'dyut'* prefixed with *'ud'*, conveyṣ the idea, "that which enlightens" and it is quite appropriate in regard to his commentaries.

This word is to be distinguished from the name *'Uddyotana'* of the commentaries written by Nāganātha and Annambhaṭṭa.[9]

Aim and Scope of the Work:

NBh, himself has given the nature aim and scope of his work in the introductory verses of the work.

He says:-

nāvistīrṇam na vistīrṇam madhyānāmapi bodhakṛd//
bhāsyapradīpavyākhyānam kurve 'haṃ tu yathāmati//

NBh's proclamation is *"bhāsyāpradīpavyakhyānam kurve"*. His work, therefore, has got the nature of a commentary. It is not an independent one if separated from the text of the *MBh* and the *Prdp*. It is not merely explanatory and discriptive but also critical.[10]

He refers to himself as *"Nāgesabhāsitārthavicaksaṇaḥ"* in the introductory verse, i.e., one adept in understanding the ideas expressed by Pat. He is quite confident that he fully knows the ideas favoured by Pat. The aim of his work is, therefore, to bring home to the mind of the reader the ideas and theories favoured by Pat, by rendering a comprehensive, but at the same time, not too elongated an elucidation. His work is intended to be comprehensive and is calculated to educate even an average student. It is not too elongated to feel bored. While Kt says that he has closely followed the lines of Bhar while commenting on *Mbh,* NBh points out that he has given priority to his own intelligence. He follows what his intellect dictates to him and that is the factor which makes his work distinctive in its nature. It is clear from the introductory verses that the scope of his work is the whole of *Mbh* and *Pradīpa* on it.

Characteristics of the Work:

As a commentary endeavouring to make the study of the *Mbh* and the *Prdp* easy and comprehensive, the *Udy* can be seen to have certain characteristics and they are noticed now:-

1. A work commenting on two works simultaneously :

A characteristic feature of the work is that it serves as a commentary for both the the *Mbh* and the *Pradp*. What the author has stated is *"bhāsyapradīpavyīkhyānam kurve"*. Here the expression *bhāsyapradīpavyākhyānam* if treated as a *sasthītatpurusa* compound by splitting it as *Bhāsyasya pradīpam bhāsyapradīpam tasya vyākhyānam bhāsya ......nam,* his work is prone to be understood as a commentary on *Pradīpa* which happens to be a gloss on the *Mbh*. But when one goes through his work it is clearly understood that his work is a commentary on the *Mbh* also.[11] The work therefore, is really an explanatory and critical study of both the *Mbh* and the *Prdp*. The part *'Bhāsyapradīpam* is to be split up as *bhāsyam ca pradīpaḥ ca bhāsyapradīpan* and then it gets compounded with the word *vyākhyānam* (i.e. *tayoḥ vyākhyānam*).[12] The reason for the fact that the *Udy* is generally referred to as a commentary of *Prdp* may probably be that it abounds more in the elucidative and critical assertions on Kṭ than those on Pat, which again may be due to the fact that NBh does not feel the necessity of commenting on all the passages in the *MBh* where Kṭ has already rendered satisfactory explanations and hence has commented upon such parts of the *Mbh* where Kṭ remains silent and NBh has thereby found scope for further elucidation. Wherever he entertains difference of opinion with Kṭ in regard to the interpretation of the *Mbh* and the like he has given his own criticism on the *Mbh*.

2. Abundance of Lucid Explanation:-

Quite befitting to his remark about his work *"madhyānāmapi bodhakrd"* in the introductory verse, it can be seen that the *Udy* abounds in explanations which are characterised by lucidity. The meanings given in the *Udy* of very short questions found in the *Mbh* like *"kassabda iti kassabdasabdābhidheya ityarthaḥ"* give clarity of the idea of the context.[13] The meaning of words are always noted down for eg. *"ātmasabdo dravyavāci bhāsye"*[14] Sentences of clumsy structure are provided with the *'anvaya'* which facilitates easy comprehension. So also ideas referred to by the phrase *'ata eva'*, those to be comprehended by the word *'ādi'* used by Pat or Kṭ and those referred to by pronouns like *'tad'*, *'tena'*, *'tatra'*, *'iha'*, etc. are always pointed out. Many passages are elucidated citing suitable *nyāyas*[15] The derivation of compounds and inflected forms are always given to make the idea of the sentence clearer. The word *'athavā'* used by Pat or Kṭ for intro-uducing a view, after citing a view already is explained significantly. So also words which occur in the *Mbh* or the *Prdp* and function as indicators (*upalaksaṇa*) are pointed out. The author always supplies the predicate, object or other suitable words that are missing in a sentences so that the idea is clarified.

Again sūtras and vārttikas are cited when the operations enjoined by them are referred to by Pat or Kṭ. The usages which come outside the scope of the rules of Pāṇ are pointed out, for example the author says *"paranipāto bhāṣyaprāmāṇyād"*.[16] The passages in the *Mbh* or statements in the *Prdp* are introduced by giving the viewpoint viz. *Jātipakṣa Kāryakālapakṣa, Vyaktipakṣa, Yathoddeśapakśa*, etc. on which the particular passage or statement is based. Again wherever Kṭ expresses his dissent by the word *āhuḥ*, the *arucibīja* is given in the *Udy*. The *Mbh* being a work in the form of dialogues, the specification of the conversant is quite welcome to the average student and the reader and we find that *Udy* abounds in statements wherein the passage is specified to be coming from the mouth of *ekadesin, siddhāntin, pūrvapakṣin siddhāntyekadesin, ācāryadeśīya, sūtrārambhavādin, pratyākhyānavādin*, etc.

3. *Originality of the author discernable in spite of the work being a commentary:*

In a work of the nature of a gloss, the commentator has scope only for the elucidation and justification of the assertions on the text on which he comments. The intellectual ability of the commentator can be discerned only when intricate passages are explained or apparent anomalies if any, in the text are justified suitably. A commentator has always thus, to adhere to what has been favoured by the author of the text on which the commentary is framed. *Uddyota*, though a commentary does not confine its scope in elucidating and justifying the statements in the *Mbh* and the *Prdp*. The text of the *Mbh* and the *Prdp* can find a critic in NBh.[17] To the intelligent reader having an objective point of view, the work of NBh presents the picture of a lawyer intent on justifying facts from the logical point of view only.

4. Citations:

Another noteworthy characteristic of the work is the citation of different views found in it. The different views related to a particular passage or assertion are always cited.[18] The individual view of the author is given by the phrases like *Pare, tu, Pare tu āhuḥ, Pare tu vadanti, vastutastu*, etc. The views of others are cited with phrases like *ityanye anye tu āhuḥ kecitu vadanti iti kecit* etc. The author does not as a rule mention the name of any grammarian whose view he cites.[19] In addition, the different readings of the text of the *Mbh* and the *Prdp* are also cited in this work.

Commentaries:

Vaidyanātha Pīyaguṇde desciple of NBh, has written a commentary by name *Chāyā* on *Udy*.[20] Pandit Rudradharajhā Śarma has recently written a commentary mainly explanatory, by name *Tattvāloka* wherein the elucidation the text of *Mbh*, the *Pradp* and the *Udy* is made.

REFERENCES

1. This fact is expressed in the statement:-
"*yathottaram munīnām prāmāṇyam*".
2. Vide *Udy* p. 2.
"Mahābhāṣyeti:- vyākhyātṛtvepyasyēṣtyādikathanenānvākhyātṛtvāditarabhāṣyavailakṣaṇyena mahatvam"
3. "Mahabhāṣya .... a critical discussion on the vārttikas of Kātyāyana, while its iṣṭis on the other hand, are original vārttikas on such sūtras of Pānini as called for his own remarks." (*Pāṇini His place in Sanskrit Literature*, p. 92) "The Mahābhāṣya is, in the first in stance a commentary on Kāt's vārttikas" (*Kātyāyana and Patañjali*, p. 51.)
4. "Param patañjaliḥ sūtrapāṭhasya vārttikasya ca mahābhāṣyam vidhāya sarvataḥ pramādaparisunyoyam pāniniyāṣṭādhyāyigrantha iti pradarśayan Kātyāyanatīvradṛṣṭeḥ rarakṣainam samādaraṇīyam grantham uttamam".
5. Vide *Udy* p.1.
6. "*Vistareṇa bharthrhariā pradarśita ūhaḥ*" (*Prdp*. p. 14.)
7. *Vide Yudhiṣṭhira Mīmāmsaka, op. cit*, pp. 387-397.
8. Vide Supra p. 10.
9. Vide Supra p. 16.
10. Sītārāma Sāstri's remark is noteworthy here.

"bhāṣyam patañjaleryattu sūtrāṇām pāṇiner mahat/
marmajñastasya nāgeśaḥ pradīpodyotakṛd yataḥ//
pratnanūtanamārgau dvau dṛśyete pāṇiner naye/
tayoḥ samanvyayaḥ sādhur nāgeśena mudā kṛtaḥ//
(Mangalśloka in his edition of *Bṛ. Śab. Śekh)*

11. Vide Infra Chapter III *Elucidation on the Mahābhāṣya* pp. 25-76.
12. Vide *"Bhāṣyeti dvandvottarm ṣaṣṭhītatpuruṣaḥ"* (Vaidyanātha Pāyanguṇde's commentary, *Chāyā* on *Udy* p. 2.)
13. *Udy* p. 8.
14. *Udy* p. 113.
15. Vide infra pp. 229-232.
16. Vide *Udy* p. 80.
17. Vide infra Chapters VI and VII pp. 139-210.
18. Vide Infra Chapter V pp. 103-138.
19. In the third *āhnika,* while commenting the first sentence in the bhāṣya under the rule *"vṛddhirādaic"* NBh refers to haradatta by name in order to cite his view regarding the interpretations of the rule *"vrddhirādaic"* (vide *Mbh* p. 103). So also, commenting on the bhāṣya passage 'naitad asti asiddho ḍhalopaḥ tasyāsiddhatvānnaitadantyam bhavati' under the rule *"iko guṇavṛddhi"* (1.1.3), he refers to Mādhava by name to cite a view held by the latter which he refutes totally (vide *Mbh* p. 126).
20. Vide Supra p. 5.

Part Two
Analytical Examination

Chapter III

Elucidiation of Mahābhāṣya

Though ordinarily viewed as the gloss on *Prdp*, the *Uddyota* can be seen to be to some extent a gloss on *Mbh* as well.[1] Many passages of *Mbh* are elucidated in regard to the particular expressions found in them and their significance. They are specified to be as that of the *siddhāntin* or of the *ekadeśin* and explained in such a way as to refute the erroneous views or interpretations pertaining to them. Some variant readings are also noted by the author.

On Certain Expressions

We find that while interpreting the sūtras every attempt is made to see whether each and every word, even a particle, in the sūtras is purposefull. But with regard to the text of *Mbh* which is a discussion on the sūtras and vārttikas every expression cannot be full of significance, but only be either befitting to the context or be explanatory. Yet there are certain expression in the *Mbh* which have particular bearing in the context and some others which requires further explanation. Among them those which are left untouched by Kṭ are dealt with by NBh.

1. *'Ayam' in "athetyayam śabdo'dhikārārthaḥ prayujyate".*

Pat says at the beginning of his work *"atha śabdānuśāsanam athetyayam śabdo'dhikāraārthaḥ prayujyate"* *NBh* brings out the significance of the pronoun *ayam* in the sentence-*athetyayam* etc. meaning that this *śabda* namely *atha* is used in the sense of commencement. He pionts out that if the sentence were without this pronoun, for example *'atheti śabdo'dhikārārthaḥ* it may mean that the *nipāta atha* possesses the sense of commencement alone and the meanings namely *ānantarya* and the like will be misunderstood to be not of the *nipāta, atha.*[2] What Pat wishes to convey is that the *nipāta atha* which is in the previous sentence *'atha śabdānuśāsanam'* is used in the sense of commencement. NBh says that it is in order to serve this purpose that the word *ayam* is used here. It specifies the fact that the sense of commencement spoken of as being expressed by *'atha'* is in the sentence *'atha śabdānuśāsanam'* and hence this does not contradict its denotation of other senses in which it may be used in other sentences.

2. *'Yājñikāḥ' in 'yājñikāḥ paṭhanti'*

This word is used many times by Pat.[3] In all his usages except the one which is to be dealt with presently, the word is elucidated by NBh as *yajñakāṇḍabhavāḥ vaidikāḥ śabdāḥ*. One such usage of Pat is quoted here - *"yājñikāḥ paṭhanti. sthūlapṛṣatīm āgnivāruṇīm anadvāhīm ālabheta iti..*[4]

In such usages NBh derives this word by the addition of the suffix *'ṭhak'* to the base *'yajña'* on the strength of the rule *"kratuyajñebhyśca"* (4-3-68). So the word means *yajñe bhavāḥ*. NBh says that the sentence *yājñikāḥ paṭhanti,* therefore means that scriptures dealing with sacrifice read thus. Since reading is an action that could be done by a person and not by *śabdas* this sentence may seem to present an ambiguity. NBh says that this is a rare usage just like *ṛṣiḥ paṭhati, śṛṇoti grāvāṇaḥ* etc. made by Pat under the rule *"dhātoh karmaṇaḥ samānakartṛkādicchayām vā"* (3-1-7). The word *ṛṣiḥ* there means *Veda* and *paṭhati* means informs.

In the *bhāṣya* passage *'Vede yājñikāḥ samjñām kurvanti'* under the rule *"vṛddhirādaic"* (1-1-1), NBh allots another sense to the word *yājñikāḥ.*[5] He says *yajñakāṇḍadraṣṭāraḥ ṛṣaya ityarthaḥ'*. The derivation of the word in this sense is worth discussion. The word cannot be derived on the strength of the rule *"kratuyajñebhyaśca* (4-3-68) since the sense allotted to *'ṭhak'* by the same is *'tatra bhavaḥ'* which does not suit here. The rule *kratūkthādisūtrānthāṭṭhak*" (4-2-60) gives to the suffix *ṭhak* the sense *'tad adhīte tad veda'*. The word *yajña* belongs to the *ukthādigaṇa* and the derivation as *'yajñam vidanti iti yājñikāḥ'* corroborates the meaning given by NBh, *yajñakāṇḍadraṣṭāraḥ ṛṣayaḥ*. Sages who have cognised the Vedas can well be considered as those who know the scriptures dealing with sacrifices.

3. 'ekaikaśaḥ' in "tadyathā ṛṣisahasram ēkām kapilām ēkaikaśaḥ....etc.[6]

Pat uses this expression in the passage *'tadyathā ṛṣisahasram ekām kapilām ekaikaśaḥ sahasrakṛtvā datvā tayā sarve te sahasradakṣināḥ sampannāḥ'* which means that a thousand of seers get the fruit of having given away in charity thousand cows, though there is only one brown cow, each giving her thousand times. NBh is of opinion that *'ekaikaśaḥ'* is an expression like *yathājātiyakaḥ* and *gārgyāyaṇī*. In *yathājātīyakaḥ* there are two suffixes namely *thāl* and *jātīyar* both of which are enjoined in the sense of *prakāra* i.e, similarity by separate rules and here they jointly express the sense of *prakāra*. So also in *gārgyayaṇī* the two suffixes *pha* and *ṅīp* jointly express the sense of *strītva*. Similarly in *ekaikaśaḥ* there are two factors namely reduplication of *eka* and the suffix *śas*, both of which are enjoined separately in the sense of *vīpsā*, by the rules *"nityavīpsayoḥ* (8-1-4) and *"saṅghyaikavacanācca vīpsāyām"* (5-4-45) respectively.

Therefore NBh says that in *ekaikaśaḥ*, these two jointly indicate the sense of *vīpsā*. However this joined indication of *vīpsā* by both the reduplication and *śas* is not seen from numerals like *dvi* since there is the *anabhidhāna* of such forms.[7] With regard to *ekaśabda*, the sense of *vīpsā* is indicated by either of these two or by both jointly. The reason is that such forms are in vogue. NBh adds that with regard to the *ekaśabda* there are instances where there are both the reduplication and *śas*, but reduplication alone indicates the sense of *vīpsā*. An instance is *'ekaikaśo dehi'*. This statement of NBh is based on the words of Pat under the rule *"nityavīpsayoḥ"* (8-1-4) *'Yatra ca taddhitenānuktā vīpsā bhavati tatra dvirvacanam, tadyathā ekaikaśo dadātīti*, commenting on which NBh establishes that this passages shows that there is a suffix *śas* which is *svārthika* and hence the rule *"saṅkhyaikavacanācca vīpsāyām"* (5-4-43) prescribes *śas* in the sense of *vīpsā* as well as in *svārtha.*[8] NBh adds that in instances like *māṣaśaḥ, śas* itself conveys the sense of *vīpsā* and reduplication also is never used for the purpose.

4. iti' in 'yat tarhi tat śuklo nīlah kapilaḥ kapota iti sa śabdaḥ'[9]

In the first *āhnika* of the *Mbh,* Pat discusses at the outset the question which is *śabda* among those concepts that appear in mind when one utters *gauḥ*. Concepts like the individuality cow, its action, its qualities and genus cow, appear in mind when one utters *gauḥ*. In the line *"yat tarthi tat śuklo nīlaḥ kapilaḥ kapota iti sa śabdaḥ"*, the colour of the cow is doubted to be the *śabda* and the doubt is refuted afterwards showing that it is not *śabda* but a *guṇa,* i.e. quality, NBh gives the significance of the word *iti* used in this line. When one utters *gauḥ* , its qualities appear in mind and the same need not be her colour alone but be other qualities also like its smell whether fragrant or otherwise, touch, gender, number etc. But in the said passage one quality namely colour alone is doubted to be the *śabda* and hence the said passage may seem to be less correct. NBh points that it is here that the word *iti* comes into play. It is used in the sense of *prakāra* i.e, similarity and by virtue of the same the question means whether colour like white, black, brown and similar other qualities (like smell, touch, gender, number, etc.) can be regarded as *śabda* and now the question becomes free from ambiguity.

5. 'Acāryaḥ' referring to Pat

Pat uses this word several times.[10] In all such instances except one which is to be dealt with presently, it is clear from the context that either Pāṇ or Kāt is referred to by this term and hence NBh keeps mum. But in the passage *"evam vipratipannabuddhibhyaḥ śiṣyebhyaḥ ācāryaḥ suhṛdbhūtvā anvācaṣṭe imāni prayojanāni adhyeyam vyakāraṇam iti."* NBh gives his comment on the word *ācārya, ācāryapadena sāstrādhyāpako bhāṣyakṛdeva vivakṣitah.*[11]

This passage is the concluding remark while giving the reason for the fact that the enumeration of the benefits accured from the study of grammar alone is made and not with regard to the study of Vedas. NBh feels that the specification of the fact that the word *ācārya* here denotes Pat is necessary since unlike this, in all other instances the term refers to Pāṇ or Kāt. Prof. Weber takes this comment, of NBh on the word *ācārya*, as a strong support to favour his theory that *Mbh* ought to be more properly be considered the work of the pupils of Pat rather than the work of their master. Kielhorn on the other hand, refutes this view and maintains that the *Mbh* is the masterly production of one and the same individual scholar, though he admits the fact that it is Pat who is referred to here by the word *ācārya.*[12]

6. 'Vakṣyāmi' in "evam tarhi aṣṭādaśadhā bhinnām nivṛttakalādikām avarṇasya pratyāpattim vakṣyāmi"[13]

In the first *āhnika* of the *Mbh,* to the question concerning the purpose to be derived from the *Māheśvara sūtras,* the *ekadeśin* replies that the said sūtras are for the understanding of correct pronounciation and in this case the necessity of uttering correct vowels like those that are grave, acute etc., no longer arises, as there is the authoritative utterance of their general forms i.e. *ākṛtyupadeśa* in the *Śivasūtras.* Here it is pointed that if *ākṛtyupadeśa* be accepted, prohibition of the comprehension of letters, that are possessed of the faults such as *saṃvṛta, kala* and the like has to laid down.[14] This necessity arises since the incorrect letters also will be comprehended by way of *ākṛtyupadeśa.* To this, the *ekadeśin* replies *evam tarhi aṣṭādaśadhā bhinnām nivṛttakalādikām avarṇasya pratyāpattim vakṣyāmi",* meaning "Well, then I shall prescribe for *'a'* such a substitute which would be characterised by its eighteen varieties, but which would be devoid of the faults such as *'kala'* and others." NBh says that there is an inconsistency in the wording *vakṣyāmi.*

Pāṇ has already framed the rule " *a a*"(8-4-68) which prescribes the correct *(saṃvṛta) a* as the substitute and so how can Pat state *'vakṣyami'* i.e. 'I shall prescribe'. NBh removes the discrepancy saying that the word *avarṇasya* here stands for all vowels. The statement therefore means that just like the rule *"a a"* (8-4-68) rules like *"i i" ū u"* etc. shall be made, so that faultless letters will substitute the faulty letters comprehended by *i u* etc. in the Śivasūtras by way of *ākṛtyupadeśa*. Since rules like *'i i'*, *'u u'* etc. are not already made by Pāṇ, Pat says, 'I shall prescribe' and so the wording *vakṣyāmi* is quite consistent.

7. upadeśaḥ

The word *upadeśa* has been used by Pāṇ in various rules like *ūpadeśe'janunāsika it"* (1-3-2) *ādeca upadeśe'śiti"* (6-1-45) etc. and is wellknown in the sense 'the first utterance of a sound to comrehend its *svarūpa'*. Both Kāt and Pat have used this word several times, but in all such usages, the word does not denote the said meaning. In such instances NBh specifies the sense in which the word *upadeśa* is used.

In the first *āhnika* of the *Mbh*, the *pūrvapakṣin* points out that if there be *ākṛtyupadeśa* of the vowels by the 14 *Śivasūtras*, there arises the necessity of the prohibition of faulty letters like *saṃvṛta kala* etc. since the same also are comprehended by the authoritative utterance of the general nature of all letters. To this the answer is that defective sounds will never be heard in aguments, substitutes suffixes, roots and bases, since all these are read correctly. Then *pūrvapakṣin* poses this question *"yāni tarhi agrahaṇāni prātipadikāni"* meaning, 'what about agrahaṇa prātipadikas? 'The answer is given *'eteṣām api svaravarṇānupūrvījñānārtham upadeśaḥ kartavyaḥ'* meaning *'the upadeśa* of these also had to be made so that the accent, letters and orders of letters can be understood'. This assertation of Pat contradicts his own assertion under the rule, *ādeca upadeśe'śiti* (6-1-45) i.e., *uddeśaśca prātipadikānām no'padeśaḥ"*[15] which means there is only *'uddeśa'* of prātipadikas and not *upadeśa* of them. In one place Pat speaks of the *upadeśa* of bases whereas in another place he asserts that there is no *upadeśa* of bases and it is thus contradictory.

NBh averts this contradiction by specifying the meaning of the expression *agrahaṇāni prātipadikāni* and of the word *upadeśdaḥ* which is used in the said assertions in the first *āhnika* and the other under the rule *ādeca upadeśe'śiti*. He says that there are bases like *garga, avaṭa,* etc. which are comprehended by means of *gaṇas* like *gargādi*. Besides these, there are also bases which, unlike the above mentioned ones, are not comprehended in any way by rules. Those are the bases known as *agrahaṇa prātipadhikas*. To quote NBh, *"kāryavidhāvakṛtanuvādānītyarthaḥ.*[16] So the question *'yāni tarhi agrahaṇāni prātipadikāni'* means 'how can the letters in bases which are not comprehended in any way by rules be understood as faultless. The answer *"eteṣāmapi..."* is that such bases are to be treated as comprehended by the expression *prātipadika* in rules like *ṅyāpprātipadikāt* (4-1-1). The word *upadeśa* here thus means *anuvādarūpeṇa grahaṇam*. So there is no contradiction since the word *upadeśa* in the passage *'eteṣām api....'* is not used in the sense in which the word is used in the passage *uddeśaśca prātipadikānām no'padeśaḥ'*. To quote NBh on the word in the latter passage, *'anirjñātasvarūpasya kāryārthas-varūpajnānārtham apūrvoccaraṇam.*[17] This is the well known sense of the word *upadeśa*, "the utterance in order to comprehend the *svarūpa*, which otherwise is unknown, of a sound, for a particular purpose. The word *uddeśaḥ* there is used in the sense *guṇaiḥ prāpaṇam* and NBh says that the word *upadeśa* is used in this sense also. In the *bhāṣya* under the rule *"ṣṇāntā ṣaṭ"* (1-1-23) Pat introduces the *vārttika ṣaṭsamjñāyām upadeśavacanam* and elucidating the same says *ṣaṭsamjñāyām upadeśagrahaṇam kartavyam. Upadeśe ṣakārānta ṇakārānta ca samkhyā ṣaṭsamjnāī bhavatīti vakatavyam.*[18]

It is argued that the word *upadeśa* is to be inserted in the rule *ṣṇāntā ṣaṭ* (1-1-23). The word *upadeśa* is here used, says NBh, in the sense *"prakṛtipratyayavibhāgena pratipādanarūpam yad guṇaiḥ prāpaṇam tad upadeśapadenātra gṛhyate"*. NBh thus says that the sense of the words *upadeśa* and *uddeśa* overlap each other and that is why Pat says under the rule *ūpadeśeja nunāsika it"* (1-3-2), *"sankīrṇāv uddeśopadesau"*. In the passage under the rule *"striyām"* (4-1-3), *"sarveṣāmeva tu prātipadikānām svaravarṇānupūr-*

vījṇānārtham upadeśaḥ kartavyaḥ the word is used in the sense of derivation i.e. *guṅaiḥ prāpaṇam.*[19] In the passage under the rule *'hayavaraṭ', "yadi ca kiñcid anyatrāpi upadeśe prayojanam asti tatrāpyupadeśaḥ kartavyaḥ,* NBh says that the word *upadeśa* means utterance alone and is not used in the sense of utterance in order to comprehend the *svarūpa* of a sound.[20]

8. 'yadi' in 'yadi tarhi sicyantaraṅgam bhavati, akārṣīt ahārṣīt guṅe kṛte raparatve cānantyatvād vṛddhir na prāpnoti.[21]

Under the rule *"iko guṇavṛddhī"* (1-1-3) Pat says that during the stage *'ni+a+nu+is+īt'*[22] of the formation of the word *'nyanuvīt'*[23] the rule *"sici vṛddhiḥ parasmaipadeṣu"* (7-2-1) is contingent to substitute the vowel *'u'* by *vṛddhi.* If the rule, *iko guṇavṛddhī"* (1-1-3) presents the word *'ikaḥ'* to this rule, this contingency can be averted by the rule 'kṅiti ca' (1-1-5) which disallows *iglakṣaṇavṛddhi.* The *pūrvapakṣin* says that the substitute *uvaṅ* taught by the rule *"aci śnudhātubhruivām yvor iyaṅnuvaṅau"* (6-4-77), here dependent on *sic* i.e *'is'* is *antaraṅga* whereas the *vṛddhi* caused by the rule *"sici..."* (7-2-1), dependent on *sic* and *parasmaipada* termination namely *'is+īt'* is *bahiraṅga.* And so *'uvaṅ'* will substitute *'u'* and there is no contingency of the substitution of *'u'* by *vṛddhi* there. Pat then says *"yadi tarhi sicy antaraṅgam bhavati akārṣīt, ahārṣīt, guṇe kṛte raparatve cānantyatvād vṛddhirna prāpnoti"*, meaning if, then, *antaraṅgaparibhāṣā* prevails in *sici vṛddhi* the forms *akārṣīt* and *ahārṣīt*[24] cannot be formed since the final element of the *aṅga* is not a vowel after the operation of the *sūtras* enjoining *guṇa* and *raparatva.*

NBh says that the word *'yadi'* at the beginning of the assertion is significant. It shows the improbability of the following assertion that *antaraṅgaparibhāṣā* prevails in instances where the rule *"sici vṛddhiḥ parasmaipadeṣu"* (7-2-1) is to operate, and prevents the same. This is because with regard to the rule *"sici..."* (7-2-1) the operation of *antaraṅga* rules cannot be accepted, since the former is *apavāda* of the rules that are *antaraṅga,.* on the basis of the maxim *'yena nāprāpte yo vidhir ārabhyate sa tasyāpavādaḥ.*[25] Therefore the further discussions trying to secure *vṛddhi* in the said instances after the operation of *guṇa,* are that of *siddhāntye-*

kadeśin and *pūrvapakṣyekadeśin*. So also are the efforts to establish the fact *'na sicyantaraṅgam'* by means of *jñāpakas* with which the discussion ends. NBh says that it is to suggest the said fact that Pat uses the word *'yadi'* here.

9. 'yān in "yān hi bhavān atra ṣaṣṭhyā pratinirdiśati eteśām anyena vyavāye na bhavitravyam'[26]

Under the rule *"halo'nantarāḥ samyogaḥ"* Pat discusses the question that when there are more than two contiguous consonants, whether every two severally gets the designation *'samyoga'* or the whole alone gets the same. This is followed by another query that whatever be the above case, whether the rule as it is now, satisfies both the cases. The answer is given that when more than two, take the designation, the word *anantarāḥ* in the rule is split *'avidyamānam antaram eṣām'* and when every two is to get the designation, it is split *'avidyamānā(ḥ) antarā eṣām*. Pat adds, with reference to the latter splitting in which the designation extends to two, *"dvayoścaivāntarā kaścid vidyate vāna vā.*[27] which means 'the existence or non-existence of anything in the middle is in relation to two alone.[28] Now it is pointed out that *"evam api bahūnāmeva prāpnoti yān hi bhavān atra ṣaṣṭhyā pratinirdiśati eteṣām anyena vyavāye na bhavitavyam"* meaning 'Even then (when the part *'anantarāḥ* is split *avidyamānāḥ antarāeṣām)* the designation extends to more than two. When those which you refer to by the sixth case, have interception by another one; they will not get the desgination." NBh here says that just after the statement of a fact about two denoted by the expression *'dvayoḥ* in the previous sentence, the same are referred to in plural number namely *yān* in the next sentence *'yān hi....'*

This may seem obscure. NBh elucidates the significance of the expression *yān* and removes this obscurity. In the sentence *'dvayoś caivāntarā kaścit vidyate vā na vā*, the word *dvayoḥ* does not denote two single letters alone. If so, these two will be the *avadhi* of the one which stands as an interception and hence these two being *niyatāvadhii* there must be accusative case from the base *dvi* and the expression ought to be the *'dvau antarā'* etc.

But Pat has used the term *dvayoḥ* in the genitive case which shows that two each of which is accompanied by another, are intercepted or not intercepted by another. These two when the number of those which accompany them are taken into account amounts to more than two and so they are referred to by the word *'yān'* in plural. The passage *"yān hi..."* etc., means that when there are three contiguous consonants they can be treated as two groups the former group constituted of the first and second letter and the latter group consisting of the second and third. Since these two groups do not have anything to intercept them, these two groups i.e, the three, will get the 'desgination and thus it can be seen that even in the splitting up as *'avidyamānā(ḥ) antarā eṣām,* the desgination relates to more than two. That is why Pat states that even then the desgination extends to more than two, since the two which are referred to by the sixth case, constitute more than two also. Thus NBh says that in the splitting up as *'avidyamanā(ḥ) antarā,* two continguous consonants as well as three contiguous consonants which can be grouped into two will get the designation and this is the import of the expression *'yān'*.

10. Adīrgaḥ in "ṅyābghrahaṇe'dīrghaḥ ādeśo na sthānivaditi vaktayam.[29]

Under the rule *"sthānivad ādeśo'nalvidhau'* (1-1-256) Kāt points out thirteen defects caused by the existence of the rule. One among them is given by the vārttika namely *'ṅyābgrahaṇe-'dīrghaḥ'*. Elucidating this Pat says *"ṅyābgrahaṇe'dīrghaḥ ādes'o no sthānivaditi vaktavyam. kim prayojanan? niṣkauśāmbiḥ atikhaṭvaḥ. Nyābgrahaṇena grahaṇāt sulopomā bhūditi"*, meaning "the non-lengthened *ādeśa of 'ṅī'* and *'āp'* should be prohibited from taking *sthānivadbhāva*. Why? So that there may not be the elision of *'su'*, the nominative singular suffix in the words *niṣkauśāmbiḥ and atikhaṭvaḥ* (on the strength of the sūtra *"halṅyābhyo dīrghāt sutisyapṛktam* hal" (6-1-68) taking the final *'ī'* and *'a'* in their stem to be *'ṅi'* and *'āp'* by *sthānivadbhāva*. NBh brings out the significance of the word *'adīrghaḥ* by way of advancing a doubt.

The adjective *'adīrghaḥ'* points out that the *dīrgha* substitute of *ṅī* and *āp* may be allowed *sthānivadbhāva*. But there is no necessity of the *sthānivadbhāva* on the *dīrgha ādeśa* of *ṅī* and *āp*. This is because in the form *khaṭvā* where *savarṇadrgha* replaces the vowel *ā* of the base *khaṭvā* and the vowel *ā* of the feminine suffix *ṭāp* the *dīrgha* substitute namely *savarṇadīrgha* can be treated as *āp* by means of *parādivadbhāva* enjointed by the rule *'antādivacca'* (6-1-85), in spite of the prohibition of *sthānivadbhāva* of the *dīrgha* substitute negating the same. Hence the adjective *adīrgha* may apparently be doubted to be non- essential,says NBh. But it is really essential, since in the absence of the same, the prohibition of *sthānivadbhāva*, being futile with regard to the substitute namely *dīrgha* in *khaṭvā* where the same can be treated as *āp* by way of *parādivadbhāva*, shall relate to the operation procured by *sthānin* by whatever means i.e, by way of *parādivadbhāva* or *sthānivadbhāva*, on *ādeśa*. Hence in order that in *khaṭvā* the *savarṇadīrgha* substitute may be treated as *āp* by way of either *parādivadbhāva* or *sthānivadbhāva*, Pat gives the adjective *adārgha* for the substitute while prohibiting *sthānivadbhāva* of the same. Thus NBh points out the purpose of the adjective *'adīrghaḥ'* to the word *ādeśa* in the bhāṣya passage.

NBh also brings to our attention the fact that to serve the said purpose, the word *hrasva* given as the adjective of *ādeśa* won't suffice. This is because in the instance, *citraḥ*, meaning *citrāyām jātaḥ*, derived by the addition of the suffix *aṇ* to the word *citrā* and wherein on account of the *luk* of the suffix *aṇ*, the feminine suffix *tāp* also has undergone elision, the substitute namely elision replacing *ā* of the feminine suffix, is contingent, by virtue of the rule," *pratyalope pratyalakṣaṇam"* (1-1-62) to procure the elision of the suffix *su* on the strength of the rule, *"haliṅyabblyo...."* (6-1-68).[30] Thus here there is the undesirable probability of the elision which being not a *hrasva substitute gets an operation, procured by virtue of its sthānin* namely *tāp*. The significance of the adjective *adīrgha* can well be understood when NBh says that elision not being *dīrgha* substitute can be prohibited from causing the *lopa* of the suffix by virtue of its *sthānin* on the basis of *pratyayalakṣaṅa*. Hence NBh says that Pat's adjective *adīrgha* to the susbstitute for prohibiting the *stānivadbhāva* is quite significant.

Signficance of Bhāṣya passages:

While commenting on the *Mbh,* NBh has given due attention to the passages in the text of the *Mbh.* He elucidates their significance.

1. The significance in the sequence of questions doubting the individuality cow,. its action, its qualities and genus cow to be the sense of śabda.

Pat beginning the discussion as to what is *śabda* when one utters *'gauḥ'* puts forward a series of questions doubting one by one, *dravya, kriyā, guṇa* and *jāti* to be the import of *śabda.*[31] Here NBh points out the significance in the sequence of these doubts. He points out that when one utters *gauḥ,* concepts like *dravya,* action, quality and genus appear in the mind. Among them *dravya* is the receptacle of *kriyā, guṇa,* etc. So first of all it is doubted to be *śabda* among all those concepts that appear in the mind of the hearer when one says *gauḥ.* The reason for doubting *kriyā* and *guṇa* to be the *śabda* before doubting genus to be the same is that genus is dependent on them. NBh finds a significance in the sequence of doubts with regard to *kriyā* and *guṇa* to be the *śabda.* In the Vaiśeṣika system of philosophy kriyās like *samyoga* and *vibhāga* are treated as *guṇas* and it is to indicate that they are *kriyā* itself, Pat gives the first preference to the doubt whether *kriyā* be the *dravya.*

2. *"santi hi yaṇaḥ sānunāsikāḥ niranunāsikāśca."*[32]

While commenting on the rule *'aiuṇ'* Pat says that in the instances *vṛkṣābhyām* and *devadatta* (3) during the stage *vṛkṣa + bhyām* and *devadatta,* when *dīrgha* and *pluta* are enjoined by the rules, *"supi ca"* (7-3-102) and *"guroranṛtonantyasyāpyekaikasya prācām"* (8-2-86) the *sthānin,* i.e. the vowel *'ā'* which is at the end and is *saṃvṛta* will never make the *dīrgha* and *pluta* substitute to be *samvṛta* as there are no *dīrgha* and *pluta* which are *samvṛta.* But with regard to the instances *sayyantā, savvatsaraḥ, yallokam* during the stage *sam + yantā, sam + vatsaraḥ, Yam + lokaṃ,* the *sthānin* namely *anusvāra* which is nasalised will necessarily make the substitutes *y, v,* and *1* enjoined by the rule, *"anusvārasya yayi parasavarṇaḥ"* (8-4-58) nasalized. This is because they have their own *anunāsika* variety. The exact words of Pat here are *"santi hi yaṇaḥ sānunāsikāḥ niranunāsikāśca"* (There are semi vowels both nasalized and non-nasalized). NBh here points out that among the semivowels *r* does not have any nasalized variety and *y, v,* and 1 alone have nasalized and non-nasalised varieties. Hence it must be understood that Pat has said *"santi..."* since the majority of letters comprehended by the *pratyāhāra yaṇ* have the said two varieties. He does never mean that *r* has got the said varieties.

3. *"Avyapavṛkte kāmacāraḥ"*.[33]

In the bhāṣya on the rules *'eoṅ'* and *'aiauṇ'* Pat gives a discussion on the question whether in letters *(ā, ī, ū, ṝ, ḷ, e, o, ai* and *au)* their parts which resemble other letters *(a, i, u, r* and 1), operate like the latter in sandhi etc, or not. Certain defects are pointed out if parts of letters operate like those which they resemble and Pat cites the vārttika *'ṇāvyavapavṛktasyāvayave tadvidhir yathā dravyeṣu'* as the answer to meet all the difficulties raised against it. He says that the ruels of those letters do not operate in the case of those which resemble them and form part of other letters, but are not taken cognisance of as separate from the whole as in *dravyas*. Elucidating the part *"yathā dravyeṣu"* Pat says *'yathā tarhi tailam na vikretavyam māmsam na vikretavyam iti vyapavṛktam ca na vikrīyate avyapavṛktam gāvaḥ sarṣapāśca vikrīyante, tathā lomanakham spṛṣṭvā śaucam kartavyam iti vyapavṛktam spṛṣṭvā niyogataḥ kartavyam, avyapavṛkte kāmacāraḥ'* (so, as, when it is said that oil should not be sold and that meat should not be sold, they are not sold, when they are separated from the whole; but the cows and mustard wherein they are not separated, are sold; as when it is said that one should purify oneself on touching hair and nail, it is obligatory to do it on touching them). Here the part *'avyapavṛkte'* is worth elucidation. It is because, in the former example the prohibition of the selling of oil and flesh is stated as not related to the selling of cows and mustards, whereas in the latter the necessity of purifying oneself is never stated, as not relating to the touching of hair and nail which are not separated from the body; and so these two examples are not equal as the clause *'avyapavrkte kāmacāraḥ'* may apparently lead one to the conclusion that *"avyapavṛkte spṛṣṭe śauce kāmacāraḥ"* NBh therefore elucidates this as *'sparśe kāmacāraḥ tena śaucābhāvaḥ'*. He points that the clause means it does not matter whether one touches or not, the hair and nail which are not separated from the body and consequently there is no need of purifying onself on touching them. Now both these examples become equal. In the former the prohibition of selling flesh does not relate to cows and flesh. In the latter the necessity of purifying onself on touching hair and nail does not relate to the touching of hair and nails not separated from the body.

4. *'yadica kiñcid antyatrāpi upadeśe prayojanamasti tatrāpyupadeśāḥ kartavyaḥ'*[34]

To the question enquiring the purpose of mentioning twice of the letter h in the *Śivasūtras*, the *vārttikakāra* says that it can be included in *pratyāhāras* like *'aṭ'* and *'haś'* as a result of the mention of the same in the rule *'hayaravaṭ'*. It can be included in *pratyāhāras* like *'val' 'ral 'jhal'* and *'śal'* as it is read in the rule *'hal'*. There Pat makes the above remark. NBh points out that the word *upadeśa* here simply means *utterance* and *anyatra* means in other *pratyāhāras*. The sentence conveys the sense that if there is any use of its being read elsewhere, there too it should be read. NBh summarises that the purpose of the mention of letters in the *Śivasūtras* is not the comprehension of their nature but for procuring several purposes by way of grouping them under different *pratyāhāras*. Therefore Pat means that the repetition of the letter *'h'* in the *Śivasūtras* is no longer a defect. The *bhāṣya* admits the fact that *'h'* can be included in other *pratyāhāras* like *aś iṇ* etc. That is why, NBh says, Pat makes under the rule, *"Pumyogād ākhyāyām"* (4-1-48) the usage *'Mañcā hasanti'* where based on the precedence of *'h'* which is being taken as *'aś'* the rule, *"Bhobhago aghoapūrvasya yo'śi"* (8-3-17) has operated. Kṭ has previously remarked that vārttikakāra has failed to note that *'h'* can be included in *aś* as a result of its mentions in the rule *"hayavaraṭ"* so as to comprehend the instance *bho hasati.*[35] Some others[36] too pointed out that *vārttikakāra failed to point out that h* can be included in the *pratyāhāra iṇ* and the instance benefitted by this is *lilihiḍhve* where *h* being treated as *iṇ* can bring the option of lingualization on the strength of the rule *"vibhāsetah"*

(8-3-79). NBh makes clear that this saying of Pat has rectified the said defects pointed out in the vārttika. NBh concludes saying that Pat in this sentence fully admits the necessity of the mention of the letter *h* twice in the *Śivasūtras.*

5. *"ya ete'kṣu pratyahārārthā anunandhāḥ kriyante eteṣām ajgrahaṇena grahaṇam kasmād na bhavati?"*[37]

With this question Pat begins the discussion regarding the non-inclusion of anubandhas like *ṇ, k* and *ṅ* in the *pratyāhāra ac.* NBh gives the reason why Pat treats this question as relating to the *pratyāhāra ac* alone and not with other pratyāhāras like *aṇ ak haś* etc. wherein also there is the contingency of the comprehension of *anubandhas* by them. *NBh* says that there is neither any purpose to be served nor any defect to be caused by the comprehension of *ṇ k ṅ* in pratyāhāras like *aṇ ak* and *aṅ.* But with regard to the *pratyāhāra ac* if it comrehends *ṇ k* and *ṅ* there is the contingency of *yaṇādeśa* in the instance *Madhu + ṅakāriyati* and the like. With regard to *pratyāhāras* like *haś yaṅ val,* etc. the anubandhas for example *ṭ ṇ* etc. will never be included in the same for the simple reason that they are uttered in the *Śivasūtras* as being devoid of a vowel which is generally added to consonants for the convenience of utterance. All the consonants desired to be included in *pratyābhāras* are uttered with a vowel. NBh says that all these facts amount to show why the question of non-inclusion of *anubandhas* is concerned with the *pratyāhāra ac* alone.

NBh points out another significance of this question. This question shows that vowel *ā* in the *laṇ sūtra* is not an *anubandha.* If it were so the questionm of its non-inclusion in pratyāhāras like *haś yaṇ* etc. ought to be discussed. Since Pat has not done so, it comes out that the vowel *ā* in *laṇ* is never an *anubandha.*

6. *"Kim punar idam tadbhāvitagrahaṇam, vṛddhirityevam ye ākāraikāraukārā bhāvyante teṣām grahaṇam āhosvid ādaijmātrasya".*[38]

Pat advances this question under the rule, *"vṛddhirādaic"* (1-1-1). It is doubted whether the term *vṛddhi* denotes only such *ā ai* and *au* that are enjoined by rules using the term *vṛddhi* or all of them irrespective of their status as being enjoined by rules or otherwise. NBh explain the basis for these two views. It is found that the term *luk ślu* and *lup* relate to the *adarśana* which occurs as a result of rules using the term *luk ślu* and *lup* alone. But the term *lopa* relates to the *adarśana* of any sound that is caused by rules without using any particular term. Hence the doubt as to whether the term *vṛddhi* denotes *tadbhāvita* alone as in the case with the term *luk* and the doubt as to whether it denotes all, as the term *lopa* does. NBh continues that the term '*ṭi*' denotes that particular portion, beginning with the last vowel, in any sound. The term '*ghu*' is enjoined to any sound having the *svarūpa* of *dā* or *dhā*. These terms thus denote only the *atadbhāvita*. Hence a doubt as to whether the term *vṛddhi* denotes only such *ā ai* and *au* that are originally there in words, may also seem to be relevant here. NBh points out that Pat does never advance such a doubt here. This is because with regard to the term like *ṭi*', '*ghu*', etc. a portion beginning with the last vowel or the *svarūpa* of '*dā*' '*dhā*' is not enjoined anywhere by any rule. Therefore in the absence of *tadbhāvita* there can be the denotation of *atadbhāvita* alone by the term '*ghu*'. But with regard to the term *vṛddhi* the case is different. In certain words like *mārṣṭi daityaḥ* and *aupagavaḥ ā, ai* and *au are enjoined by rules namely "mṛjervṛddhiḥ"* (7-2-114) *"taddhiteṣvacāmadeḥ"* (7-2-117) using the term *vṛddhi*. In bases like *bāla rai* and *glau* the *ā, ai* and *au* are originally there. So there being both *tadbhāvita* and *atadbhāvita*, the doubt naturally arises as to whether the term *vṛddhi* denotes *tadbhāvita* alone or both of them. He then adds that if it be *tadbhāvitagrahaṇa* we have to accept the mention of the word *vṛddhi* in rules like *"mṛjervṛddhiḥ" (7-2-114) to be tantra nirdeśa*. If it be *atadbhāvitagrahaṇa* there is no such necessity.

7. *"evam tarhi vṛddhir bhavati guṇo bhavatīti yatra bruyātika ityetattatropasthitam draṣṭavyam"*[39]

NBh points out that there is a maxim *"anuvāde paribhāṣā nopatiṣṭhate.*[40] Though this maxim has not been orally stated anywhere by Pat it is this passage that forms the source of this maxim and gives its scope. The above passage occurs under the rule *"iko guṇavṛddhī"* (1-1-3) after the refutation of the view that the rule is *taccheṣa* or *tadapavāda*. It means that "if so whenever it is said that *vṛddhi* appears or *guṇa* appears one should take that the word *ikaḥ* presents itself."

NBh says that in the said rule there is the word *'guṇavṛddhī'* and there are also the words *guṇaḥ* and *vṛddhiḥ* got by *anuvṛtti.*[41] If these only be the words got by *anuvṛtti,.* the rule is liable to mean "where there is the sound *guṇa* and *vṛddhi* there the word *ikaḥ* presents itself". This is because the words got by *anuvṛtti* denote in the previous rule the sounds *guṇa* and *vṛddhi.* Consequently there is the contingency of the supply of the word *ikaḥ* to rules like *"ato guṇe"* (6-1-97), where there is the sound *guṇa,* though the rule does not enjoin *guṇa.* However one cannot say that the words got by *anuvṛtti* denote the sense, since it involves an effort of *śabdādhikāra.*[42] Therefore as a result of the words got by *anuvṛtti* and the word *guṇavṛddhī* present in the rule we get the sense *guṇaśabdavān guṇaḥ* and *vṛddhiśabdavatī vṛddhiḥ.* We accept the predicate here to be *bhavati* which denotes the sense of *vidhīyate.* We cannot take the predicate it to be *vartate,* since the rule may mean *"yatra guṇaśabdavān guṇaḥ vartate tatra ikaḥ ityetad upatiṣṭhate"* and to arrive at such a sense there is no need of the mention of the word *'guṇavṛddhī'* in this rule in addition to the ones got by *anuvṛtti.* Moreover *'bhavatikriyā'* is *antaraṅga* than *astikriyā.*[43] Therefore also, the predicate ought to be *bhavati.* Thus the rule means where *guṅa* and *vṛddhi* are prescribed by the terms *guṇa* and *vṛddhi* there the word *'ikaḥ'* presents itself. The *paribhāṣā sūtra "iko guṇavṛddhī"* does not therefore supply the word *'ikaḥ'* to rules like *"ato guṇe"* (6-1-97) where *guṇa* is only *'anuvādya'* and not 'vidheya'. This paves the way for the maxim *'vidhau paribhāṣopatiṣṭhate nānuvāde'.* Thus NBh points out that it is the mention of the word *guṇavṛddhī* in the rule in addition to the words got by *anuvṛtii* that becomes the source of the said maxim. Based on the same reason, this maxim relates to the rules *"iko guṇavṛddhi"* (1-1-3) and *"acaśca"* (1-2-28) among which the latter supplies the word *acaḥ* to rules that enjoin *hrasva dīrgha* and *pluta* by using the same terms.

8. *"ādeśastarhīme bhaviṣyanti anāgamakānām sāgamakāḥ tat katham? sarve sarvapadādeśā dākṣīputrasya pāṇineḥ/ ekadeśavikāre hi nityatvam nopapadyate".*[44]

Under the rule *"dādhāghvadāp"* (1-1-19), Pat says that an augment is taken to be the very part of the original to which it is enjoined. A doubt in regard to the propriety of the prescription of augments to sounds which are *nitya* and should be made up of letters everexisting, undying and not allowing elision, augmentation and substitution. To the counter-question whether the prescription of substitutes, to sounds, which are nitya is proper, it is answered that it is quite correct. Substitutes should be taken here as different śabdas and it is but proper that the substitute becomes the object of cognition instead of the original. Now Pat removing the doubt in regard to the propriety of the prescription of augment, says, "In that case, words with *āgama* replace those without *āgama*. How is it? In the opinion of Pāṇini,. the son of *Dākṣī*, all are the *ādeśas* of all the padas, for the *nityatva* will be marred even if there is slight change (of the word)."

NBh elucidates this passage which deals with the substitutes. It is pointed out here that the there is no impropreity in their prescription since there is only change of cognition of the original and substitute. It is to be understood that augments though enjoined as additional elements to sounds, are alike substitutes. As a result of the *ekavakyatā* of the ruels *"ārdhadhātukasyeḍvalādeḥ"* (7-2-35) and *"ādyantau" ṭakitau"* (1-1-46) one may derive the idea that the *ārdhadhātuka* suffixes like *tavya* are added with the element *'i'* at the beginning. But as this is contradictory to the *nityatva* of sounds, the idea that instead of the cognition of the suffix *tavya* the cognition of the sufgfix *itavya* is to be accepted, is arrived at. Hence as in the case of substitutes, here also there is only change of cognition and not any addition of new elements to sounds. Considering that, instead of the cognition of the suffix *tavya*, we get the cognition of a sound *itavya* which has an element *'i'* at its beginning, the *'i'* can be named as augment. Therefore the contention that if change of cognition is accepted with regard to augments, there will not be anything which can be called augment, is baseless.

NBh then elucidates the verse which is the basis for the acceptance of change of cognition in instances where substitutes and augments are enjoined. Though rules like *"eruḥ"* (3-4-86) enjoin the substitution by *'u'* of the final element *'i'* of the termination *ti*, there is the acceptance of *sthānyādeśabhāva* between the two wholes i.e, between *ti* and *tu* as otherwise it is contradictory to the *nityatva* of sounds. Similarly though augments are enjoined as additional elements to sounds there is the acceptance of *sthanyādeśabhāva* between the sound devoid of the augment and the sound having the augment, i.e, between *tavya* and *itavya*, and hence augments too can be designated as *ādeśas* *though not primarily but secondarily, so that nityatva* of sounds may not be contradicted. Again with regard to substitutes, though a *sthānyādeśabhāva* between *ti* and *tu* is conceived, the direct relation of *sthānyadeśa* between *i* and *u* is never left out and that is why rules like *"acaḥ parasmin pūrvavidhau"* (1-1-57) enjoin the *sthānivadbhāva* of the substitute that replace an element i.e, vowel. Similarly though augments are secondarily treated as substitutes, *stānivadbhāva* does not relate to *itavya* and *tavya* as the element i is always the component element of *tavya* and there the maxim *"yadāgamāḥ...."* i.e 'an augment is taken not to vary from the original', operates, and in the rule enjoining *sthānivadbhāva,* there is the word *sthānivat* which relates only to the originals like *i* pointed out by the rule *"eruḥ"* (3-4-86) and so on.

9. *"Bhavateścāpi na vaktavyaḥ; astisico'pṛkte iti dviśakārako nirdeśaḥ asteḥ sakārāntād iti".*[45]

Under the rule *"sthānivad ādeśo 'nalvidhau'* (1-1-56) vārttikakāra points out 13 defects caused by *sthānivadbhāva*. One among them is that in the form *'abhūt'* there is the contingency of the augment *'iṭ'* to the termination *t* on account of *sthānivadbhāva*. The root *as* in the aorist first person singular, becomes *"as + ti"* and takes *sic* after it. The root gets the substitute *bhū* by the rule *"asterbhūḥ* (2-4-52) and the augment *aṭ* by the rule *"luṅlaṅlṛṅṣvaḍudāttaḥ"*. (6-4-71). A stage like *a+bhū+s+ti* is arrived at. *Sic* as well as the vowel of the termination elides on the strength of the rules *"gātisthāghupābhūbhyaḥ...."* (2-4-77) and *"itaśaca"* (3-4-100). In the resultant form *a+bhū+t*, the substitute *bhū* may be treated as *'as'* on account of *sthānivadbhāva* and hence there is the contingency of the augment *iṭ* to the termination *t* by the rule *"astisico'pṛkte"* (7-3-96). Hence *vārttikakāra* argues that *sthānivadbhāva* need be prohibited in this instance. Refuting this Pat says "It (the prohibition of *sthānivadbhāva)* need not be mentioned with reference to *bhū* also. The *sūtra astiscio'pṛkte"* (7-3-96) is read with two *sakāras*, so that it may mean 'after the root *as* which ends in *s*'.

Elucidating this assertion, NBh says that the form of the rule read with two *sakāras is 'astissico'pṛkte'*. If the rule is read in some other way as possessed of two *sakāras*, the significance of the word *'nirdeśaḥ'* shall be lost.[46] NBh says that *vārttikakāra* too favours this form of the rule. In this case the *s* can be treated as an adjunct of *sic* and so in instances where there is the elision of *sic*, there cannot be *iḍāgama* since even by *pratyayalakṣaṇa* or *sthānivadbhāva* we cannot get a *sic* which ends in *s*. That is why *vārttikakāra* does advance the necessity to prohibit *pratyalakṣaṇa* or *sthānivadbhāva* in instances where *sic* has been elided. NBh says that the rule therefore being *"astissico'pṛkte*, Pat has resorted to its relation with both, namely *asti* and *sic* in the rule. This is by what is known as *madhyamaṇiṇyāya*. Just as a gem in the midst of a garland beautifies both the strings on either side, so also the *s* between *asti* and *sicas* in the rule refers to both the root *as* and the suffix *sic*.

Establishment of Ekadeśibhāṣya

The *Mbh* of Pat seems, on its surface, to be an easy book as the discussions therein take the form of a dialogue and are full of short questions and answers of charming and short sentences possessed of simple words. But it will be bewildering and confusing when questions and answers coming from various members of a debate as it were, are alone given without specifying the person from whom the assertions come. Again in certain instances more than one solution is offered to solve a particular problem. Among them, some solutions though they establish the *siddhānta* in the particular context are contradictory to the statements of Pat elsewhere. So also on certain rules Pat makes certain assertions whereas quite an opposite idea is established elsewhere. In such isntances one is at a loss to know for certain, the idea actually favoured by Pat.[47] The elucidiation of the passages of *Mbh* becomes perfect only when passages which present an ambiguity as such or otherwise,. are specified on the basis of sound reasoning, to be that of *siddhāntin* or that of *siddhāntyekadeśin*. This factor has also been given due attention by NBh, in his elucidative assertions of the text of *Mbh*.

1. *"Athavaikayogaḥ kariṣyate, 'vṛddhirādaijaden guṇaḥ' tataḥ 'iko guṇavṛddhī, iti. na caikayoge'nuvṛttir bhavati"*[48]

In the bhāṣya under the rule *"iko guṇavṛddhī"* (1-1-3) the *anuvṛtti* of the word *vṛddhiḥ* is sought in the *sūtra "iko guṇavṛddhī"* from the sūtra *"vṛddhirādaic"* (1-1-1). The *pūrvapakṣin* raises the objection that in that case, invariably there shall be the *anuvṛtti* of the word *vṛddhiḥ* in the intermediate *sūtra "aden guṇaḥ"* (1-1-2) and so the term *vṛddhi* is liable to be connected with *aden* also. Pat offers six solutions to avoid the connection of the term *vṛddhiḥ* with *aden* and thus establishes that there is no contingency of *aden* being designated as *vṛddhiḥ*. The above passage is one among these six. It means "ōr else it shall be made an *ekayoga* namely *"vṛddhirādaijaden guṇaḥ"*. Next, *"iko guṇavṛddhī"*. There cannot be *anuvṛtti* in an *ekayoga*". the import of the passage is as follows. The two rules *"vṛddhirādaic"* (1-1-1) and *"adenguṇaḥ"* (1-1-2) are to be treated as a single rule namely *'vṛddhirādaijadenguṇaḥ'*. As it is now a single rule, there cannot be the *anuvṛtti* of the word *vṛddhiḥ* in the part *'Adenguṇaḥ'* of the same rule. This is because by mentioning the word *tad* a second time in the rule *"tad adhīte tad veda"* (4-2-59), it is made known that there cannot be the *anuvṛtti* of a word from the part of a rule in another part of the same rule. Otherwise the repetition of the word *tad* in the said sūtra is prone to be to be effete. This fact has been pointed out by Pat under the rule *"tad asminnastīti deśe tannāmni"* (4-2-67).

But NBh points out that one has to accept the *anuvṛtti* of a word in an *ekayoga* on the authority of Pat's final statement on the said point under the same rule and so the passage here is to be treated as that of *siddhāntyekadeśin.*[49] There Pat has stated that since in the rule *"tadasyāstyasminniti matup"* (5-2-94) which enjoins the suffix *matup* in the sense of *tad asya asti* and *tad asmin asti,* the word *tad* is mentioned only once, it follows that there can be the *anuvṛtyti* of a word in an *ekayoga.*[50] Pat has added that the repetition of the word *tad* in the rule *"tad adhīte tadveda"* (4-2-59) is only for the clear grasping of the meaning by students. NBh therefore comes to the conclusion that the above passage, *'athavā...bhavati'* is to be treated to be that of *ekadeśin* and not that of the *siddhāntin.* However since the solution helps to establish that there will not be the connection of the term *'vriddhiḥ'* with *aden* and admits the *anuvṛtti* of the word *vṛddhiḥ* in the rule *"Iko guṇavṛddhī"* and the same being the *siddhānta,* the passage is reasonably characterised by NBh as coming from the mouth of *siddhāntyekadeśin.*

2. *"Lakṣaṇam hi nāma dhvanati bhramati muhūrtam api nāvatiṣṭhate"*[51]

Under the rule *"Iko guṇavṛddhī"* it is argued that the rule must necessarily present the word *ikaḥ* to the rule *"sici vṛddhiḥ parasmaipadeśu"* (7-2-1) as otherwise a consonant at the end of an *aṅga* followed by *sic* is liable to undergo substitution by *vṛddhi* in instance like *abhaitsīt* and *achaitsīt.*[52] The *pūrvapakṣin* says that the rule *'vadavrajahalantasyācaḥ'* (7-2- 3) will cause *i* to be substituted by *vṛddhi* and save the consonant *d* from being susbtituted by *vṛddhi*. Now, again it is argued that in instances like *akoṣīt*[53] where the rule *'vadavrajahalantasyācaḥ'* is superseded by the rule *"neṭi"* (7-1-4) the rule *"sici vṛddhiḥ parasmaipadeṣu"* may cause the consonant *s* to be substituted by *vṛddhi*. To this answer given is that the Rule *Neṭi* forbids the rule *"sici vṛddhiḥ parasmaipadeṣu"* also. The reason is given in the passage *"lakṣaṇam hi nā nāma dhvanati bhramati muhūrtampai nāvatiṣṭhate"*. (The Rule *(Niṣedha)* suggests vaguely, wanders everywhere and does not stand still for a moment). NBh states that the assertion here that the rule *"neṭi"* (7-2-4) prohibits the *vṛddhi* enjoined by the rules *"vadavrajahalantasyācaḥ"* and *"sici vṛddhiḥ parasmaipadeṣu"* as well, is in accordance with the view known as *'bādhyasāmānyacintā'* i.e., the general consideration of what must be superseded, whatever it may be. He points out this view with regard to the rule *"neṭi* is that of the *ekadeśin* and not of the *siddhāntin*. This is because in the ensuing discussion that the rule *"iko guṇavṛddhi"* ought to present the word *ikaḥ* to the rule *"sici vṛddhiḥ parasmpaipadeṣu"* in order to bring the same under the scope of the prohibition enjoined by the rule *"kṅiti ca"* (1-1-5), instances like *nyastārīt* and *nyadārīt*[54] are cited and it is stated that if *antaraṅga kārya* namely *guṇa* operated[55] formerly than the *vṛddhi* caused by *sic*, the forms would become only as *nyastarīt* and *nyadarīt* and now the rule *"sici vṛddhiḥ parasmaipadeṣu"* cannot operate on the *a* before *r,* since *a* is not the final element of the *aṅga*. The rule *"vadavrajahalantasyacaḥ"* cannot cause the *a* before *r* to be substituted by *vṛddhi* since the same is prohibited by the rule *"neṭi"*. If the rule *"neṭi"* were to prohibit the *vṛddhi* enjoined by both the rules *"sici vṛddhiḥ parasmaipadeṣu"* and *"vadavrajahalantasyacah* this assertion will be contradicted. Hence NBh says the view, that the said rule prohibits both on the basis of the view point known as *'badhyasāmānyacintā'*, is that of *ekadeśin*.

3. *"Athavā sici vrddhiḥ parasmpaipadeṣu iti sici vṛddhiḥ prāpnoti. Tasyā halantalakṣanā vṛddhir bādhikā tasyā api neṭi iti pratiṣedhaḥ"*[56]

This passage immediately follows the passage *'lakṣaṇam...'* dealt with just above. There it is pointed out that based on the view *'bhādhyasāmānyacintā* the rule *"neṭi"* (7-1-4) is stated as preventing the *vṛddhi* enjoined by both the rules *"sici vṛddhiḥ parasmaipadeṣu"* (7-2-1) and *"vadavrajahalantasyācaḥ"* (7-2-3). In the passage based on the view i.e. *bādhyaviśeṣacintā* (the consideration of what particular rule is to be superseded) a different solution is given to prevent the *s* of the root *kuṣ* from being substituted by *vṛddhi*. The passage means *'Or vṛddhi* before *sic* is enjoined by the *sūtra "sici vṛddhiḥ parasmaipadeṣu"*, it has its *apavāda* in the *sūtra "vadavrajahalantasyācah"* and it has its *apavāda* in *"neṭi"*. the idea is that when the rule *"vadavrajahalantasyācaḥ"*, which is the *apavāda* of and hence supersedes the rule *"sici vṛddhiḥ parasmaipadeṣu"* is prohibited by the rule *"neṭi"*, the general rule *"sici vṛddhiḥ"* is also automatically prohibited by the same rule *"neṭi"*. Instances like *'sujāte eśvasūnṛte'* where the dipthong followed by vowel when prohibited on the strentgh of the rule *"nāntaḥ pādam avyapare"* (6-1-115) from *pūrvarūpa* enjoined by the rule *"eṅaḥ padāntād ati"* (6-1-109) are prohibited from being substituted by *ay* which is enjoined by the rule *"ecoyavāyaḥ"* (6-1-78). NBh says that this kind of thought is according to the *nyāya* known as *'bhraṣṭāvasaro na pravartate'*. But the fact that when *pūrvarūpa* is prohibited, *ayādeśa* too is consequently prohibited, cannot be accepted. This is because Pāṇ has made usages like *'saṅghoddhau'*[57] and *'tau'*[58]. In these expressions the *aṅga* ending in *a* is followed by the dual suffix *'au'* and there the rule *"nāaici"* (6-1-102) which is the *apavāda* of the rule *"prathamayohpūrvasavarṇah"* has opperated. But however *"nādici"* has not prohibited the rule *'vṛddhireci'* since in the said expressions *vṛddhi* is found taking place. If the said maxim were resorted to by Pāṇ these expressions of his cannot be explained. Hence on the authority of these expressions it is undersetood that the maxim *bhraṣṭāvasaro na pravartate,* according to which something does not take place when the occasion for the taking place of it has once gone by, is not resorted to in the science of grammer by Pāṇ. In the instance *'sujāte asvasūnṛte'* the dipthong does not undergo the substitution by *ay.* This is not because of *bhraṣṭavasaranyāya* but because of the fact that there is the *anuvṛtti* of the word *eṅah* in the rule *"nantaḥ pādam avyapare"* (6-1-115) and the rule means that whatever is contingent to substitute a dipthong preceded by *a,* is prohibited. Hence NBh says that this assertion is that of *ekadeśin.*

4. The problem of sthānivadbhāva of the substitute that replace laṅ, luṅ and lṛṅ.

After the discussiuon of the essentiality of the insertion of the word *nimitta* in the rule *"kṅiti ca"* (1-1-5) a contingency[59] is brought to the attention, that the substitute *mip* that replaces *laṅ, liṅ, luṅ* and *lṛṅ* attains the status of *ṅit* by means of *sthānivadbhāva* and thereby it may prevent on the strength of the rule *"kṅiti ca"* (1-1-5) the *guṅa* on the final element of the *aṅga* in the stage *aci+nu+am*[60] during the process of formation of words like *acinavam*[61] and so on. The solution gfiven is that the *ṅitva* assigned by the rule *"yāsuṭ parasmaipadeṣūdātto ṅicca"* (3-4-103) to *yāsuṭ* which is the augment of the substitute of *liṅ,* brings forth the remedy. The assignment of *ṅitva* to *yāsuṭ* which is augment of the substitute of *liṅ,* is futile as it cannot make the substitute (here the *āgamin) ṅit.* Besides, the susbtitue of *liṅ* is already *ṅit* by way of *sthānivadbhāva.* Hence the same indicates that no substitute of *ṅit* can, by virtue of the *ṅitva* obtained by *sthānivadbhāva,* cause any operation on that which follows the referred to susbtitute, however, the substitute *ṅit* can bring forth any operation caused by *ṅitva* itself.

In the context *guṅa* is an operation on the final element of the *aṅga* and so it is unwarranted by the *ṅitva,* derived by *sthānivadbhāva* on the substitute. Anyhow in forms like *acinot* and *acinva*[62] the *lopa* of the *i* and *s* of *ti* and *vas* (*the parasmaipada* terminations) respectively are operations on the substiute itself. The *ṅitva*, by means of *sthānivadbhāva* being alert in such cases, brings forth *lopa* on the strength of the rules *"itaśca"* (3-4-10) and *"nityam ṅitaḥ"* (3-4- 99). NBh points out that the question of the contingency pointed out above is prompted by the *ekadeśin* (*pūrvapakṣyekadeśin)* and the answer too comes from the mouth of the *siddhyāntyekadeśin*. This is because Pat has framed the formula *"pit ṅinna bhavati"* and *"ṅit pinna bhavati"*. Therefore, in instances like *acinavam* the substitute *mip* being originally *pit* can never be *ṅit* even if there be *sthānivadbhāva* and so there is no contingency of the prohibition of *guṇa* on the basis of *ṅitva*. Similarly the removal of this contingency resorting to an indication too cannot stand careful scrutiny. this is because NBh says that, there is no inefficacy of *ṅitva* to give rise to an indication. The *ṅitva* of *yāsut* is fruitful, in spite of the *ṅitva* of the substitute. During the process of formation of words like *stuyāt*[63] a stage like *stu* + *yā* + *t*[64] the part *yāt* is contingent to bring forth, on the strength of the rule *ūto vrddhir luki hali"* (7-3-89) *vṛddhi* on the vowel *u*. This *vṛddhi* is not *iglakṣana* so as to be prevented by *ṅitva* on the strength of the rule *"kṅiti ca"* (1-1-5). In such circumstances the assignment of *ṅitva* to *yāsuṭ* which is the augment of a *ṅit* substitute serves the purpose of prohibiting the *vṛddhi* even though the same is not *iglakṣana*. The *ṅitva* of *yāsut* is fruitful in another respect also. It prevents the *guṇa* caused by the rule *"Jusi ca"* (7-3- 85) in forms like *cinuyuḥ*.[65]

Here the *ṅitva* derived by *sthānivadbhāva* on the substitute cannot prevent the *guṇa*, since *"Jusi ca"* (7-3-85) is a rule that supersedes the rule *"kṅiti ca"* (1-1-5). Therefore it can be said that to defeat the rule *"jusi ca"* (7-3-85) *ṅitva* is enjoined to an already *ṅit* substitute and by this reaffirmation of *ṅitva*, *guṇa* is prevented by the rule *"kṅiti ca"* and the rule *"jusi ca"* (7-3- 85) does not supersede it. Thus no indication can be made since the basis of the same i.e., the inefficacy of the *ṅitva* of *yāsuṭ*, is lacking here. Therefore the answer too based on this indication is that of the *ekadeśin*. However it must be remembered that in view of the *siddhāntin* who maintains the statement *"ṅit pinna bhavati"*, the *yāsuṭ being ṅit* cannot be treated as *pit*. The Rule *'uto vṛddhir luki hali"* (7-3-89) will not therefore operate on the *u* of *stu* since the same is followed by *yāsuṭ* which is *ṅit* and not *pit*. With regard to the form *cinuyuḥ* there is no contingency of *guṇa* since the rule *"jusi ca"* (7-3-85) by the *anuvṛtti* of the word *aci* from the rule *"ksyasyāci"* (7-3-72) enjoins *guṇa* only when the *ik* is followed by the suffix *jus* beginning with a vowel and in *cinuyuḥ* the suffix *jus* as is possessed of the augment *yāsuṭ*, is devoid of *ajāditva* and the rule does not operate here. Thus it is clear that the conception of Pat *"ṅicca pinna, picca ṅinna"* avoids the complication in the event of the *sthānivad-bhāva* of the substitutes of *laṅ*. The solution on the basis of indication too cannot be correct since it is pointed out above that no such indication is possible. Hence NBh concludes that this passage suspecting this contingency and giving the solution for the same is that of *ekadeśin*.

5. *"ārdhadhātukasyeḍ valādeḥ ityatra iḍityanuvartamāne punariḍgrahaṇasya prayojanam ideva yathā syād yad anyat prāpnoti tan mā bhūditi"*[66]

In the *bhāṣya* under the rule *"dīdhīvevīṭam"* (1-1-6) just after the establishment of the idea that the roots *"didhī"* and *vevī* need not be mentioned in the rule, there is a statement *'iṭaścāpi grahaṇam śakyamakartum'* which means, 'The mention of the augment *iṭ* in the *sūtra* also can be dispensed with." To the subsequent question how the forms *akaṇiṣam, araṇiṣam, kaṇitā* and *raṇitā* wherein *iṭ* is contingent to undergo *guṇa*, can be explained in the absence of the prohibition of *guṇa* to it by this rule; the answer is given, "when it is possible to take *iṭ* by *anuvṛtti*, *Paṇini* has read *iṭ* in the rule *"ārdhadhātukasyeḍ valādeḥ"*. The motive underlying it is that it should stand as *iṭ* under any circumstance and should never change into another. What can come instead? *guṇa*". The idea is that the *anuvṛtti* of the word *iṭ* from the rule *"neḍvaśikṛti"* (7-2-8) is quite possible, to the rule *"ārdhadhātukasyeḍvalāḥ"* (7-2-35), and the mention of *iṭ* in the latter rule is an excess. There is no room for the apprehension that in the absence of the word *iṭ* in the latter rule the word *na* also, from the rule *"neḍvaśi kṛti"* (4-2-8) along with *iṭ* is due in the rule *"ārdhadhātukasyeḍvalaādeḥ"* (7-2-35) by way of *anuvṛtti*. This is because on the basis of the maxim *'kvacid ekadeśo'pyanuvartate'*, it can be taken by *anuvṛtti*. Hence the excess mention of *iṭ* in the rule specifies the fact that it will ever be retained as *iṭ* and as such no change like substitution by *guṇa* occurs on it. Therefore on the basis of this *niyama* the mention of the word *iṭ* in the rule, to serve the purpose that *guṇa* may be prohibited to *iṭ*, can be dispensed with.

After thus explaining the passage NBh establishes that this view is that of *ekadeśin*. He points out that the refutation of the mention of *iṭ* in the rule *"dīdhāveviṭām"* (1-1-6) is made on the strength of the mention of the same in the rule *ārdhadhātukasyeḍ valādeḥ* (7-2-35) whereas the mention of *iṭ* in the said rule is refuted by Pat under the rule *"neḍvaśi kṛti"* (7-2-8) on the strength of the mention of *iṭ* in the rule *"neḍvaśi kṛti"* (7-2- 8). It is quite clear that these two refutations are not independent and only one of them can be explained. Hence the problem arises as to which one among the refutations of the word *iṭ* in the two rules namely *"ārdhadhātukasyeḍvalādeḥ"* and *"dīdhīveviṭāam"* (1-1-6) is favoured by Pat. NBh's keen intellect discerns lack of effort in the refutation of the mention of the word *iṭ* in the rule *"ārdhadhātukasyeḍ valādeḥ"* (7-2-35). In order to refute the mention of *iṭ* in the rule *"dīdhīveviṭām"* (1-1-6) one has to resort to the *niyama* whereas the refutation of the same in the rule *"ārdhadhātukasyeḍ valādeḥ"* (7-2-35) never involves such a necessity.

Again in the existence of the *niyama* as such, it is difficult to get the lengthening of *iṭ* in frorms like *"pipaṭhīh"*[67] To remove this difficulty a clause has to be added in the *niyama* that operations that are *āṅga* i.e, taught in *aṅgādhikāra* alone, are prevented to *iṭ*. It is noteworthy that the word *āṅga* cannot ordinarily convey the sense 'taught in *aṅgādhikāra*'. NBh continues that if in order to obtain the lengthening of *iṭ*, the rule *"pūrvatrāsiddham"* (8-2-1) is resorted to and hence the lengthening enjoined by the rule in *tripādi* becomes null and void in the point of view of the *niyama* which falls within the scope of *sapādasaptādhyayī*, there is yet the difficulty to get the substitution by *savarṇadīrgha* of *iṭ* in instances like *alāvīt*[68] since *savarṇadīrgha* that operates on *iṭ* is enjoined in the *sapādasaptādhyāyī* and cannot be null and void in the view of the *niyama*. Hence to bring forth *savarṇadīrgha* on *iṭ* in the said instance at the existence of the *niyama*, there is yet the cumbrousness of resorting to the vārttika *"sijlopa ekādeśe siddho vaktavyaḥ"*. One has to say that *savarṇadīrgha* will substitute *iṭ* in spite of the *niyama*, since it is in order to secure *savarṇadīrgha,* the *vārttika* declares the elision of *sic* as known to *savarṇadīrgha.* Thus it can be seen that refutation of the *iḍgrahaṇa* of the rule *"dīdhīvevīṭam"* (1-1-6) is arduous and the refutation of the same in the rule *"ārdhadhātukasyeḍ valādeḥ"* (7-2-35) involves no effort. NBh, therefore, comes to the conclusion that the discussion and establishment of the assertion that *'iṭascapi grahaṇam śakyamakartum'* is that of *ekadesin.*

6. "samjñādhikāro'yam ādyantau ceha samkīrtyate takārakakāravitāvudādriyete. Tatrādyantayoṣṭakārakaravitāau samjñe bhaviṣyataḥ. Tatra ārdhadhātukasyeḍ valādeḥ ityupasthitamidam bhavati ādiriti. tenekarādirādeso bhaviṣyati"[69]

Under the rule *"ādyantau ṭakitau"* (1-1-46) there is the discussion as to whether the *ṭit* and *kit* that respectively occur at *ādi* and *anta,* are *āgamas* or *ādesas.* To the answer that they are *āgamas,* the propriety of the prescription itself of *āgamas* to sabdas which are *nitya,* is questioned. It is replied that the same is certainly proper since *ādesas* are sabdas, which are different from sabdas which are *sthānin* and by prescribing *ādesas,* in instances where the *sthānisabda* chances to be the object of cognition, *Pāṇ* allows the *adeśaśabda* to be the object of cognition. The question doubting the propriety of the prescription of *āgamas* to *śabdas* that are *nitya* remains as such and it is answered by Pat as *'ādeśātarhīme bhaviṣyanti anāgamakānām sāgamakā ādeśāḥ'* NBh points out that this statement has already been dealt with in the *bhāṣya,* under the rule *"dādhāghvadāp"* (1-1-19)[70]. It follows that when a suffix like *tavya* chances to be the object of cognition, *Pāṇ* by the rule *"ārdhadhātukasyeḍ valādeḥ"* (7-2-35) allows the form *itavya* to be the object of cognition. Hence it is with forgetfulness that the following question *tat katham',* is raised and an answer is given to it.

NBh specifies the answer to be the assertion of *ekadeśin.* The answer is as follows. "The *sūtra* is within the the section where samjnas are enjoined.

The expression *ādyantau* is mentioned first and *ṭakāra* and *kakāra* which are *it* are mentioned next. Hence *ṭakara* which is *it* and *kakāra* which is *it* are respectively the *samjñas* of *ādi* and *anta.* When the *sūtra ārdhadhātukasyeḍ valādeḥ"* has to operate, it means *ikārādi* and hence the word which has *i* at the commencement becomes the *ādeśa* to the same word which does not have *i*. This assertion means that the expression *iṭ* is a *bahuvrīhi* compound and means a substitute which has *'i'* as the former element. The idea is that the suffix *tavya* gets the substitute *itavya*. NBh argues that if *'ṭ'* and *k* are the *samjña* of *ādi* and *anta* there is no necessity of their being an *it*. So the word *itau* in the rule *ādyantau ṭakitau* becomes futile. The rule need only be *ṭakau*. Moreover, as *'ṭ'* denotes the word *ādi* and *k* denotes the word *anta*, the *ṭuk* enjoined by the rule *"ṅṇoh kukṭuk śari"* (8-3-28) would be defective since it possesses both *ṭ* and *k*. There is thus the contingency of *ṭuk* being alternatively the former and final element. Thus being defective, this assertion is that of *ekadeśin*, says NBh.

Moreover taking *ṭ* to be the *samjña* of *ādi*, the *ekadeśin* adds that in the rule *"luṅaṅlṛṅsvaḍudāttaḥ"* (6-4-71) the part *aḍudāttaḥ* is a *tripada bahuvrīhi* and means *'akāraḥ ṭ (ādiḥ) udāttaḥ yasya'*. Though in the rule *"āḍajādīnām"* (6-4-72) such an explanation cannot be given, there is no harm since this rule has been discarded by the vārttika *'ajādīnām aṭā siddham'*. NBh points out that the *sūtrakāra* who has framed the rule *"āḍajādīnām"* (6-4-72) would never have dreamt of such a *samjñā* and that is why another answer which is in concordance with the statement *anāgamakānām sāgamakā ādeśāḥ* is given next by the *siddhāntin*. Hence this assertion is definitely that of *ekadeśin*.

7. *"Yadyevam adeso 'visesito bhavati, ādeśaśca viśeṣtaḥ katham dvitīyam sthānegrahaṇam prakṛtamanuvartate. Tatraivamabhisambandhaḥ kariṣyate 'uḥ sthāne aṇ sthāne uḥ prasaṅge aṇ prasajyamāna eva raparo bhavati'"*[71]

In the rule *"uraṇ raparaḥ"* (1-1-51) Pat says that *aṇ* which has a chance to replace *ṛ*, is followed by *r*. To the question whether a statement to this effect is to be newly made, Pat points out that there is no such necessity since the idea is meant by the rule itself as there is the *anuvṛtti* of the word *sthāne* form the rule *"ṣaṣthīsthāneyogā"* (1-1-49). Now a difficulty is pointed out "If so the *ādeśa* is devoid of the restrictive adjunct". This assertion means that the word *sthāne* got by *anuvṛtti* relates to the word *uḥ* in the rule in which case the rule will mean that the *aṇ* that replace *ṛ* is followed by *r* and so, the idea that *aṇ* which chances to replace *ṛ* is followed by *ṛ*, is not derived. Or if the word *sthāne* relates to the substitute *aṇ* which chances to replace *r* and so the *niyama* that the *aṇ* which chances to replace *r* alone, becomes *rapara,* is not understood. Thus this assertion takes for granted that the *paribhaṣā* rule "*ṣaṣṭhīsthāneyogā*" (1-1-49) does not present itself here in spite of the genitive case and this is due to the fact that *'vidhau paribhāṣopatiṣṭhate nānuvāde'*. A *paribhāṣā* presents itself only when there is *vidhi* and in the rule "*uraṇ raparaḥ*" (1-1-51) since it does not enjoin any thing in the place of *ṛ*, the genitive case in *uḥ* is only *anuvāda* and hence the maxim *ṣaṣthīsthāneyogā* does not operate there. Hence by the *anuvṛtii* of the word *sthāne*, only one word *sthāne* is got. This is clear from the answer "*ādeśa* too has the restrictive adjunct. In what manner? There is here the *anuvṛtti* of another (second) *sthāne* (from the rule "*sthānentaratamaḥ*) (1-1-50) and the sentence is thus construed i.e, *ūḥ sthāne aṇ sthāne*" which means the *aṇ* which has a chance to replace *ṛvarṇa* in the course of happening is followed by *r*." NBh points out that these two assertions are of the *ekadeśin* since the rule "*śaṣṭhīsthāneyogā*" operates in *anuvāda* also. For example in the rule *ūdāttāsvaritayor yaṇaḥ savarito'nudāttasya" (8-2-4) the genitive case is anuvāda* since the word relates to *yaṇaḥ* and not to the *vidheya* of the rule, namely *svarita.* So also in the rule "*laḥ parasmaipadam*" (1-4-99) the designation *parasmaipadam* is enjoined to the substitutes which come in the place of *l*. Here the word *laḥ* is *anuvāda* since it does not relate to *vidheya* namely *parasmaipadam.* Yet there the rule "*ṣaṣthīsthāneyogā*" functions. So these assertions which takes for granted that the rule '*ṣaṣṭhīsthāneyogā* does not present itself here, are that of *ekadeśin.* NBh has already established that the maxim *'vidhau paribhaṣopatiṣṭhate nānuvāde'* relates only to the rules "*iko guṇavṛddhī* (1-1-3) and "*acaśca*" (1-2-28)[72]

8. "Naiṣa doṣaḥ - "svaravidhau vyañjanam avidyāmānavad bhavati" iti nāsti vyavadhānam"[73]

In the rule "*uraṇ raparaḥ*" (1-1-51) Pat discusses the question that the *r* enjoined by the rule, is to be considered whether *pūrvanta* or *parādi* or *abhakta* (an element which is neither related to the *pūrva* or *pāra*). Among the difficulties in case *r* is treated as *abhakta,* one is that in instances like *gīryate (svayameva),* enjoined by the rule *"acaḥ kartṛyaki"* (6-1-195) when *ac* is followed by *yak* in the sense of *kartṛ*, cannot be accomplished; since the vowel is intercepted from *yak* by *r* enjoined by the rule *ūraṇ raparaḥ"* (1-1-51). A solution to this difficulty is given i.e, "This objection cannot stand, since there is no interception on the basis of the dictum that consonants are considered to be non-existant in *svaravidhi"*. The idea is that the rule *acaḥ kartṛyaki"* (6-1-195) is *svaravidhi* and so *r* being a consonant need not be treated as an existing interception between the vowel and *yak*. NBh, points out that this solution is offered by *ekadeśin*. This is because the dictum *"svaravidhou..."* means that a consonant is to be treated as non-existant in instances where something is enjoined with regard to an accent (i.e, in *svaroddeśyakavidhi)* and when a consonant is contingent to obtain an accent. The maxim *"svara..."* does never mean that when an accent is enjoined, the consonants need be treated as non-existant. If it were so; there is no necessity of the word *acaḥ* in the rule *"acaḥ kartṛyaki"* (6-1-195) since in that case the accent enjoined by the rule, will relate only to the vowels on account of the treatment of consonants as non-existing when an accent is enjoined. Therefore the dictum *'svaravidhau....'* means that consonants can be treated as non-existant when something in regard to accent is prescribed. Since the rule enjoins an accent and not anything to an accent, the consonants cannot be treated as non-existant. Hence the solution offered on this basis, can rightly be characterised as that of *ekadeśin.*

9. *"Aparavidhaviti tu vaktavyam"*[74]

Under the rule *"acaḥ parasmin pūrvavidhau"* (1-1-57) the *pūrvapakṣin* brings the suggestion that the rule may be read as *'acaḥ parasmin aparavidhau'* instad of *'acaḥ parasmin pūrvavidhau'* By this change, *sthānivadbhāva* can be taken recourse to in *'pūrvavidhi'* as well as *'svavidhi'* since both are not *paravidhi*. As a result of *stānivadbhāva* in *svavidhi ādeśa* is admitted *sthānivadbhāva* if some *kārya* is enjoined to itself. The benefits from this can be seen in forms like *āyan, āsan, dhinvanti, kṛṇvanti, dadhyatra, madhvatra, cakratuḥ and cakruḥ*. The *purvapakṣin* says that in *āyan* and *āsan*[75] where the root *i* takes *yaṇādeśa* and the root *as* loses its *a* respectively, there is no chance for *āḍāgama* to be got by the rule *"āḍajādīnām"* (6-4-72) since *yan* and *san* do not commence in a vowel and it is secured through *sthānivadbhāva*. With regard to *dhinvanti* and *krṇvanti*[76] during the stage *dhi + nu + anti* and *kṛ + nu + anti*[77] where *u* of *nu* takes *yaṇādeśa* and becomes *v*, there is chance for *iḍāgama* before *v*, but the contingency can be avoided on account of *sthānivadbhava* of *v* whcih is *svavidhi*. In the instances *dadhyatra, madhvatra, cakratuḥ* and *cakruḥ* also it is pointed out that the contingency of the operation of the rule *"samyogāntasya lopaḥ"* (8-2-23) and the non-operation of the reduplication by the rule *"liṭi dhātoranabhyāsasya"* (6-1-8) can be averted by admitting *sthānivadbhāva* in *svavidhi*. It is also pointed out that the necessity of the change in the rule as *acaḥ parasmin aparavidhau* arises on account of the fact that in the wording of the rule *"acaḥ parasmin pūrvavidhau"* (1-1-57) the word *pūrva* relate to the *ādeśa* and the rule enjoins *sthānivadbhāva* only when something is enjoined to that which is *pūrva* to *ādeśa* and not when something occurs to *ādeśa* itself which is referred to here as *svavidhi*. Pat refutes this suggestion of change in the wording of the rule, on the basis of the word *vidhi* in the rule. The word *vidhi* is derived by adding the *kṛt* suffix *i* in the sense of *karman*, to the root *dhā* preceded by the *upasarga vi* so that it means that which is enjoined. It can also be derived by adding the same suffix to the same root to denote *bhāva*, so that it means the state of existing. Thus the word *vidhi* which is *bhāvasādhana* is taken here. So the *ādeśa* becomes *sthānivad* in the case of the existence of anythying previous to it. Since there is the *āḍāgama* before *v* and *s* in *āyan* and *āsan* and the absence of *iḍāgama* before *v* in *dhinvanti* and *kṛṇvanti, sthānivadbhāva* is admitted by the rule *"acaḥ parasmin pūrvavidhau"* (1-1-57). With regard to *dadhyatra* and *cakratuḥ* Pat offers other solutions.[78]

NBh here points out that the suggestion is raised by the *ekadeśin*. This is because the *āḍāgama* in *āyan and āsan* can be easily obtained by the non-validity of *yaṇādesa* in *āyan* and *lopa* of *a* in *āsan* on the basis of the rule *"asidddhavadatrābhāt"* (3-4-22). In *dhinvanti* and *kṛṇvanti*, the *v* though *valādi*,. is not an *ārdhadhātuka suffix*. To become an ārdhadhātuka suffix, it has to resort to the *sthanin u* by the rule *"sthānivadadeśa'nalvidhau"* (1-1-56). Hence the suggestion of change in the rule, so as to arrive at the forms *āyan*,. *āsan, dhinvanti, kṛnvanti*, etc., is of no avail. Hence this suggestion is that of *ekadeśin* says NBh. Here one may doubt as to why Pat does not refute the suggestion on this basis itself and NBh gives the reason for this also. It is in order to point out that the word *vidhi* is treated here as *bhāvasādhana* also, in addition to treating it as *karmasādhana* that Pat does not refute on the above said basis the suggestion of the change in the wording of the rule. Thus NBh concludes that the passages beginning with *"aparavidhāviti tu vaktavyam"* and ending with *"yāni tarhi svavidhau sthānivadbhāvasya prayojanāni"* are that of *ekadeśin.*

10. *"Na kartavyaḥ anenaiva praklptir bhaviṣyati tasminniti nirdiṣṭe pūrvasya ṣaṣthī tasmādityuttarasya ṣaṣṭhīīti"*[79]

Under the rule *"tasminniti nirdiṣṭe pūrvasya"* (1-1-66) Pat says that the rule effects a *niyama* that the locative case in sūtras can have the relationship of *pūrvatva* alone and the rule *"tasmādityuttarasya"* (1-1-67) effects the *niyama* that ablative case can have the relationship of *paratva* alone, since both these can have equally the relationship of *pūrvatva* and *paratva*. Now a question ensues,. when both these cases are mentioned in a *sūtra* whether the operation relates to that which precedes or that which follows. The answer given is that the rule *"tasmādityuttarasya"* (1-1-67) will operate through *vipratiṣedha* when there are both the cases, as in *sūtras* like *"tāsyanudāttet...."* (6-1- 186) *bhū ca bahoḥ"* (6-4-158) *"goto ṇit"* (7-1-90) *"rudādibhyaḥ sārvadhātuke"* (7-2-76) *"īdasaḥ"* (7-2-83) *"āmi sarvanāmnaḥ suṭ"* (8-3-32). Now it is pointed out that *vipratiṣedha* is not proper here since the *saptamī* in all these *sūtras* has been made use of in the previous or latter rules, while the ablative case is *anavakāśa* and it is on that score that the operation relates to the latter This is followed by a suggestion made under the *vārttika 'yathārtham vā ṣaṣthīnirdeśaḥ kartavyaḥ'*. To quote it, *"yathārtham vā ṣaṣthinirdeśaḥ kartavyaḥ yatra pūrvasya kāryam iṣyate tatra pūrvasya ṣaṣṭhī kartyavyā yatra parasya kāryam iṣyate tatra parasya ṣaṣṭhī kartavyā*, which means there is need to use *ṣaṣṭhī* after every *viṣaya.*[80] *Ṣaṣṭhī* should be suffixed to the former, if there is *kārya* to it and *ṣaṣthī* should be suffixed to the latter if there is *kārya* to it. NBh says that this view is that of *ekadeśin* since it involves cumbrousness to mention both the words ending in genitive and locative cases, and is only *prauḍhivāda*. To the following assertion that genitive case is to be used as told, reply is made 'No', it need not. It is decided by this itself. Where there is the mention of locative case, (the same assigns) genitive case to that which precedes and when there is the mention of ablative case, (the same assigns) genitive case to that which follows". The idea is that the rule *"tasminniti nirdiṣṭe pūrvasya"* (1-1-66) gives genitive case to that which precedes and the other gives genitive case to that which follows. This is by way of the *anuvṛtti* of the word *ṣaṣṭhī* in these rules from the rule *"ṣaṣṭhi sthāneyogā"* (1-1-49) whereby the words of the rules are *tasminniti nirdiṣṭe pūrvasya ṣaṣṭhī and tasmādityuttarasya ṣaṣṭhī*. NBh says that this is also the *prauḍhivāda* of the *ekadeśin* since in this view, also there is the cumbrousness of the *anuvṛtti* of the word *ṣaṣṭhī*. Again in instances where there are both these cases and hence there being the contingency of both cases assigning genitive case to the *pūrva* and *para*, one has to resort to the *anavakāśatva* itself of the ablative cases in the sūtras cited above and *paratva* where there is *vipratiṣedha* in rules like *"ḍaḥ si dhuṭ"* (8-3-29) where both the cases are *anavakāsa*. Hence this assertion is correctly characterised as that of *ekadeśin* by NBh.

Anticipation of Objections:

While elucidating the text of the *Mbh* NBh anticipates doubts on certain assertions of Pat and then wards off the same with clear and correct solutions.[81] A good effect that has resulted from this process is that the statements of Pat are simultaneously elucidated and established.

1. "Evam tarhi sāmarthyāt purveṇa, na pareṇa. Yadi pareṇa syād aṇgrahaṇam anarthakam syād, uraj raparaḥ ityeva brūyāt"[82]

Under the rule *laṇ* Pat discusses the question whether the *pratyahāra aṇ* is coined with the *ṇ* of the Śivasūtra *'a iu ṇ'* or with that of the rule *'laṇ'*. It is pointed out that with regard to the rule *ūraṇ raparaḥ"* (1-1-51) such a doubt exists and that if the *pratyāhāra aṇ* there, be with the *ṇ* of the rule *laṇ* there is the contingency that the lengthened vowel which is enjoined by the rule *"supi ca"* (7-3-102) and is to substitute *r*, may become *rapara* in instances like *mātṝṇām*. To this Pat gives the answer in the above quoted passage meaning "If so by *sāmarthya*, it is with the former and not with the latter, the reading of *aṇ* would be of no avail since he would have read *uraj raparaḥ*" By *sāmarṭhya* Pat means that if the *aṇ* in the said rule be with the latter *ṇ*, it will comprehend all vowels and consonants *h, y, v, r* and *l*; but among these, *ac* i.e, vowels alone are contingent to replace *ṛ* and Pāṇ would have read the rule as *uraj raparaḥ*. Since he has not done so, the *pratyāhāra* can be only with former *ṇ*.

NBh here cites an instance *gamḷ* + *ā*.[83] Here the rule *"iko yaṇaci"* (6-1-51) enjoins *yaṇ* as the substitute of *ḷ* and it is the consonant *l* that is to replace *ḷ* which is a *savarṇa* of *ṛ* and hence comprehended by *ṛ*. So how can there be the statement that vowels alone are contingent to replace *ṛ* and hence liable to become *rapara*? In this instance the consonant *l* is also contingent to be *lapara* by the rule *ūraṇ raparaḥ*" (1-1-51).[84]

NBh clears the doubt saying that the rule *ūraṇ raparaḥ*" (1-1-51) will not operate in the instance like *gamḷ* +*ā*. He gives the reason. Among the consonants comprehended by *aṇ, h* and *y* will never be liable to become *rapara* as they never replace *ṛ*. Now the question is concerned with *r* and *l*. With regard to *r*, in the instance *kartṛ* + *artham r* replaces *r*. If it becomes *rapara* there will be two *r* as *kartrrartham* and one of them will be elided by the rule *"ro ri"* (8-3-14). Thus it can be seen that precedance by *r* of the consonant *r* has no standing effect, when the rule *ūraṇ raparaḥ*" operates on the consonant substitute that replace *ṛ*. Therefore the rules *ūraṇ raparaḥ*" (1-1-51) will not operate on the consonant substitute of *ḷ* also which is a *sahacarita of ṛ*. Thus NBh esetablishes that vowels alone are contingent to replace *ṛ* and liable to become *rapara* thereby and hence the above statement of Pat.

NBh points out that some others give a different solutiuon to this problem. They opine that even if *l* becomes *lapara* one of them will be dropped by the rule *"ro ri"* (8-3-14) itself since *r* and *l* are having *samānaśruti*. He adds that still others give a difference solution. On the authority of this *bhāṣya* passage that vowels alone are liable to replace *r* and become *rapara*, instances like *gamḷ ā* which contradict the same must come under the scope of *anabhidhāna*, i.e, forms like *gamlā* are to be treated as not in vogue.[85]

2. *"satām ādaicām samjñāyā bhavitavyam, samjñayā cādaico bhāvyante tad etad itaretaraśrayam bhavati"*[86]

Under the rule *"vṛddhirādaic"* (1-1-1) the *pūrvapakṣin* points out that there is interdependance in rules like *"mṛjervṛddhiḥ"* (7-2-114) which enjoin *vṛddhi.* He says, *"samjñā* is to (indicate) the *ā, ai* and *au* which are existant, (but in rules like *"mṛjervṛddhiḥ")* they are made to exist by means of the *samjñā*. There is thus interdependence. What he means is this, a *samjñā* presupposes the existence of those that are designated by it and it is by the rule *"mṛjervṛddhiḥ"* (7-2.114)(having the *samjñā vṛddhi* in it that we get *ā* in the root *mṛj,* and this is interdependence since a *samjñā* presupposing the existence of the *samjñin,* is made to bring the *samjñin* newly. NBh anticipating a doubt with regard to the existence of interdependence here and removing the same establishes the idea of the said passage that there is interdependence in the rule mentioned. The *vṛddhiśabda* can by virtue of *sāmānyalakṣaṇā,* be well expressive of all the *ādaic* that are lost or existant or yet to come. If *lakṣaṇā* be not accepted of the word *vṛddhi* it may denote only those particular *ā, ai* and *au* mentioned in the rule and not the same others in other instances, which are not present in the mind of the reader of this rule. Therefore *lakṣaṇā* being accepted of one word *vṛddhi,* the word denotes all the *ā, ai* and *au* i.e., lost existant and yet to come and so the rule *"mṛjervṛddhiḥ"* (7-2-114) can quite possibly denote the *ā that is to substitute the r* of the root *mṛj* which is not originally there, and hecne there is no problem of interdependance here. Besides,. even if *sāmānyalakṣaṇā* in the word *vṛddhi* is not accepted, there is no interdepndance here. The expressive power i.e, *śakti* of the word *vṛddhi* has within its scope the genus i.e, *ātva aitva* and *autva.*It is a generally accepted fact that the *śaktigraha* of a particular *śabda,* causes to be derived from the *śabda,* a *śabdabodha* involving the same particular characteristic. Therefore the word *vṛddhiḥ* in the rule *"mṛjervṛddhiḥ"* (7-2- 3114) denotes the genus i.e, *ātva* on the phoneme that is to replace *ṛ* of the root *mṛj* and so also there is no interdependance h 2ere. After thus entertaining a doubt with regard to the existance of interdependence here, NBh removes the same. It is true that if there be the *śaktigraha* of *vṛddhiśabda* on the genus, the word can denote all the letters having the genus. But with regard to the root *mṛj*, there is no letter to be pointed out at present as having the said genus and so the word *vṛddhiḥ* in rules like *"mṛjervṛddhiḥ"* cannot have connection with the genus of a phoneme that is yet to come. Since a phoneme which is yet to come is unknown to be possessed of any particular genus, the denotation of that unknown genus by the word *vṛddhiḥ* in rules like *"mṛjervṛddhiḥ"* (7-2- 114) is also quite improbable. Therefore, the prescription of *ā*, *ai* and *au* by the term *vṛddhiḥ* which presupposes their previous existence is definitely an anomaly. Moreover it is impossible to have *śaktigraha* on those that are yet to function as the word *vṛddhiḥ* in *"mṛjervṛddhiḥ"* (7-2-114) is quite satisfied by having, under the scope of its expressive power, the *ā*, *ai* and *au* that are already in the mind of the reader. Hence letters which are enjoined by rules and yet to function can never come under the scope of the expressive power and hence the prescription of *ā*, *ai* and *au* as substitute by the term *vṛddhi* in rules like *"mṛjervṛddhiḥ"* (7-2-1214) is explicitely an interdependence here.

3. *"Evam tarhi gamerapyayam ḍo vaktavyaḥ gameśca guṇaḥ ucyamānaḥ āntaryataḥ okāraḥ prāpnoti. Tasmād iggrahaṇam kartavyam"*[87]

Under the rule *"iko guṇavṛddhī"* (1-1-3) Pat says that the word *ikaḥ* is necessary in the said rule to ward off the contingency of *guṇa* replacing consonants. The prescription of the suffix *ḍa* having the *anubandha ḍ* cannot be an indication to this effect. This is because the same suffix by means of *anuvṛtti*, is enjoined by the rule, *"anyeṣvapidṛśyate"* (3-2-1012) and hence this suffix may be added to the root *gam*. Consequently in the formation of the word *nagaḥ*, *agaḥ*, etc., if there be the absence of the word *ikaḥ* in the said rule, the consonant *m* of the root *gam* is liable to be susbtituted by the *guṇa o* as it is *antaratama* to the original from the point of view of the place of articulation and thereby the forms *nagaḥ*, etc. cannot be arrived at. Therefore the *anubandha ḍ* of the suffix *ḍa* is prupuseful by bringing the elision of part *am*, of the root *gam*, known as *ṭi* on the strength of the rule *"ṭeh"* (6-4-143) whereby the form *nagaḥ* can be arrived at, and it cannot indicate the fact that consonants will not be replaced by *guṇa*. NBh brings an objection to the statement that there is no factor to indicate the said fact. He points out that the suffix *ḍa-a-u* is enjoined by the *Uṇādi* rule *"tanoter ḍa-a- uḥ sanvacca"* (5-730) to the root *tan*. This suffix has got the *anubandha ḍ*. This can be an indication of the fact that consonants will not be replaced by *guṇa*. If *guṇa* can replace consonant, *ḍitkaraṇa* will be of no use for in the formation of the word *titau, ti + tan + au* will become *ti + ta + a + au* if *guṇa* replaces the consonant *n* and then this will change into *ti + ta + a + u* by the operation of the rule *"ato guṇe"* (6-1-97) on the first two *a* and *a* then by the operation of the same rule on the remaining two *a* and *a* the form *titau* will result. Hence the *anubandha ḍ* being futile can indicate the said fact.

After thus giving an objection to the assertion of Pat, NBh removes the same saying that the word *titau* is treated as non-derivative stem and so no indication is possible, and hence Pat's statement that the word *ik* is necessary to ward off the contingency of *guṇa* replacing consonants. NBh adds that there may be a further objection that the word *ik* is not necessary since *guṇa*, viz. *a, e* & *o* will never replace consonants as the same (*a, e* and *o*) have got *a, i* and *u* as their *antraratama sthānin*. This objection is baseless, says NBh, since the a which is *guṇa* has got the consonant *s* as *antaratama sthānin* in instances like the root *īs'*. Both *i* and *ś* are palatals and have the effort viz. *vivṛta* from the point of view of *Pāṇ* to whom sibilants and vowels have the same effort viz. *vivṛta*.[88] Again the selection of an *antaratama sthānin* by a substitute is quite improbable since Pat has refuted the wording of the rule *"sthānentaratame"* (1-1-50) which gives rise to the said selection and accepted the rule with the wording *"sthānentharatamaḥ"* (1-1-50).

4. *"athavā-āhayam "adaso māt" iti, na ca ītvotve staḥ, nāpi makāraḥ tata evam vijñāsyāmaḥ mārthādīdādyarthānām iti"*[89]

Under the rule *"adaso māt"* (1-1- 12) it is pointed out that in the rule the designation *pragṛhya* is enjoined to *ī* and *ū* after *m* in *adas*, and there is the necessity of the prohibition of *ayādeśa* and *ekādeśa (pūrvarūpa)* since the consonant *m* that replaces *d* and the vowels *ī* and *ū* that replace *e* and *au* are non-valid by the function of the rule *"pūrvātrāsiddham"* (8-2-1) in instances like *amī + atra, amī + āsāte, amū + atra, amū + āsāte* which appear to the *sapādasaptādhyī* as *ade + atra, ade + āsāte, adau + atra* and *adau + āsāte.* Different solutions are given to avoid the necessity of such a prohibition. One among them, is given under the *vārttika "mārthadīdādyarthānām vā"*. "Or the *sūtrakāra* has said *"adaso māt"*. There is no *ī* or *ū* or *m*. Therefore we take to mean *"mārthāt īdādyarthānām"*. The idea is that the word *māt* in the rule is taken to be *mārthād* and *īdūt* in the rule to be *īdūdartha.* The word *mārtha* denotes that which stands for *m* i.e, *d* the original of the substitute *m*. *Idūdartha* denotes that which stands for *e* and *au* i.e, the originals of the substitutes *ī* and *ū*. Thus *e* and *au* in *adas* are designated as *pragṛhya* by the rule *adaso māt,* whereby they get *prakṛtibhāva* and there is never a necessity for a prohibition of *ayādeśa,* etc. on them.

NBh says that there is a difficulty in this interpretation. It is the forms *ade* and *adau* that get the designation *pragṛhya* and when they become *amī* and *amū* by the substitution by *m* of *d* and by the substitution by *ī* and *ū* of *e* and *o* etc. the *ī* and *ū* would not get the designation and so there will be the contingency of other euphonic combinations here instead of *prakṛtibhāva.* The *samjnā* relating to *e, o* etc., is *alvidhi* in which *sthānivadbhāva* is prohibited.

After anticipating such a difficulty NBh gives the import of the passage which averts the objection. The word *pragṛhya* in all the rules in which it is used denotes not only *e, ō aī* and *āū* but also the originals (*ī* and *ū*) of these substitutes. The denotation of ī and ū is by virtue of the acceptane of *lakṣaṇā* in the word *pragṛhya.* So where *ī* and *ū* are to be provided with the operations relationg to the term *pragṛhya,* the term *pragṛhya* in the rule enjoining that particular operation is taken to denote them by virtue of *lakṣaṇā* in the word *pragṛhya.* Therefore there is the designation *pragṛhya* to the *e* and *au* as well as *ī* and *ū*. Therefore there is no necessity for a prohibition of *ayādeśa* etc. in this interpretation.

5. "tasmin kriyamāṇe ihaiva syāt-papāca papāṭha; iyāya āra ityatra na syāt. vyapadeśivadekaśmin kāryam bhavatītyatrāpi siddham bhavati"[90]

Under the rule *"ādyantavadekasmin"* (1-1-20) Pat discusses the need for remodelling the said rule as *vyapadeśivadekasmin,* so that operations shall be made on a single unit by taking recourse to *vyapadeśivadbhāva.* To the question about the purpose of this remodelling he says, *"vakṣyati-ekāco dve prathamasyeti bahuvrīhi-nirdeśa iti". tasmin kriyamāṇe ihaiva syād - papāca papāṭha; iyāya āra ityatra na syād. Vyapadeśivadekasmin kāryam bhavatityatrāpi siddham bhavati"* which means "He (*Vārttikakāra*) is going to say under the *sūtra ēkāco dve prathamasya"* (6-1-1), the vāritika *ēkāco dve prathamasyeti bahuvrīhinirdeśaḥ* (by which it is clear that the word *ekāc* is a *bahuvrīhi* compound and not a *karmadhāraya* compound). According to it the roots *pac* and *path* will be reduplicated, but reduplication cannot take place with reference to the roots *ī* and *ṛ* (to go). The object is achieved thereto by adopting the principle that what happens to the primary *ekāc* happens even when there is only one vowel. The idea is that by virtue of the rule *"ādyantavadekasmin"* (1-1- 20), roots like *ī* and *ṛ* can be treated as *ajādi* or *ajanta.* To get the reduplication enjoined by the rule *"liṭi dhātor anabhyāsasya"* (6-1-8) where there is the *anuvṛtti* of the word *ekācaḥ,* the roots need be *ekāc.* But these roots each of which is a single vowel cannot be treated as possessed of a single *ac* by the rule *"ādyantavadekasmin"* (1-1-20). Hence reduplication relates only to roots like *pac, paṭh,* etc. which are possessed of a single vowel and not to roots *ī* and *ṛ.*

NBh here brings an objection to the statement that roots like *pac* will get reduplication even without *vyapadeśivadbhāva.* He says that the rule enjoins reduplication to the *ekāc* which is first in a root (i.e, *Prathama*). With regard to the roots *pac* and *paṭh* the root itself is a single *ekāc* and not the first *ekāc* in a rule. Hence with regard to these roots also in order to treat them as the first *ekāc* of the root, which cannot be effected by the rule *"ādyantavadekasmin"* (1-1-020) there is the necessity of *vyapadeśivadbhāva* and so the assertion of Pat may seem obscure.

But this statement of Pat, NBh says, is correct. This is because the word *prathama* Is a synonym of the word *ādi* and so the treatment of an *ekāc* as the first *ekāc* i.e, *ādi* is well nigh achieved by the rule *"ādyantavadekasmin"* (1-1-20) and so is not a unique purpose to be served by the said remodelling of the rule.

6. "Evam tarhi ācāryapravṛttir jñāpayati sthānivad ādeśo bhavati yadayam 'yuṣmadasmador anādeśe ityādeśe pratiṣedham śāsti. Katham kṛtvā jñāpakam? Yuṣmadasmador vibhaktau kāryamucyamānam kaḥ prasaṅgo yad ādeśepi syād: Paśyati tu ācāryo sthānivadādeśo bhavati iti-ataḥ ādeśe pratiṣedham śāsti"[91]

In the rule "sthānivad ādeśo'nalvidhau" (1-1-56) Pat doubts the necessity of the said rule. The argument that ādeśa plays the same part as the sthānin just according to what we find in the world, i.e, one who comes in the place of another takes to his work, is refuted by pointing out that this worldly example does not apply in the science of grammar on account of the rule "svam rūpam śabdasyāśabdasamjñā" (1-1-68). According to this rule śabdas like han shall denote han alone that is the sthānin and not vadh which is the substitute. Pat then establishes the non-essentiality of the rule by citing an indication for the rule. He says "If so Ācārya Pāṇini suggests that ādeśa becomes sthānivad since he has used the word anādeśe in the sūtra "yuṣmadasmador anādeśe" (7-2-86) prohibiting the lengthening of a of yuva and āva before halādivibhakti which is anādeśa (not being substituted by another). Under what conception does it become jñāpaka.? What happens to yuṣmad and asmad when case suffix follows them, may not happen to them when an ādeśa to the case-suffix follows. Acārya prohibits it when ādeśa follows them seeing that ādeśa may play the same part as sthānin". Thus the part anādeśe of the rule is resorted to as an indication by Pat. NBh advances an objection here and by way of clearing it confirms the indication pointed out by Pat. He presents a contingency for the word anādeśe. The rule "yuṣmadasmador anādeśe" (7-2-86) prohibits the lengthening of yuva and āva when preceded by vibhakti which is not a substitute. Vibhakti is a technical term in the science of grammar and so the rule "svam rūpam śabdasyāśabdasamjñā" (1-1-68) cannot apply here on account of the part aśabdasamjñā in the same rule. Technical terms do not denote the svarūpa but the sense. The term vibhakti need not denote the svarupa vibhakti but the sense namely su au jas, etc. Hence in the absence of svarūpavidhi the substitute of su au jas etc., can play their part just as in the world one who is in the place of another takes to his work. NBh thus states that in the absence of the word anādeśe qualifying the word vibhaktau, the prohibition of lengthening will apply to the precedence of *vibhakti* which is even an *ādeśa. The word anādeśe* is therefore fully satisfied in avoiding the lengthening when preceded by suffixes which are substitutes.

NBh now establishes the superfluity of the word *anādeśe*. The technical term *vibhakti* indicates *su au jas*, etc., mentioned in the rule *"svaujasamuṭ..."* (4-1-2) and *"tiptasjhi..."* (3-4-78). In these rules, however there is the application of the rule *"svam rūpam śabdasyāśabdasamjñā* (1-1-68). Therefore sounds having the *svarūpa* namely *su au jas*, etc., can be designated as *vibhakti* and the substitute which have a different *svarūpa* can never be termed as *vibhakti*. Hence there is no need for the prohibition of lengthening in the precedence of a *vibhakti* which is not a substitute. Hence the superfluous word *anādeśa* is rightly taken for the indication of the *sthānivadbhāva*.

7. *"Kim prayojanam? Śobhanā dṛṣado'sya brāhmaṇasya sudṛṣad brāhmaṇaḥ, sor manasī alomoṣasī ityeṣa svaro mā bhūditi"*[92]

Vārttikakāra maintains that the rule *"pratyayalope pratyayalakṣaṇam"* (1-1-62) is necessary to operate in instances where *sthānivadbhāva* is prohibited on the score *alvidhi*. He enumerates the merits and demerits of the rule. Pat shows that the merits to be accrued by the said rule can be achieved even otherwise and so there is no need for the rule (as *vidhisūtra*). Yet he says that there is the necessity of the sūtra. It has to effect a *niyama* as follows:- 'that which is enjoined with reference to *prataya* may come within the range of *pratyaykhlakṣaṇa* and that which is enjoined with reference to a word may not come within its range.' To the further question enquiring the purpose of this *niyamā*, he replies that the *bahuvrīhi* compound *sudṛṣad*, which becomes an adjunct of *brāhmaṇaḥ* may not take *ādyudātta svara* enjoined by the rule *"sor manasī alomoṣasī"* (6-2-117) that enjoins *ādyudātta svara* to the sound ending in *au* or *as*, but not the sounds *loman* and *uṣas* and is contingent to bring forth the *svara* on the part *dṛṣad*. This is because of *pratyayalakṣaṇa* of the elision of *as*. If the rule effects the said *niyama*, there is no such contingency here since in the rule *"sormanasī alomoṣasī"* (6-2-117), the suffix *jas* is not referred to, but only the sound *as* which may comprehend both the suffix as well as the nonsuffix sound.

NBh brings a doubt here. In the said rule, *svara* is prohibited to *loman* and *uṣas* by the part *'aḷomoṣasī*. By the prohibition of *svara* to *uṣas* a similarity of this may be drawn to *as* which is being endowed with *svara*, i.e, a sound ending in *as*, must actually be heard as ending in *as* and not sounds like *dṛṣad* in the cited instance which is not heard to end in *as*. This is by virtue of the prohibition, known as *paryudāsa* and consequently here is no necessity to a *niyama* to avoid *svara* on *dṛṣad* in *sudṛṣad*.

After expressing the doubt, NBh establishes the statement of Pat. He says that there is a difficulty in resorting to the prohibition known as *paryudāsa*. Based on the similarity with *uṣas*, the sound ending in *as*, may be taken to be that ending in *as* which is a suffix itself and so in the word *suvaḥ* the ending of which though is *as*, is not a suffix, we cannot get the *svara* by the rule. Hence it is in order to avoid *svara* in *dṛṣad* and to procure the same in *suvaḥ* also that Pat takes the rule *"pratyayalope pratyayalakṣaṇam"* (1-1-62) to give rise the said *niyama*.

Readings

While elucidating the text of the *Mbh*, NBh has given great attention to the readings in the same. He specifies and justifies certain readings, points out variant readings for some others and brings to our attention certain incorrect readings found in the text. Most of his assertions in this regard are supported by strong and logical reasoning based on grammar.

Specifications and justifications of the readings in the text of the Mbh

1. *"atha mukhasukhārthastakaraḥ akāropi"*[93]

Here NBh specifies that the expression *'mukhasukhārthaḥ;* in the above reading, should be treated as a compound formed by the rule *"mayūravyamsakādayaśca"* (2-1-72). This is because the idea conveyed by the compound *mukhsukhārathaḥ* relates to the *uccāraṇakriyā* which is implied but not expressed in the sentence and if the compound *mukhasukhārthaḥ* is treated as regularly derived (i.e, *mukhasukhāya ayam mukhasukharthaḥ*) by the rule *ēaturthī tadharthā..."* (2 - 1- 36) then by virtue of the masculine gender in it, the compound will relate to the masculine word *takāraḥ* in the sentence in the strength of *vārttika* under the same rule, *'arthena saha samāso viseṣyanighnatā ceti vaktavyam'*. Therefore in order to relate the sense of the compound word with *uccāraṇakriyā* itself implied in the sentence, NBh specifies that *mukhasukhārthaḥ* should be treated as a compound formed on the strength of the rule *"mayūravyamsakādayaśca"* (2-1-72) in which case it is not necessary that it should relate to the word *takāraḥ* and hence can be taken as relating the *uccāraṇakriyā* implied in the sentence and which can be expressed by the masculine word *upadeśaḥ*. Thereby NBh implies that, if the reading be *mukhasukhārtham,* it can be treated as formed by the rule *ēaturthī tadarthārtha...."* (2-1-36) and also will relate to the neuter word *uccāraṇam* the sense of which is implied in the sentence.

2. *"mātrakālo'tra gamyate, na ca mātrikam vyañjanam asti. anupadiṣṭam sat katham śakyam vijnatumasacca katham śakyam pratipattum"*[94]

NBh brings to our attention the fact that in certain versions of the *MBh,* the sentence *'asacca....pratipattum'* is not seen. However it may be noted that the absence of the same does not obstruct the clarity of idea in the context.

3. *"katamasmimstāvad aṇgrahaṇe sandehaḥ"*[95]

NBh points out that if the reading be *"katarasmimstīvad...sandehaḥ"*, i.e, with the word *katarasmin* in the place of *katamasmin* there is no defect since the expression *katarasmin* derived by the addition of the sufffix *ḍatarac* to the base *kim* is grammatically quite correct in the context. It may be pointed out here that the rule *"kimyattadornirdhāraṇe dvayorekasya ḍataracca"* (5-3-92) enjoins the suffix *ḍatarac* to the base *kim* and the like, when the mention of one among two (*dvayoḥ ekasya nirdhāraṇam*) is to be made and the rule *"vā jātipariprasne ḍatamacca"* (5-3-93) enjoins the suffix *ḍatamac* to the base *kim* and the like, when mention of one among many (*bahūnām ekasya nirdhāraṇam*) is to be made. The question *'katamasmimstāvad...."* follows the statement that there is a doubt in regard to the expressions *aṇ iṇ* etc., since the same letter *ṇ* is made use of in the two *Sivasūtras 'aiuṇ'* and *'laṇ'*. Such expressions being many in number, the *pūrvapakṣin* says, "*tatraāṅgrahaṇeṣu ingrahaṇeṣu ca sandeho bhavati - pūrveṇa vā syuḥ pareṇa veti*". Now, it is asked: 'In which *aṇgrahaṇa* does the doubt arise? Since, many expression of *aṇ* are being stated be to be doubtful previously, this question is: "which one among these is doubtful' and so here in this question mention is to be made of one among many and so the expression *ktamasmin* with the suffix *ḍatamac* may appear to be more proper here. And one may feel that the reading *katarasmin* with the suffix *ḍatarac* in the sense of the *nirdhāraṇa* of one among two, may apparently be not proper. But NBh justifes this reading also saying that the condition that *ḍatarac* is to be used only when there is the mention of one among two, is refuted by Pat and so *ḍatarac* can also be made use of when there is *nirdhāraṇa*, irrespective of the fact that the same is of one among two or many.

4. "*yadi parigaṇanam kriyate, syadaḥ praśrathaḥ, himaśrathaḥ ityalrāpi na prāpnoti*"[96]

Here NBh specifes that if the reading be "*yadi..ityalrāpi prāpnoti*', then, the verb *prāpnoti* should be supplied with the agent *vṛddhiḥ*. If the reading be '*yadi...ityatrāpi na prāpnoti*' as cited above, the agent to be supplied to the predicate *na prāpnoti* is, '*niṣedhaḥ*'.

5. "*kim ca syāt yadyekasya halaḥ samyogasamjñā syāt? iyeṣa uvoṣa 'ijādeśca gurumatonṛcchaḥ ityām prasajyeta*"[97]

NBh points out that in the above reading mention of the word *uvoṣa* is made quite accidentally. But it cannot be cited as an example along with *iyeṣa* to illustrate the undesired contingency of the suffix *ām* to roots, since the addition of the suffix *ām* to the root *uṣ* is desired (though optionally) by the rule *ūṣavidajāgṛbhyo' nyatarasyām*" (3-1-38). NBh continues that the reading may be "*kim ca....syāt? iyeṣa uvokha. Ijādeśca...prasajyeta*" i.e, the example cited may be the form *uvokha*. In this case it is quite appropriate to cite the same as an illustration for the contingency of the suffix *ām* to roots in case a single consonant is treated as possessed of the term *samyoga*.

6. "ṛkāraḷkārayoḥ savarṇavidhiḥ ṛkāralkārayoḥ savarṇasamjñā vidheyā"[98]

NBh specifies that in the part *ṛkāraḷkārayoḥ* in the *vārttika* and *bhāṣya* cited above, the rule *"ṛtyakaḥ"* (6-1-128) which enjoins *prakṛtibhāva* has operated and hence the reading as such and there is no function of any rule on the *a* and the following *ḷ* there.

7. ūpadāstāsya svaraḥ'śikṣkasyeti. ātve kṛte "sthāghvoricca" itītvam prāpnoti"[99]

NBh points out that the reading is *"sthāghvoricceti kitvam prāpnoti"* Even in the reading *"sthāghvoricca itītvam"* (as cited above) he says that *"itvam"* means *'kitvasahitam itvam'*. This is because the rules *"sthāghvoricca"* (1-2-17) enjoins *kitva* and *itva* and in the context here in the bhāṣya where it is referred to, the reference is to the *kitva* enjoined by the rule.

8. "naiveśvara āñjāpayati, nāpi dharmasūtrakārā paṭhanti asambhave'pavadairutsargā bādhyantām iti"[100]

NBh points that the word *apavādaiḥ* in the above reading has as its precedant the word *'asambhave'* and adds that in certain editions of the *Mbh,* as in the above, the reading itself is *"asambhave'pavādair.....iti"*. This shows that there is also the **read**ing *"naiveśvara āñjāpayati nāpi dharmasūtrakārā paṭhanti - apavādairutsargā bādhyantām iti"*, in certain editions of the *Mbh.*

9. "Parādau guṇavṛddhyautvadirgha-nalopānusvāraśibhāvenakārapratiṣedhāh"[101]

NBh specifes that in the *vārttika* cited above the readings is *"sībhavenakārapratiṣedhāḥ"* as cited above and the non-elision of the locative suffix is *ārṣa.*

10. "yo hi bhuktavantam brūyāt mā bhukthāḥ iti, kim tena kṛtam syād?"[102]

Here NBh specifies that the reading of the verb *"bhukthaḥ"* is dvoid of the *anuṣvāra* as cited above.

11. *"rāyi chāndasaḥ"*[103]

NBh specifies that the part *'rayi'* in the bhaṣya quoted above, is to be separated as *rāḥ* (which means *raiśabda*) + *yi* (which means *yakārādau*) and the reading is *rāyi* i.e, without the *visarga* and thus averts the doubt that the reading *rāyi* is not correct since the *śabda 'rai'* cannot entertain both the *ātva* enjoined by the rule *"ādeca upadeśe'śiti"* (6-1-45) and the *'ik'* which is usually added to roots. NBh points out that it is the nominative case suffix *'su'* that is added to the *śabda rai*.

Variant Readings:

1. *"Tatra cāsyāgamakālenaivāyuḥ kṛtsnam paryupayuktam syāt"*[104]

NBh points out that there is a variant reading *'paryavasannam'* as against the reading *'paryupayuktam'*. But the variant reading noted by NBh does not effect any change in the idea expressed by the sentence.

2. *"Tathā vākyānyapi dviṣṭhāni bhavanti, śveto dhāvati alambusānām yāteti"*[105]

NBh states there is a variant reading *'pātā'* as against the reading *yātā*, in the sentence above quoted. He specifies that the word *pātā* is derived from the root *pā* meaning to protect.

3. *"āmramayam - śālamayam, vṛddhilakṣaṇo mayaṇ na prāpnoti"*[106]

NBh makes clear that the suffix *mayaṭ* is enjoined by the rule *"nityam vṛddhaśarādibhyaḥ"* (4-3-144) to a base having the designation *vṛddha* which itself is brought about by an initial vowel having the designation *vṛddhi* and in the quoted passage, *mayaṭ* is, therefore, spoken as being caused by *vṛddhi*. He adds that there is a variant reading *'vṛddhalakṣaṇo mayaṇ na prāpnoti'* whch means that the suffix *mayaṭ* is caused by the designation *vṛddha* possessed by a base.

4. *"Sambandhamanuvartiṣyate - "vṛddhirādaic" "adeṅguṇaḥ" vṛddhirādaic tataḥ "iko guṇavṛddhi" iti. guṇavṛddhigrahaṇam anuvartate, ādaijadeṅgrahaṇam nivṛttam"*[107]

NBh points out that in the passage quoted above, the assertion *"vṛddhirādaic adeṅguṇaḥ"* corresponds to the rules 1-1-1 and 1-1-2 in the *Aṣṭ*. The next assertion *'vṛddhirādaic'* denotes the *anuvṛtti* of the same in the rule *'adeṅguṇaḥ'*. The next sentence means that just as the word *guṇa* alone and not the word *aden* is got by *anuvṛtti* in the rule *'iko guṇavṛddhi'*, so also *'vṛddhiḥ'* alone is got by *anuvṛtti* and *'ādaic'* is not got by *anuvṛtti* in the rule *'iko guṇavrddhi"*. NBh adds that there is a variant reading *"ādaijgrahaṇam nivṛttam'* as against *ādaijadeṅgrahaṇam nivṛttam'*.

Incorrect Readings:

1. *"nanu ca bhośchandogānām sātyamugvirāṇāyanīyā ardhamekāram ardhamokāram cādlītyate - sujāte eśvasūnṛte, adhvaryo odribhiḥ sutam-śukram te enyat, rajatam te enyat - iti*[108]

Here NBh points that in the above sentence in the part *eśvasūnṛte"*, there is an incorret reading including the letter *'a'* as *sujāte a eśvasūnṛte* and such a reading is caused by carelessness (*pramāda*).

2. *"kim vaktavyam etat? nahi kathamanucyamānam gamsyate? ekādeśe kṛte dvivacanaparao'yam antadivadbhāvena"*[109]

NBh points out that the passage cited above is an incorrect reading found in the text of the *Mbh*. This passage occurs after the vārttika *"avacanādapi tatparavijnānam"* and the bhāṣya on it, *"antareṇāpi vacanam āpi dvivacanaparo'yam bhaviṣyati"*. It is stated in the vārttika and bhāṣya that the feminine word *ubhe* formed by the addition of the nominative dual suffix *au* to the feminine base *ubhā* which is derived by the addition of the feminine sufffix *ṭāp* to the *prātipadika ubha*, can be treated as endowed with *dvivacana* at the end, even without making a specific statement to that efect. The idea is that when the feminine suffix *ṭāp* is added to *ubha*, the resultant form *ubhā* can be treated as *ubhaśabda*, by virtue of the *pūrvāntavadbhāva* of the *ekādeśa ā of ā + a*, on the strength of the rule *"ādyantavadekasmin"* (1-1-20). Thus *ubhā* being treated as *ubhaśabda*, it goes without saying that *ubha*, formed by the addition of the dual suffix *au* to *ubhā*, becomes *dvivacanānta* and there is no necessity of making a specific statement to that efffect. Hence the passage cited above, meaning "Is this to be mentioned? No. How can that which is not mentioned, be understood? This (*ubhe*) will be treated as being endowed with dual suffix at the end on account of *antādivadbhāva* when the *ekādeśa* is made" is not correct since a discussion of the necessity of a specific statement becomes out of place when it has been pointed just previously that the same is not necessary.

However, NBh ads that, the said reading may be treated as correct if in the said passage, the discussion arises out of the misundertanding that a statement as *'avacanādapi tatparvjñānam'* is necessary.

3. *"asti veha kaścit puruśārambhaḥ"*[110]

NBh points out that the passage cited above is a question and hence the reading with *ca* in the place of *vā*, i.e, *asti ceha kaścit puruśārambhaḥ* is incorrect since the use of the *nipāta, ca* is not appropriate here in the statement which is in the form of a question.

REFERENCES

1. Vide Supra p 18.
2. Vide *Amarakośa: "mangalānantharārambhapraśnakārtsnyeśvatho atha"*
3. Vide *Mbh* pp. 20, 29 and 37.
4. Vide *Mbh* p. 20.
5. *Mbh* p. 106.
6. *Mbh* p. 68.
7. Vide Infra p. 232.
8. Vide *Mbh*, Vol. III p. 286.
9. *Mbh* p. 11
10. Mbh pp. 41, 49, 82, 100, 116, 128, 139.
11. *Mbh* p. 41.
12. Vide 'Notes on the Mahābhaṣya', *Indian Antiquary*, Vol. V p. 241.
13. *Mbh* p. 61.
14. Though *'a'* is *saṃvṛta* and the same is not a fault with regard to *'a'*, it is definitely a fault in regard to letters like *ā, i, ī,* etc. (vide Udy p. 60. *"ākarādināṃ saṃvṛtatvam doṣaḥ na tvakārasya saṃvṛtaguṇatvād"*)

15. *Mbh* Vol. II p. 707.
16. *Udy*. p. 62.
17. Vide *Mbh* Vol. II, p. 707.
18. *Mbh* p. 263.
19. Vide *Mbh* Vol. II, p. 300.
20. *Mbh* p. 87.
21. *Mbh* p. 127
22. *ni=upasarga, a = aḍāgama, is = sic* preceded by *iḍāgama t=* parasmaipada termination.
23. *nyanuvīt = Aorist Third person singular of the root 'nu'* prefixed with the *upasarga 'ni'*.
24. Aorist Third person singular of the roots *'kṛ'* and *'hṛ'*.
25. *Udy* p. 127.
26. *Mbh* p. 147.
27. *Mbh* p. 147.
28. P.S. Sāstri has however gone wrong in interpreting the meaning of this passage. He takes this to be a question i.e. "Is there anything between the two or not?" Vide *letures on the Mahabhāṣya of Patañjali* Vol. II, p. 43 and *Udy* p. 147.
29. *Mbh* p. 299.
30. Vide *"Luk taddhitaluki"* (1-2-49)
31. *Mbh* pp. 9-11
32. *Mbh* p. 66
33. *Mbh* p. 83
34. *Mbh* p. 87.
35. Vide *Prdp* p. 57
36. *Udy* p. 87.
37. *Mbh* p. 94
38. *Mbh* p. 104.
39. *Mbh* p. 124.
40. Vide *Par.Śekh, "Paribhāṣā* No. 101 *"Vidhau paribhāṣopatiṣṭhate nānuvade"*.
41. The previous rules are *"vṛddhirādaic"* (1-1-1) and *"Aden guṇaḥ"* (1-1-2)
42. A kind of *anuvṛtti* by which a word denotes in the rule in which it is got by anuvṛtti a sense, different from the same denoted by that word in the rule where it originally was.
43. NBh here is probably referring to the six *'bhāvavikāras'* mentioned by Yāska, Vide *Nirukta*, (Chapter I, Para I), p. 8.
44. *Mbh* p. 184.
45. *Mbh* p. 301.
46. NBh probably refers to the view of Daṇḍin here. He takes the first word of the rule to be *astisicas* wherein a *sakāra* has been elided by the rule *"saṃyogāntasya lopaḥ"* (8-2-23) and

the remaining word *astisicas* in combination with the word *apṛkte*, becomes *astisicopṛkete*. (See *Mbh* with the commentary *Tatvāloka* p. 424).

47. Vide *Vākyapadīya kāṇda* II alabdhagāthe gāmbhiryād uttāna iva sauṣṭhavād/tasminnakṛtabuddhīnām naivīvasthirthinirṇayaḥ.
48. *Mbh* p. 118.
49. Vide *Mbh* Vol. II, p. 427.
50. Vide *Mbh* Vol. II, p. 427, the passage under the rule (4-2-67) "ekayoge" nuvṛttiḥ bhavati. Katham jñāyate? Yadayam 'tadasyāstyasminniti matup' iti dvihḥ tadgrahaṇam, karoti. Katham' tadadhīte tadveda'? Pramādakṛtam ācāryasya śakyamakartum. (Kṭ on 'Pramādakṛtam:- siṣyāṇām sukhabodhāya lāghavam prati anavadhānalakṣaṇena kṛtamityarthaḥ'.)
51. *Mbh* p. 127.
52. The aorist third person singular of the roots *bhid* and *chid*.
53. The aorist third person singular of the root *kuṣ*.
54. Aorist third person singular of the roots *stṛ* and *dṛ*
55. Vide Supra p. 32.
56. *Mbh* p. 127.
57. Vide *"saṅghoddhau gaṇapraśamsayoḥ"* (3-3-86)
58. *'Tau sat'* (23-2-127)
59. Vide the passage beginning with "lakārasya ṅitvād ādeśeṣu sthānivadbhāvaḥ prāpnoti" and ending with "ṅitam cainam karoti, tasyaitad prayojanam - ṅito yat kāryam td yathā syād ṅiti yat kāryam tan mā bhūt". (*Mbh* pp. 140 - 141)
60. *a* = *adāgama ci* = root, *nu* = the *vikaraṇa am* = *parasmaipada* termination first person singular.
61. Imperfect First person singular of the root *ci*.
62. Imperfect third person singular and first person dual respectively of the root *ci*.
63. Third person singular of the benefictive mood of the root *'stu'*.
64. *stu* = the root, *yā* = *yāsuṭ*, *t* = *parasmaipada* termination *ti* with the *i* in it being elided.
65. Benedictive third person singular of the root *'ci'*
66. *Mbh* p. 143.
67. Nominative singular of the base *pipaṭhiṣ*.
68. Aorist third person singular of the root *lū*.
69. *Mbh* p. 254.
70. Vide *Mbh* p. 184.
71. *Mbh* p. 277.
72. Vide Supra pp. 40 & 41.

73. *Mbh* p. 281.
74. *Mbh* p. 308.
75. The imperfect third person plural of the roots *'i'* and *'as'*
76. Present tense first person plural of the roots *'dhiv* and *'kṛv.*
77. *dhi* = the root, *nu* = the *vikarana śnu*, and *anti* = the *parasmaipada* termination (plural)
 kṛ = the root, *nu* = the *vikaraṇa śnu*, *anti* = the *parasmaipada* termination (plural)
78. *Mbh* p. 310.
79. *Mbh* p. 363.
80. *Mbh* p. 363.
81. Such doubts are more or less based on the view entertained by scholars. Vide Infra p. 137 Ref No. 29..
82. *Mbh* p. 98.
83. The base *gamḷ* preceded with the instrumental singular case ending.
84. *'Ra'* in the rule *"uraṇ raparaḥ"* is taken as a *pratyāhāra* comprehending *r* and *l*.
85. Vide Infra p. 232.
86. *Mbh* p. 110.
87. *Mbh* p. 117.
88. Vide *Pāṇinīyaśikṣā* - *"Vivṛtamūṣmanām svarāṇāmca"*.
89. *Mbh* p. 171.
90. *Mbh* p. 148.
91. *Mbh* p. 291.
92. *Mbh* p. 347.
93. *Mbh* p. 81.
94. *Mbh* p. 86.
95. *Mbh* p. 97
96. *Mbh* p. 133.
97. *Mbh* p. 149.
98. *Mbh* p. 148
99. *Mbh* p. 230.
100. *Mbh* p. 258.
101. *Mbh* p. 259
102. *Mbh* p. 271.
103. *Mbh* p. 279.
104. *Mbh* p. 43.
105. *Mbh* p. 62.
106. *Mbh* p. 104.
107. *Mbh* p. 118.
108. *Mbh* p. 79.
109. *Mbh* p. 253.

Chapter IV

Elucidation of the Pradīpa

In his work *Uddyota,* NBh elucidates the *Pradīpa,* which is a gloss on the *Mbh.* He explains the expressions of Kṭ and elaborates Kṭ's assertions on the expressions found in the text of the *Mbh.* He supplements the views held by Kṭ on various points. The elucidative assertions of Kṭ on the different passages in the text of the *Mbh* are also dealt with by NBh. The method of elucidation by way of answering the objections and doubts raised by himself, is followed while dealing with Kṭ also and this helps NBh to justify the assertion of Kṭ.

Certain Expressions

While Commenting on the *Prdp,* NBh pays attention to the explanation given by Kṭ to the various expressions in the sūtras and passages in the text of the *Mbh.* He gives additional information on them and elucidates the expressions used by Kṭ himself.

1. *'Tāvad'*

The word *'tāavad'* used by Kṭ and Pat in two different places, has been explained significantly by NBh. He specifies the two distinctly-related yet different senses in which the same word is used by them. Kṭ used the word in the sentence, *"svavākyam vyākhyātum tadavayavam athaśabdam tāvad vyācaṣṭe"*[1] NBh says that the word *'Tāvad'* used by Kṭ here means 'first of all', *Tāvad" prathamam"*[2] Pat in answer to the questions, *"kaṣām śabdānām?""*, says, *"laukikānām, vaidikānāñca. Tatra laukikāstāvad".* Here the word *'Tāvad'* is used by Pat and NBh says: *'tāvacchabdo 'nukrame'* i.e, *'tāvad'* is used in the sense of priority.

In the former instance, the sense given to the word is significant, because it is meant that Pat intends to explain all the words in the sentence *'athaśabdānuśasānam'* and took first of all the word *'atha'* for explanation. That may be due to the of t-quoted saying *'prathamātikramaṇe mānābhāvāt'*. In the latter context, the sense of priority is significant. Among the Vedic and non- Vedic words though the Vedic words are more important, Pat with a view to show his equal regard to non- Vedic words, begins to cite the examples for non-Vedic words before giving the same for Vedic words. This may be due to the fact *"bahūnāmanugraho nyāyyaḥ"*. Thus the two meanings of the word i.e, 'first of all' and 'prior' (*prāthamya* and *anukrama*) have only a narrow distinction between themselves, since the former relates to number and the latter relates to the sequence. This subtle difference has been clearly pointed out by NBh.

2. *'Bhūyah'*

Commenting on the word 'bhūyah' used by Pat in the sentence *'imānica bhūyah śbdāanusāsanaprayojanāmi* Kt says *"bhuya iti punarityarthaḥ"*. NBh points out the significance of this explanation.[3] In the sentence there is the word *'prayojanāni* used in the plural number and the word *bhūyah* ordinarily used to denote the sense of many, may seem to be an adjective of *prayojanāni*. There is thus the scope for a doubt as to how can the word *bhūyaḥ*, nominative singular of the neuter base *bhūyas*, can correspond to the word *prayojanāani* used in the plural number. NBh says that it is to avert this obscurity that Kṭ gives the meaning of the word *'bhūyaḥ'* as *'punaḥ'* which shows that the word *bhūyaḥ* is an indeclinable here, meaning 'again' and hence it is not an adjective qualifying *'prayojanāni'*. This sense suits the context. After dealing with the main purpose to be achieved by the study of *Vyākaraṇa*, Pat again deals with the purposes, of the study of *Vyākaraṇa*, which are accessory.

3. *'Pramattagītaḥ'*

Pat uses the expression *'pramattagītaḥ'* in the sentence *'pramattagīta eṣa tatrabhavataḥ'*.[4] By the word *'eṣah'*, he refers to a verse cited previously. In this sentence the derivation of the word *'pramattagītaḥ'* presents an ambiguity. If the suffix *'kta'* in the part *'pramatta'* of the compound, is used in the sense of agent, it will correspond to the word *'tatrabhavataḥ'* and so cannot be compounded with the word *'gītaḥ'*. NBh says that it is to point out the correct derivation, that Kṭ splits up the compound as *'pramādena vipratipannatvena gīta ityarthah'*. The idea is that the suffix *'kta'* in *pramatta* is in the sense of *'bhāva'* whereby *pramatta* means *pramāda* and the compound means, recited by a dunce.

4. *Dharmaniyamaḥ*

The compound word *'dharmaniyamaḥ'* in the vārttika,
siddhe śabdārthasambandhe lokato'rthaprayukte śabdaprayoge/
śāstreṇa dharmaniyamaḥ kriyate yathā laukika vaidikeṣu//,
is given different derivations in the bhāṣya i.e., dharmāya niyamaḥ dharmaniyamaḥ. dharmartho vā niyamaḥ *dharmaniyamaḥ, dharmaprayojano vā niyamaḥ - dharmaniyamaḥ.*[5] Kṭ says that the explanation *dharmāya niyamaḥ* must not lead one to the misunderstanding that *'dharmaniyamaḥ'* is a *'caturthītatpuruṣa'* compound enjoined by the rule *'caturthī tadarthārtha'*, etc. (2-1-36). The relation between *dharma* and *niyama* is *'tādarthya'* whereas *'caturthīsamāsa'* is restricted to those having *'prakṛtivikṛtibhāva'* as their relation. The compound is an example of *ṣaṣṭhīsamāsa* enjoined by the rule *'ṣaṣṭhī'* (2-2-8) and the genitive case after *dharma* shows the relation between *dharma and niyama* and the same is explained as *'dharmāya niyamaḥ'*. NBh here says that this statement of Kṭ shows that the sense *tādarthya* comes under the scope of genitive case. He continues that Kṭ is quite justified when he takes the word *'dharmaniyamaḥ'* as an example of *ṣaṣṭhīsamāsa* in spite of the explanation *'dharmāya niyamaḥ'*. He points out that the derivation of the compound as *'caturthītatpuruṣa'* cannot be sanctioned by the *yogavibhāga* of the rule *"caturthī tadarthārtha...."* (2-1-36) into two, one compraising the word *'caturthī'* alone, considering that such a *yogavibhāga* is mentioned nowhere in the text of the *Mbh.* The splitting up of the compound as *'dharmāya niyamaḥ'* with a view to treat the same as a *'caturthīsamāsa'* cannot be justified even by the rule *'saha supā'* (2-1-4)[19] since it is the last resort in the absence of any other explanation and hence cannot be a

strong support to establish the purpose. Therefore, NBh strongly supports the view of *Kṭ* that even in the explanation *dharmāya niyamaḥ,* the compound word is an example of *ṣaṣṭhīsamāsa.*

Kṭ says that in the second interpretation *dharmārtho vā niyamaḥ dharmaniyamaḥ,* the expression *dharmaniyamaḥ* is an example of *karmadhāraya* compound. *Dharma and niyama* are identical here. The *niyama* that the meaning is to be denoted by correct words alone, is to procure *dharma*. Thus the *niyama* is *'dharmārtha'*. The component word 'dharma' of the compound is in the sense of *'dharmārtha'* and as the words *'dharma'* and *'niyama'* denote identical ideas they are compounded by the rule *"viśeṣaṇam viśeṣyeṇa bahulam"* (2-1-56). K*ṭ* continues saying that the third interpretation of Pat i.e., *dharmaprayojano vā niyamaḥ dharmaniyamaḥ* means that *niyama* is effected by *'dharma'* known in the name of *'niyoga'* which is the scope of *liṅ* and the like.

NBh points out that the difference which Kṭ wants to bring out between the second and third interpretation is that in the former *dharma* is treated as the consequence of *niyama* whereas in the latter *niyama* is treated as being effected by *dharma*. He specifies that the explanation given by Kṭ to the third interpretation is in accordance with the view of Mīmāmsakas. According to them, the *liṅ*, i.e., *'yajeta'* in the injunction *'svargakāmo yajeta'* denotes *apūrva*. This *apūrva* causes man to be engaged in the same and hence is called *'niyoga'* NBh makes clear that this *'niyoga'* is the one referred to as *dharma* by *Kṭ* here and it effects the *niyama* of excluding incorrect words. Hence the explanatory assertion *dharmaprayojanaḥ* is an example of *ṣaṣṭhīsamāsa* with the derivation *dharmasya* (the genitive case after *dharma* being in the sense of agent) *prayojanaḥ,* wherein the part *prayojanaḥ* has the suffix *lyuṭ* in the sense of *karman,* and by this derivation the compound denotes the idea effected by *niyama*. Hence the compound *dharmaniyama* used in this sense means the *niyama* caused by *dharma*. In this way NBh clarifies the difference suggested by Kṭ between the second and third interpretation given by Kṭ himself.

5. *Iglakṣaṇaḥ*

Pat and Kṭ use this expression as an adjunct to *guṇa* and *vṛddhi*. In the bhāṣya under the rule *"na dhātulopa ārdhadhātuke"*

(1-1-4) the objector asks how the forms *'upeddhaḥ* and *'preddhaḥ'* can be arrived at, if the word *'ārdhadhātuke'* is treated as an adjunct of *lopa*.[6] What he means is that in the form *'iddhaḥ'* which is derived from the root *'indh'* with the addition of the suffix *'kta'*, there is the elision of the element *'n'* of the root caused by the suffix *'kta'* and so when the form is prefixed with *'upa' or 'pra'*, there may be the undesirable prohibition of *guṇa* from replacing the *'a'* of the prefix and *'i'* of the form *'iddhaḥ'*. Kṭ says that as the *guṇa* is *aniglakṣaṇa* and the rule prohibits such *guṇa and vṛddhi* that are *iglakṣaṇa*, there is actually no difficulty like the contingency of the prohibition of *guṇa* here and yet the question is put forward to bring another solution to this problem. NBh here explains the idea conveyed by the word *iglakṣaṇa* and the circumstance under which such an idea is got. In the said instance, the *guṇa* as it replaces *'i'* can be desccibed as *iksthānika*, but it is not *iglakṣaṇa*. This is because the expression *iglakṣaṇa* means that caused by the *paribhāṣā* rule *"iko guṇavṛddhīī* (1-1-3). The rule *"iko guṇavṛddhī"* is got by *anuvṛtti* in the rule *"na dhātulopa ārdhadhātuke"* (1-1-4) and the latter means :- the prohibition i.e., *'na dhātulopa ārdhadhātuke'* presents itself in the rules where the rule *"iko guṇavṛddhī"* presents itself. Thus the rule *"na dhātulopa..."* (1-1-4) too is treated as a *paribhāṣā*. We thus find that the prohibition is only to those *guṇa and vṛddhi* that are caused by the rule *"iko guṇavṛddhī"*. NBh gives another interpretation of *"na dhātulopa....."* for arriving at the idea of the prohibition of *guṇa and vṛddhi* that are *iglakṣaṇa*. The rule prohibits the *guṇa and vṛddhi* enjoined by rules wherein there is the function of the rule *"iko guṇavṛddhī"*. NBh quotes the words the Kṭ under the vārttika *'ikprakaraṇānnumlope vṛddhiḥi'*. They are *"tena yatrekparibhāṣā sthānyantaranivṛttaye vyāpriyate tatrāyam niṣedhaḥ"*.[7] Without treating the rule *"na dhatulopa......"* (1-1-4) as a *paribhāṣā*, NBh suggests another way by which the rule prohibits *guṇa and vṛddhi* that are *iglakṣaṇa*. The word *ikaḥ* in the rule *"iko guṇavrddhī"* denotes the word *ikaḥ* and with this meaning it is got by *anuvṛtti* in the rule *"na dhatulopa...."* (1-1-4) and so the rule prohibits the *guṇa and vṛddhi* that have their operation specified by the word *ikaḥ*.

6. The word 'ūdāttaḥ' in the rule "asthi dadhisakthyakṣṇām ananudāttaḥ" (7-1-75)

Pat says that the word *udāttaḥ* in the rule *asthidadhisakthyakṣṇām anaṅudāttaḥ* (7-1-71) indicates that guṇas are treated as abhedakas in the science of grammar.[8] In case *guṇas* were non-differentiating elements of phonemes, there is no need for the mention of the word *udāttaḥ* in the rule. Pāṇ could have uttered the *akāra* with the *udāttasvara* and *anaṅ* will ever be treated as *udātta*. Kṭ elucidates the *jñāpaka*. *Guṇas* are non- differentiating elements and since the utterance of a letter is not without a *svara*, the particular *svara* of a phoneme can be taken into account only when there is a specific effort for its sake. That is why Pāṇ has mentioned the word *udāttaḥ* in the said rule. Now, Kṭ anticipates an objection here. As the utterance of a letter is not without a particular *svara* and as a *svara* can be taken into account only if there is a specific effort for the same, how can Pat resort to *udāttanipātana* for serving different purposes? He speaks of the *udāttanipātana* of the substitute *vadha* of the root *han* so that the part *ekācaḥ* in the rule *"ekāca upadeśe nudāttād"* (7-2-10) can be dispensed with. Kṭ clears this inconsistency pointing out that the *udāttanipātana* itself is an effort in instances where by virtue of *sthānivadbhāva* another *svara* is contingent to be used in a letter. The *han* is *anudātta* and *vadha* being its substitue ought to be uttered with the *anudāttasvara* and in this circumstance the *udāttanipātana* in the substitute becomes a specific effort. So also the *nipāta uñ* is not nasalized and its substitute need be non-nasalized and the nasalization (*ū*) of the same in the rule (1-1- 18) is an effort to take the vowel substitute as nasalized.

To establish what has been stated by Kt. NBh advances a doubt here. In the rule *"asthidadhisakthyakṣṇām anaṅudāttaḥ"* (7-1-75) the *a* of *anaṅ* need be uttered as *anudātta* since the svara of the *sthānin 'i'* in *asthi* etc. is *anudātta* and the utterance itself of *a* with the *udātta svara* can be treated as an effort, in the light of Kṭ's explanation, to indicate that *guṇas* are *adhedakas*. Therefore the doubt that the word *udāttah* in the rule is still superfluous, arises. NBh continues that this doubt cannot stand careful scrutiny. In instances like *paramāsthi, paramadadhi,* etc., the *sthānin 'i'* is *udātta* and so in accordance with the *sthānin,* the *'a'* of *anaṅ* has to be *udātta*. Thus considering that the *sthānin* is one having varied *svaras* in varied instances, there is no certainty that the *sthānisvara,* is ever *udātta* in which case the utterance itself of a with *udāttasvara* would have become a specific effort. Therefore it is the mention of the word *udāttaḥ* that is, as pointed out by Kṭ, the *jñāpaka* for the fact that *guṇas* are *abhedakas*.

Here one thing may be asked, says NBh. The substitute *catasṛ* prescribed by the rule *"tricaturoḥ striyām tisṛcatasṛ"* (7-2-99) need be *ādyudātta* and it cannot be a specific effort since the *sthānin catur* is *ādyudātta* by the rule *"uraḥ saṅkhyāyām"*.[9] At the same time Pat speaks of *ādyudāttanipātana* of *catasṛ* to serve the purpose of averting the *antodātta* of *catasṛ* in the instance *catasraḥ* that is contingent to be uttered there by the rule *"caturaḥ śasi"* (6-1- 167). NBh says that it is this discrepancy that presuaded Kt., to introduce another view with the statement *anye tvāhuḥ*. Kṭ says that some are of opinion that *udāttanipātana* in an instance becomes a specific effort as the rules are read in *ekaśruti*. NBH explains it saying that the rule (1-2- 36) *"vibhāsā chandasi"* enjoins *ekaśruti* optionally. Hence the *udāttanipātana* i.e., the utterance of a syllable with a particular svara becomes a specific effort (for taking the *udāttasvara* into account) where on account of *ekaśruti* no particular *svara* need by uttered. However, the mention of the word *udāttaḥ* in the rule (7-1-75) becomes an indication to the *abhedakatva* of *guṇas* in the *traisvaryapakṣa* according to which a syllable cannot be uttered without a *svara*. Hence if the guṇas were differentiating elements, Pāṇ could have more conveniently uttered the *a* of *anaṅ* with the accent *udātta* and the superfluous mention of the word *udāttaḥ* becomes the *jñīpaka* to show the non-differentiating capacity of *guṇas*.

NBh says that the view cited by Kṭ with the statement *'anye tu āhuh'* is expressive of Kṭ's disagreement with the same and he brings out that point. There is no authority to point out that all the rules are read in *ekaśruti*. In the bhāṣya under the rule *"dāṇḍināyana....."* (4-7-4) Pat says that the word *aikṣvāka* in the said rule is read in *ekaśruti*. Again though students read the whole of Aṣṭ in *ekaśruti*, we are informed from the *vyākhyāna* (interpretation of the learned), of the sounds that are nasalised and the like. Hence we cannot wholly accept the view that all the rules are read in *ekaśruti* in which *udāttanipātana* can be treated as a specific effort. Again NBh, adds that the *udāttanipātana* in the rule *"tricaturoḥ striyām tisṛcatasṛ"* (7-2-99) can well be treated as a specific effort in the *traisvaryapakṣa*.

This is because *nipātana* means a particular usage of the *ācarya* where another kind of usage is contingent in the natural course. In the rule *"tricaturoḥ striyām tisṛcatasṛ"* (7-2-99) the accent on the *a* of *catasṛ* ought to be *anudātta* since *tisṛcatasṛ* is a *dvandva* according to which *a* can be only *anudātta*. Thus, the *udāttanipātana* on the *a* of *catasṛ* when it ought to be *anudātta* is a specific effort and hence it averts *anudāṭṭa* contingent to be given to *'a'* in the instance *catasraḥ* by the rule *"caturaḥ śasi"* (6-1-67) NBh therefore says that the mention of the word *udātta* as the *jñāpaka* to the non- differentiating capacity of *guṇas* and the *udāttanipātana* incidentally resorted to by Pat is well justified by Kṭ.

7. Sāmānādhikaraṇya

Pat says that *"vṛddhirādaic"* (1-1-1) is a rule defining the technical term *vṛddhi*, as there is *sāmanādhikaraṇya* and *ekavibhaktikatva* in the rule.[10] Kṭ cites two different views with regard to what the expression *sāmānādhikaraṇya* means. *"Tattu sāmānādhikaraṇ-yam śabdāyoreva kecid iccahanti, dvābhyām bhinnapravṛttinimittābhyām ekasyābhidheyasya pratipādanān viśeṣaṇaviśesyārthapratipādanācca viśeṣaṇaviśeṣyatvam. Anye tu nīlamutpalam iti pravṛttinimittayoḥ jātiguṇayor ekam adhikaraṇam aśraya iti sāmānādhikaraṇyam viśeṣaṇaviśeṣyabhāvam cārthayor eva manyante"*.[11] NBh explains these views on *sāmānādhikaraṇya*. When two *śabdas* of varied *pravṛttinimittas* denote one and the same object, those *śabdas* can be called *sāmānādhikaraṇa*. In a *samjñābodhakaśabda*, the *pravṛttinimitta* is that *śabda* itself whereas in a *samjñibodhakaśabda* the *pravṛttinimitta* is the quality i.e., *dharma* that rests on the *samjñin*. Accordingly the *pravṛttinimitta* of *vṛddhisamjñā* is *vṛddhiśabda* itself and that of *ādaic* is *ādaictva*. These two *śabdas* of varied *pravṛttinimittas* thus, denote one, by virtue of the rule *"vṛddhirādaic"* (1-1- 1). Hence there is the *sāmānādhikaraṇya* of these two words. The *śabdabodha* derived from the rule is *vṛddhiśabdavadabhinnāḥ ādaicaḥ*. The other view cited by Kṭ is that *sāmānādhikaraṇya* relates to the senses denoted by sounds, and not to the sounds. NBh says that according to this view the senses of words *vṛddhiḥ and ādaic*, are treated as *samānādhikaraṇa* since the *pravṛttinimitta* of these two, namely, *vrddhiśabda* and *ādaictva* rest in one object. (*Vṛddhiśabda* rests in the *samjñin* and that relation is known as *tādātmya*). NBh adds that this view cited by Kṭ with the statement *anye tu āhuḥ* is expressive of his dissent with that view and he brings out that point of disagreement. If as according to this view *sāmanādhikaraṇya* relates to the sense and not to the sounds the expression *pratītapadārthakayoḥ* of Pat in the passage *"dvayor hi pratītapadārthakayor loke viśeṣaṇaviśeṣyabhāvo bhavati na cādaic-chabdaḥ pratītapadārthakaḥ tasmat samjñāsamjñināveva"* cannot be explained.[12] In this passage the expression *pratītapadārthakayoḥ* is a *bahuvrīhi* compound meaning,'of those two, which have their sense well-known'. Pat speaks of sounds alone in this passage in order to establish that the word *vṛddhiḥ and ādaic* are *samjñā and samjñin* and are *samānādhikaraṇa*. If the *sāmānādhikaraṇya* relates to objects, he would not have used the *bahuvrīhi*, but stated *pratītapadārthayoḥ (karmadhāraya* compound). Hence the usage of the *bahuvrīhi* compound by which sounds are taken into consideration, does not seem to favour the idea that *sāmānādhikaraṇya* relates to the sense and not to the sound.

8. *'Ekayoga'*

In order to secure the non-connection of the word *vṛddhiḥ* of the rule *"vṛddhirādaic"* (1-1-1) with *aden* of the rule *"adenguṇaḥ"* caused by the *anuvṛtti* of the word *vṛddhiḥ* from the rule *vṛddhirādaic* to the rule *"ikoguṇavṛddhi"* (1-1-3) which is immediately preceded by the rule *"adenguṇaḥ"* (1-1-2) Pat says that *"vṛddhirādaic"* and *"adenguṇaḥ"* are to be made an *ekayoga* i.e., *vṛddhirādaijadenguṇaḥ* and as there cannot be the *anuvṛtti* of a word within an *ekayoga* there is no problem of the connection of the word *vṛddhiḥ* with *aden*.[13] Kṭ maintains that *ekayoga* means a simple sentence. NBh points out the basis of Kṭ's conception of *ekayoga*. *Ekayoga* cannot be a rule possessed of single prediction, since *vṛddhirādaijadenguṇaḥ* which is the *ekayoga* mentioned here, conveys the predication of two *samjñās* namely *vrddhi* and *guṇa* that are distinctly separate in as much as they relate to different *samjñins*.

Ekayoga cannot be the closest utterance of words. If it were so, even before the solution that *vṛddhirādaic and adenguṇaḥ* are to be made an *ekayoga*, is offered, they are uttered in close proximity and hence the future tense in *kariṣyate* in the passage giving this solution cannot be explained and it is prone to be regarded as superfluous.[14]

Again in the rule "*ṇerаṇau yat karma ṇau cet sa kartā nādhyāne*" (1-3-67) which is a single sūtra, there is the *anuvṛtti* of the words *aṇau, yat, karma, ṇau, cet*. This rule is possessed of four clauses namely, (1) *ṇeḥ ātmanepadam (syād)*; (2) *aṇau yat karma (tat) ṇau cet* (3) *aṇau yat karma as ṇau kartā cet and (4) anādhyāne (cet)* and among these four, the first is the principal clause. From this it is clear that *ekayoga* cannot also mean a signle sūtra. Pat has stated that there cannot be the *anuvṛtti* of words within an *ekayoga* and in the said rule there is the *anuvṛtti* of words within itself. NBh points out that it is after taking into consideration all these factors that Kṭ upholds the view that *ekayoga* means a simple sentence. Kṭ says that by supplementing a word denoting the idea of *bhavathikriyā* a simple sentence is obtained. Though this predicate namely, *bhavatikriyā* may relate separately to *guṇa* and *vṛddhi* in the *pratipattikāla*, the connection of *guṇasamjñā* with *aden* and that of *vrddhisamjñā* with *ādaic* is understood simultaneously and therefore, *vrddhisamjñā* cannot correlate to *aden* which is already connected with *guṇasamjñā*. NBh elucidates this assertion of Kṭ also. He points out that Kt. derives a simple sentence i.e., *vrddhirādaij adenguṇobhavati*, by means of *ekayoga*. The word *pratipatti* used by Kt. means *vakyārthabodha* derived from the sentence and it is here that which is known as *samoohālambanajñāna* and hence there is no problem of the connection of the word *vṛddhiḥ* with *aden*. Or the *vākyārthabodha* derived from the sentence may be as *vṛddhirādaic adenguṇaḥ ca bhavataḥ* and as such also there is no connection of the word *vṛddhiḥ* with *aden*. NBh points out that Kṭ is quite justified in assuming *ekayoga* to be a simple sentence and it is because of the complex nature of the rule "*ṇeraṇau....*" (1-3-67) that the *anuvṛtti* of the words within itself is accepted.

9. The compohent word 'ādi' in the rule "vānyasya samyogādeḥ" (6-4-68).

In the *bhāṣya* under the rule "*halo'nantarāḥ" samyogaḥ*" (1-1-7) Pat discusses the question whether the word *saha* is to be added at the end of the *sūtra* so that when there are two contingous consonants, the whole may get the designation samyoga collectively. If otherwise they get the designation individually, there is the difficulty that in instances like *niryāyāt* and *nirvāyāt,* the *ā* after the first *y* in the former and after *v* in the latter can optionally change to *e* by the rule *"vānyasya...."* (6-4-68), as the *y* and *v* can be designated as *samyoga* as there are two contiguous consonants namely, *r* and *y* in the former and *r* and *v* in the latter.[15] The solution given is that this defect cannot stand careful scrutiny by virtue of the word *ādi* in the compound word *samyogādeḥ* of the rule. The compound word *samyogādeḥ* is to be split up in the dual number as *samyogau ādī yasya so'yam samyogādiḥ* and not in singular number *samyogaḥ ādiḥ yasya so'yam samyogādiḥ tasya samyogādeḥ* so that the optional substitution by *e* shall function on the vowel *a* of such *aṅga* alone that begins with two *samyogas* and not with one.[16] Here *Kṭ* points out how the word *ādi* helps to arrive at this meaning. He says that if the optional replacement by *e* is to influence the *a* of an *aṅga* beginning with a single consonant the wording of the rule need only be as *vānyasya samyogāt* from which even without the word *ādi* by virtue of the *paribhāṣā sūtra "tasmādityuttarsya"* (1-1-67) the idea, that the vowel *a* following a single *samyoga* undergoes the optional replacement by *e,* can be easily arrived at. The word *ādi* being thus superfluous helps in splitting the compound in the dual number.

To justify Kṭ NBh says that the word *'ādi'* is not even necessary to get the idea that, in order to get the optional sibstitution of *ā* by *e,* the single *samyoga* which is to precede the *'a'* should be the former element of the *aṅga.* It may be said that if there is no specification that the single *samyoga* ought to be the former element of the *aṅga,* there is the contingency of the optional substitution by *e* of *ā* in the instance *khatvāyāt* where the single samyoga *v* is not the former element of the *aṅga.*[17] But this contingency can easily be avoided by the *anuvṛtti* of the word *upadeśa* from the rule *"syasicsīyuṭtāsiṣu bhāvakarmaṇorupadeśe.."* (6-4-42) to the rule *"vānyasya samyogādeḥ"* (6-4-68) so that those which are roots in the *upadeśa* itself are taken into consideration in this rule and not those which are nominal roots. Therefore, there is no problem in the instance *khatvāyāt* as the same is derived from a nominal root. Moreover, NBh says that a form like *khatvāyāt* need not be taken into consideration as it is understood from the bhāṣya under the rule "*āto dhātoḥ*" (6-4-140) that there is the *anabhidhāna* of the forms derived by the addition of *kvip* in the sense of *ācāra*, from bases like *khatvā*. Therefore, the word *ādi* in the rule is quite unnecessary to prevent the optional substitution by *e* of the vowel *ā* in the said instance. Kṭ is, therefore, quite correct in saying that it is by virtue of the word *ādi* that one gets the compound having the components in the dual number.

NBh however, adds that in the *siddhānta* that the designation *samyoga* relates to two or more contiguous consonants, the word *ādi* in necessary to get the idea that the *samyoga* by which two or more contiguous consonants are meant, must be the former element of the *aṅga* of the root for the function of the rule, so that in instance like *niryāyāt*, the *aṅga* i.e., *yā* being devoid of *samyoga* at the beginning won't undergo the optional substitution of *ā* by *e*.

10. The expressions mahiṣī rūpam iva and brāhmaṇī rūpam iva in Samānādhikaraṇeṣu ghādiṣu ityucyamāne iha prasajyeta mahiṣī rūpam iva, brāhmaṇī rūpam iva iti[18]

Under the rule "*taraptamapau ghaḥ*" (1-1-21) Pat says that in the rule "*gharupakalpaceladbruvagotra....*" (6-3- 43) which enjoins *hrasva* to a *pūrvapada* ending in *ṅī* when followed by an *uttarapada* like *gha* etc., the *uttarapada* must be treated as feminine in gender for the function of the rule. If on the other hand the *uttarapada* like *gha* etc., is interpreted to be *samānādhikaraṇa* with the *pūrvapada*, therein is involved the difficulty of the contingency of *hrasva* in *mahiṣī rūpam iva* and *brāhmaṇī rūpam iva*". The exact words of Pat are *Strīliṅgeṣu ghādiṣu ityevam tad. Avaśyam caited evam vijñeyam. Samānādhikaraṇeṣu ghādisu ityucyamāne iha prasjyeta mahiṣī rūpam iva, brāhmaṇi rūpam iva iti.* Meaning "It is interpreted thus, followed by *ghādi* which is feminine in gender. It must be necessarily interpreted so: If it is said that it takes place when followed by *ghādi* which is *samanādhikaraṇa*, it will operate in *mahiṣī rūpam iva, brāhmaṇī rūpam iva* also. With regard to the expressions '*mahiṣī rūpam iva*' and '*brāhmaṇī rūpam iva*' Kṭ says that the word *iva* in these, is to be put after the words *mahiṣī* and *brāhmaṇī* respectively. He points out that the expression means *mahiṣī iva iyam ākṛtiḥ* and says that there is the contingency of *hrasva* by the rule *"gharūpa ...."* (6-3-43) on the word *mahiṣīī* when the two words *mahiṣī* and *rūpam* are compounded by the rule *"saha supā...."* (2-1-4). NBh gives the significance of Kṭ's explanation. He points out that Kṭ is quite justified in considering *mahiṣī rūpam iva*, which is in the sense of *mahiṣī iva iyam īkṛtiḥ*, to be the *vigrahavākya* of a compound. The words *mahiṣī rūpam iva* cannot be treated as an expression wherein separate words are used without composition and the same cannot be a compound expression also. There cannot be the contingency of *hrasva* as pointed out by Pat in *mahiṣīī*, if the said expression gives separate words without composition, considering that it (the word *mahiṣīī*) is not followed by an *uttarapada* since *rūpam* is a separate word and the rule enjoins *hrasva* only when a *pūrvapada* ending in *ṇī* is followed by *uttarapada* as the rule falls within the jurisdiction of the *adhikārasūtra "alug uttarapade"* (6-3-1). Again since the word *rūpam* means *ākṛti* and since it is in anticipation of that, the *ākṛti* of which is equal with *mahiṣīī*, it will not even correspond to the word *mahiṣīī*. *Mahiṣī rūpam iva* cannot even be a compound expression since in that case also there cannot be the contingency of *hrasva* which is pointed out by Pat. The same, if it were a compound expression, is to be accepted as the *ṣaṣṭhītatpuruṣa* compound in which case the components will never be *samānādhikaraṇa* and what Pat has stated is that it is when the *uttarapada* is treated as *samānādhikaraṇa* with the *pūrvapada* that there is the contingency of *hrasva*. Thus it can be the *vigrahavākya* of a compound in which case is implied an *upamānopameyabhāva*. However the compound cannot be the one enjoined by the rule *"upamānāni sāmānyvacanaiḥ"* (2-1-55) as there is not the mention of *sāmānyadharma* here. Again it cannot be the one enjoined by the rule *"upamitam vyāghrādibhiḥ sāmānyāprayoge"* (2-1-56) since *rūpa* being the *upameya* is to be placed before the word in the compound. If it (*rūpa*) is treated as *upamāna* it will always anticipate that, of which it is (*i.e., kasya rūpam*), and hence being related to that, it cannot undergo a *vṛtti* like *samāsa*, with *mahiṣīī* with which it does not correspond. NBh says that it is after taking into consideration all these facts that Kṭ says that the words *mahiṣī and rūpam* are compounded by the rule *"saha sūpā"* (2-1-4).

On the Views of Kaiyaṭa

1. The reason for the absence of vibhakti from a, i etc. in the Śivasūtras

Kṭ asserts that the absence of case-endings from *a, i* etc. in the Śivasūtras is due to the fact that they are not prātipadikas after which alone case-endings are added. Though by virtue of *svarūpa and anukārya* they can be treated as *'arthavat'* that *'arthavatva'* is not taken into consideration and hence being not *arthavat* they are never *prātipadikas* after which case-endings are added. NBh elucidates the view of Kṭ. As a rule, the *svarūpa* of a *śabda* can be treated as its *'artha'* since it is being cognised on hearing the *śabda*. The *a, i* etc. in the *Śivasūtras* give a cognition in which their *svarūpa* is also involved. Hence *a, i* etc. are well *arthavat*. Or else *a, i* etc. are the *anukaraṇa* of the *a, i* etc. in the worldly usages. An *anukaraṇa* always denotes the *anukārya* and hence it is the *artha* of the *anukaraṇa*. Therefore *a, i* etc., being imitative of *a, i* etc. are *arthavat*. Yet they do not come under the scope of the word *arthavat* to which the term *prātipadika* is given by the rule *"arthavadhātur...* (1-2-45). This is because the word *arthavat* in the rule denotes a *śabda* having a sense i.e., *artha* denoted by its expressive power known as *vṛtti*. *Svarūpa* and *anukārya* are not this kind of *artha*. There is no need of the function of the expressive power of the sound in understanding its *'svarūpa'*. It will be cognised simply when the sound becomes the object of hearing. So also an *anukaraṇa* indicates the *anukārya* not by its expressive power, but by virtue of its similarity with the *anukārya*. *a i* etc. being thus indicative of no sense by its expressive power cannot be characterised as *arthavat* and so cannot entertain case-suffixes after them. Moreover if the suffixes are added to it, its imitative power as an *anukaraṇa* may be disturbed. Hence the absence of case- suffixes after each letter in the *Śivasūtras*. NBh says that the same can be justified by treating the same as *'sautra'* i.e., peculiarity found in *sūtras* alone.

2. The correctness of the word 'ḷtaka'

While enumerating the benefits of the enunciation of the letter *'ḷ'* it is pointed out in the bhāṣya that the same is for the sake of *yadṛcchāśabdas* i.e., for words coined at random. These words like *ḷtaka, ḷphiḍa* and *ḷphiḍḍa* are words of casual utterance and form one group among the four divisions of standard words. The vārttikakāra points out that these are not correct and it is the words *ṛtaka ṛphiḍa and ṛphiḍḍa* that are correct. They are the regularly derived forms and consequently grammatically correct forms. They are only three kinds standard words i.e., *jātiśabda, guṇaśabda* and *kriyāśabda*. The objector attacks this view saying that this kind of argumentation is not fair. He argues that the utility of the mention of *'ḷ'* in *Śivasūtras,* is shown on the strength of the view that there are *yadṛcchāśabdas* and the same is disproved by denying the existence of *yadṛcchāśabdas*. Besides a *śabda* formed according to rules debars the other one not so formed, only when both are used in the same sense. Here the words *ṛtaka* and *ḷtaka* do not have the same sense, the former meaning truthful and the latter being the designation of a person. The answer given to this argument is that refutations are made even on the basis of different views. This means that the view admitting the existence of three groups of standard *śabdas* is the one to be accepted. Thus according to *vārttikakāra* the regularly derived words like *ṛtaka* alone are to be used. NBh says that, one can refute the utility of the mention of *'ḷ'* for the sake of *śabdas* like *ḷtaka* even by admitting the existence of yadṛcchaśabdas. Words like *ḷtaka* are debarred from usage since they are not accepted by *śiṣṭas*. Correct words include those which even though not regularly derived are sanctioned by the usage of śiṣṭas. NBh points out that, this fact, though not stated orally by Pat, is noted by Kṭ who for the sake of average students says that *"avyutpannasamjñāsabdapakṣe'pi pāramparyagatāḥ śiṣṭaprayuktā eva samjñāḥ kartavyāḥ"*.[20].

3. The problem of substitution of 'ā' by hrasva ***in the absence*** *of the upadeśa of 'a' as vivṛta in the rule 'aiuṇ'*

Under the Śivasūtra *'aiuṇ'* Pat says that the vārttika *'akārasya vivṛtopadeśaḥ ākāragrahaṇārthaḥ'* points out the inclusion of *ā* by *a* as the purpose of the actual utterance of the letter *a* in the said rule and the vārttika does never advise the mention of *a* as *vivṛta* instead of the usual *saṃvṛta* which is actually made there.[21] The rule *"a a"* (8-4-68) is an indication to this effect since it enjoins the substitute namely *saṃvṛta 'a'* in the place of *'a'* which is *vivṛta*. To contradict this indication, the objector says that the rule *'a a'* (8-4-68) is not at all redundant to bring forth such an indication. It has got the specific purpose of making the *hrasva* substitute namely *a* enjoined by the rule *"gostriyor upasarjanasya"* (1-2-48) in instances like *atikhaṭvaḥ*, to be *saṃvṛta*, which otherwise is contingent to be *vivṛta* on account of the similarity with the *sthānin* namely *ā* and so it cannot indicate the fact that there is *vivṛtopadeśa* of *a* in *'aiuṇ'*. The words of Pat are here *"naitadasti jñāpakam". asti hyanyad etasya vacane prayojanam. kim? atikhaṭvaḥ atimālaḥ ityatrāntaryato vivṛtasya vivṛtaḥ prāpnoti, saṃvṛtaḥ syād ityevamarthā pratyāpattiḥ*. Kṭ suspects an inconsistency in this assertion. If there is no *vivṛtopadeśa* of the letter *'a'* in the rule *'aiuṇ'*, it cannot comprehend *'ā'* and so *'ā'* will be devoid of the designation *'ac'*. *Hrasva* substitute can only be *'ac'* since in rules like *"gostriyor......"* (1-2-48) enjoining a *hrasva* substitute, the rule *'acaśca'* (2-1-28) presents itself and points out *'ac'* as the *sthānin* of the *hrasva* substitute. *'A'* will not therefore be a substitute for *ā*. Thus at a stage when the substitution by *hrasva* of *ā*, in instances like *atikhaṭvaḥ* is impossible, how can it be said that the rule *'a a'* (8-1-68) can serve the purpose of making the *hrasva 'a'* substituting *'ā'* to be *vivṛta*? *Kṭ* clears this doubt on the strength of the rule *"udīcām ātaḥ sthāne yakapūrvāyāḥ"* (7-3-46). This rule enjoins short *'i'* in the place of *a* which has substituted *ā*. As the substitution of *ā* by *a* is impossible in the above circumstance and the mention of such as *'a'* in this rule indicates that *'ā'* even if devoid of the designation *'ac'* will be substituted by *a*. NBh fully agrees with the view of Kṭ and to confirm Kṭ's assertion anticipates a doubt on the same and then gives the answer. It may be pointed out:- The rule *"āponyatarasyām"* (7-4-15) prescribes *hrasva* to the *ā* of the feminine suffix *cāp, ḍāp and ṭāp*. In the examples of this rule we get a short *a* that is spoken of in the rule *"udicāmātaḥ....."* (7-3-46). Therefore it cannot be the basis for the indication that *a* even if devoid of the designation *'ac'* is substituted by *hrasva*. Therefore, the inconsistency, that in the absence of *vivṛtopadesa* in the rule *'aiuṇ'*, *hrasva* i.e., short *a* cannot substitute *ā* in instances like *atikhaṭvaḥ* still remains as such. Now the answer is given by NBh to justify Kṭ's statement. If the rule *"udīcām ātaḥ....."* (7-3-46) functions only in instances where the rule *"āponyatarasyām"* (7-4-15) has brought *a* in the place of *ā*, the rule is actually being restricted in its scope. This must be avoided. Hence it is better to accept the substitution by *hrasva* i.e., *a* of *ā* even devoid of the designation *'ac'*. Again it can be established that the rule *"acaśca"* (2-1-28) does not exert its influence on the rule *"gostriyor....."* (1-2-48). Among the *gośabda* and the feminine suffix mentioned in this rule, the vowel *o* in *'go'* will be substituted by *hrasva* even in the absence of the function of the rule *"acaśca"* (2-1-28) as there is only one vowel there and so the rule *"acaśca"* does not present the word *'acaḥ'* with regard to *'go'*. The rule does not present the word *acaḥ* to the feminine suffix also. Since it is read along with *'go'* in the said rule and being its *sahacarita* the rule *"acaśca"* does not refer to it. Thus in the rule *"gostriyor....."* the feminine suffix is not presented with the word *acaḥ* and so the *ā* of the feminine suffix even devoid of the designation *'ac'* gets the *hrasva* substitute in instances like *atikhaṭvaḥ*.

4. *The insertion of the word 'nimitta' in the rule "kṅiti ca" (1-1-5)*

Under the rule *"kṅiti ca"* vārttikakāra suggests the insertion of the word *nimitta* in the rule. Kṭ is of opinion that such an insertion is necessary only if in the interpretation of the rule, the word *kṅiti* relates to the word *ikaḥ* got by *anuvṛtti*. This is because the rule *"tasminniti nirdiṣṭe pūrvasya"* (1-1-66) will exert its influence on the word *kṅiti* and the rule may teach the fact that *ik* which is adjunctly previous to the suffix shall get the prohibition of *guṇa* and *vṛiddhi* substitutes. Hence the *ik* which is the last element of the *aṅga* in instances like *citam, stutam,* etc. alone gets the prohibition and the penultimate *ik* in instances like *bhinnam,* cannot get this prohibition as the same cannot be adjunctly previous to the suffix and to secure the same the insertion of the word *nimitta* becomes an essential factor. But Kṭ says that if the word *kṅiti* relates to the word *guṇavṛddhī* got by *anuvṛtti,* the locative case in *kṅiti* will be *nimittasaptamī* as the rule *"tasminniti nirdiṣṭe pūrvasya"* (1-1-66) will not exert it influence and so there is no need of the insertion of the word *nimitta* in the rule.[22] NBh elucidates this assertion of Kṭ. He points out that the locative case in *kṅiti* is to be interpreted as the one taught by the rule, *"yasya ca bhāvena bhāvalakṣaṇam"* (2-3- 37) by which the action of one expressed in the locative case indicates the action of another. By virtue of this locative case in the word *kṅiti* which relates to the word *guṇavṛddhī*, it is understood that the existence of *kṅit* suffix indicates the existence of *guṇavṛddhī*. This is possible only if there is some connection between them and that relation is none other than *nimittanimittibhāva*, since rules like "*Sārvadhātukārdhadhātukayoḥ*" "*mṛjervṛddhiḥ*" etc., that enjoin *guṇa* or *vṛddhi*, offer *sārvadhātuka and ārdhadhātuka* suffix as the *nimitta*. Thus the rule *kṅiti ca* by virtue of the locative case taught by the rule "*yasya ca....*" (2-3-37) prohibits the *guṇa* and *vṛddhi* that are indicated by the existence of *kṅiti* suffix on account of their *nimittatva* to the same. That is why, says NBh, Kṭ feels the non- essentiality of the insertion of the word "*nimitta*" in the rule "*kṅiti ca*".

NBh here cites a view of some scholars elucidating the assertion of Kṭ in a manner different from that of NBh. These scholars maintain that the locative case in *kṅiti* that relates to the word *guṇavṛddhī*, is the one taught by the rule "*yasya ca bhāvena bhāvalakṣaṇam*" (2-3-37). But it is on the basis of the dictum *siddhasādhyasamabhivyāhare siddham sādhyāya kalpate* that the *kṅiti* suffix is being treated as the *nimitta* of *guṇavṛddhī* in this rule. This dictum known a *siddhasādhyasamabhihārasyāya* points out that when there is the coherence of something which is *siddha* (already accomplished) and some other which is *sādhya* (to be accomplished) the *siddha* paves the way for (becomes the *nimitta* of) *sādhya*. In the rule *kṅiti ca*" that, which is predicated and hence *sādhya*, is the prohibition of *guṇavṛddhī* and that which is *anuvādya* and hence *siddha*, includes the *kṅit* suffix. Therefore, on the strength of this *nyāya* it can be said that the *kṅit* suffix brings forth the absence of *guṇavṛddhī* which results in the *nimittatva* of *kṅit* suffix of *guṇa* and *vṛddhi*. The rule therefore means "*kṅinnimitte guṇavṛddhī na bhavataḥ*".

5. Yathotharam hi munitrayasya prāmāṇyam

This is a remark made by Kṭ while commenting on the last statement of Pat in the bhāṣya under the rule "*na bahuvrīhau*" (1-1-28).[23] The discussion there is concerned with the fact whether the rule is necessary to prohibit *sarvanāmasamjñā* to *sarvādi* that occur in the *alaukikavigrahavākya* of *bahuvrīhī* i.e., the words which convey the sense of *bahuvrīhīī* and since being for *bahuvrīhī* compound can be designated as *bahuvrīhī*.[24] The benefit derived from this prohibition is that in the *bahuvrīhī* compound formed from the two components *yuṣmad* and *pitṛ*, the *sarvādi* namely *yuṣmad* won't entertain the suffix *akac* prescribed by the rule "*avyaya sarvanāmnām akac prāk ṭeḥ*" (7-3-71) and it enjoins the suffix *ka*. The resultant form of this *bahuvrīhī* is *tvatkapitṛkaḥ* and not *tvakatpitṛkaḥ*. Now it is stated in the bhāṣya "*Gonardīyastu āha:- akacsvarau tu kartavyau pratyaṅgam muktaśamśayau tvakatpitṛko, makatpitṛka ityeva bhavitavyam iti.*[25] In the opinion of *Gonardīya*, the sūtra '*na bahuvrīhau*' (1-1-28) is not necessary and the form *tvakatpitṛkaḥ* and *matkapitṛkaḥ* are treated as correct and desirable words. Kṭ says that with this assertion Pat is discarding the rule which is made to arrive at the form *tvatkapitṛkaḥ* and *matkapitṛkaḥ*. Thus it is found that in the opinion of the sūtrakāra who frames the rule '*Na bahuvrihau* (1-1-28) the form *tvatkapitṛkah* is desirable whereas to Pat who refutes the sūtra it is the form *tvakatpitṛka* that is favourable. Kṭ says that we have to adhere to the opinion of Pat since "*yathottaram hi munitrayasya prāmāṇyam*", "superiority goes to the latter among the three sages, in matters of controversy".

NBh commenting on this assertion of Kṭ says that the reason for the acknowledgement of superiority to the latter among the three sages is that the latter is the one familiar with more forms in the progress of language. Therefore the view, that in order to make the sūtra significant the examples like *tvatkapitṛka* given by the Vṛttikāra is to be accepted, need not be paid attention to. NBh adds that the superiority of Pat as pointed out in the statement is clear from the bhāṣya under the rule "*dhinvikṛṇvyor a ca*" (3-1-87). The rule enjoins the substitute *a* to the final element of the roots *dhiv* and *kṛv* and the suffix *u* to these roots when there is the possibility of the suffix *śap* from these. Pat discusses the purpose of prescription of the substitute *a* to the *v* instead of enjoining *lopa* to the same. To the argument that the rule even if it enjoins *lopa* to *v* the root will get prohibition of *guṇa* by the rule "*na dhātulopa ārdhadhātuke*" (1-1-4) Pat says that the rule "*na dhatulopa*". (1-1-4) will bestow the prohibition of *guṇa* only when the *lopa* is caused by an *ārdhadhtuka* and the *lopa* desired to be enjoined is not such a one. Pat adds that the rule "*na dhātulopa...*" (1-1-4) is a sūtra already discarded. Hence the contingency of *guṇa* can be prohibited only by the prescription of the substitute *a* which even when elided by the rule *"āto lopaḥ"* (6-4-48) can prohibit *guṇa* by means of the *sthānivabdhāva* of *lopa*. The exact words of Pat are *"na caiṣa ārdhadhātukanimitto lopaḥ api ca pratyakhyāyate khalvapi sa yogaḥ Tasmin pratyākhyāte guṇaḥ syādeva tasmād atvam vaktavyam"*. Here NBh says that it is clear from the above passage that the view of Pat who refutes the rule is more prominent than that of Sūtrakāra. He says that this is the source for the statement *yathottaram munīnām prāmāṇyam*.[26]

Bhāṣya Passages

1. *"atha gaurityatra kaḥ śadaḥ?"*

After stating the fact that the science of grammar is concerned with correct words both Vedic and non-Vedic Pat puts forward the question *"atha gauritratra kaḥ śabdaḥ?"*[27] Kṭ says that the idea of the question is as follows:-

"gauriti vijñāne pratibhāsamāneṣu vastusu kah śabda ityarthaḥ (what, among the concepts that appear in mind on the cognition *gauḥ*, is denoted by the word *śabda?*) Commenting on the word *pratibhāsamāneṣu* NBh says that the concepts that appear in mind on the cognition *gauḥ* are the sound, the genus cow, the individual cow, etc. Hence these concepts are doubted by Pat to be the *śabda*. NBh says that in the light of the explanation given by Kṭ, it may seem that *guṇa* and *kriyā* cannot be doubted to be *śabda* as these concepts do not appear in mind on the cognition *gouḥ*, but Pat introduces questions doubting *guṇa* and *kriyā* to be the *śabda*. NBh adds that it can be shown that these doubts are quite concordant with the explanation given by Kṭ. He points out that the relation between *guṇa* an *guṇin* and the same between *kriyā* and *kriyāvat* is *abheda* and so quality and the individual cow, as well as action and the individual cow are identical with each other. It is also to be noted that the sound *gauḥ* and the individual cow are identical as the relation between the sound and sense is *abheda*. Therefore by the application of the *nyāya, 'tadabhinnābhinnasya tadabhinnatvam'* (one thing which is identical with a particular thing, is identical with another thing which is identical with the one mentioned second-

ly) the sound identical with the individual cow is identical with *guṇa* and *kriyā* that are identical with the individual cow and hence they are also doubted to be the *śabda* by Pat.

2. *"atha kimartham antasthānām ansūpadeśaḥ kriyate?"*[28]

While commenting on the rule *hayavarat* Pat puts forward this question and Kṭ says that this question does not enquire the purpose of the mention of the letter *y, v, r* and *l* in the Śivasūtras *"hayavaraṭ"* and *"laṇ"*. The mention of these letters is quite necessary there for including them in *pratyāhāras* like *iṇ*. Kṭ hence says that the idea of the question is why the rule *"aṇuditsavarṇasya cāpratyayaḥ"* (1-1-69) is not read as *ajuditsavarṇasya cāpratyayaḥ*. Apparently it may seem quite far-fetched to take the question as conveying this idea. NBh with his brilliant interpretation justifies the explanation of Kṭ. The part *'aṇsūpadeśaḥ'* of the question is a single compound word and not two separate words like *aṇsu upadeśah*. The compound is to be split as *aṇaḥ s – ūpadeśaḥ* and means the utterance of the word *aṇ*. So the words *'Anthasthānām aṇsūpadeśaḥ* means the utterance of *aṇ* to indicate anthasthās. Such an utterance of the word *aṇ* to the indicate anthasthas is seen in the rule *"aṇuditsavarṇasya cāprutyayaḥ'd* (1-1-69). The rule teaches the ability of *aṇ* to comprehend its cognate. Among the consonants denoted by *aṇ, h and r* does not have any cognates and it is the letters *y, v and l* known as anthasthas that are given the ability to comprehend their cognates and Pat enquires in this question the purpose of the comprehension of cognates by anthasthas. Thus the question results in the sense pointed out by Kṭ why the rule *"aṇudit...." (1-1-69) is not read as ajuditsavarṇasya cāpratyayaḥ*.

3. *"chandovat sūtrāṇi bhavanti"*[29]

In order to explain the non-substitution by *k* of the letter *c* in the rule *"vṛddhirādaic"* (1-1-1) Pat says that the word *ādaic* is endowed with *bhasamjñā* by the rule *"ayasmayādīni chandasi"* (1-4-20). To the subsequent objection that the said rule is concerned with Vedic words alone whereas *ādaic* is a non-Vedic word, Pat makes the above assertion. "Sūtras are to be regarded as equal to Vedas". Kṭ says that this is an *iṣṭi* of Pat. The status of Vedas is such that the Vedic words are not fettered by the rules of grammar. This privilege is extended to the expressions in sūtras also by this *iṣṭi* of Pat. Kṭ points out that the *sūtras* mentioned in this *iṣṭi* are not those of *Vaiśeṣika* system of philosophy or the like, but those of the science of grammar as it is one among the Vedāṇgas. Here NBh says that this reason given by Kṭ is significant. It points out why the sūtras of the science of grammar are treated like the Vedas. The science of grammar as it helps in understanding the Vedas by explaining the words and their meaning, is treated as an accessory to the Vedas. It is regarded as the face of the Vedas personified as a human being, Pat too has stated that the science of grammar is the principal one among the four Vedaṇgas.[30] NBh favours the reason given by Kṭ for treating the s{ūtras of the science of grammar to be equal of Vedas. NBh adds that Pat has pointed out under the rule *"yū strkhyau nadī"* (1-4-3) that the assertion *'chandovat kavayaḥ kurvanti'* is not an *iṣṭi* of Pat.[31] Pat does not recognise the fact that writers can make usages, uncontrolled by the rules of grammar, like those in the Vedas which are free from the clutches of grammar. Hence NBh draws the conclusion that the basis for the *iṣṭi, 'Chandovat sūtrāṇi bhavanti'* is not that the rules of the science of grammar are *ārsa* but that the sūtras are of the science of grammar which is the *aṇga* of the Vedas. Thus it is because of this *iṣṭi* of Pat the sūtras of the science of grammar get the freedom enjoined to Vedas in regard to word formation.[32]

4. *"kim prayojanam?"*[33]

Under the rule *"dādhāghvadāp"* (1-1-20) Pat begins the discussion regarding the essentiality of the insertion of the word *prakṛtayaḥ* in the sūtra with the assertion *ghusamjñāyām prakṛtigrahaṇam kartavyam dādhāprakṛtayo ghusamjñā bhavantīti vaktavyam* (Mention of the word *Prakṛti* is needed in the sūtra enjoining *ghusamjñā*. It needs be said that *dādhāprakṛtayaḥ* gets the designation). Now a question is raised *"kim prayojanam"* meaning What is the benefit (of the insertion of the word *Prakṛtayaḥ*)? Kṭ says that the idea behind this question is that in the reading of the rule as *ddhghvadp* itself, all the six roots desired to be benefitted by this designation namely *du dañ* (3rd conj) *dāṇ* (1st conj) *do* (4th conj) and *deṇ* (1st conj) *dudhāñ* (3rd conj) and *dheṭ* (1st conj) can get the designation and he points out how these get the said designation. The word *dādhāḥ* in the rule is to be regarded as a *dvandva* compound of the two components *dā* and *dhā* each of which in its turn is the expression by *ekaśeṣa* i.e., *dāśca, dāśca, dāḥ, dhāśca dhāśca dhāḥ*. One among each of these two similar groups, namely, *dā* and *dhā* are the *anukaraṇa* of the roots *dudāñ daṇ* and *dudhāñ*. Among the other ones, *dā* is arrived at by the substitution by *a* of the final element of the *anukaraṇa do de* of the roots *do* and *deṅ* ending in *ec* and *dhā* is arrived at by the same process from the *anukaraṇa dhe* of the root *dhe* ending in *ec* devoid of the *anubhanda ṭ* having been elided. Elucidating the assertion of Kṭ NBh says that the *anukaraṇa do* and *dhā* of the roots ending in *ec* get the substitution by *a* enjoined to the originals by virtue of the maxim *'Prakṛtivad anukaraṇam'* by which these *anukaraṇas* can be treated as the originals. So also in the rule *"ādeca upadeśeśiti"* (6-1-45) which enjoins *ātva*, there is a word namely *aśiti*, and the *nañ* there is to be treated as *prasajya pratiṣedha* whereby the rule *"ādeca upadesiśiti"* (6-1-45) enjoins *ātva* to the roots when they are not followed by a suffix which is *śit*. Since the *anukaraṇas* are not followed by any siffix, they get the substitution by *a* of the final element. One may doubt that on the strength of the maxim *'lakṣaṇapratipadoktayoḥ pratipadoktasyaiva grahaṇam'* the forms *dā* and *dhā* in the rule may not comprehend the same arrived at by the substitution by *a* in the *anukaraṇas*, as the latter are *lākṣaṇikas*. It may also be doubted that on the basis of the maxim *'niranubandhakagrahaṇe na sānubandhakasya'* the roots *dheṭ* and *deṅ* may not be comprehended as they are possessed of anubandhas whereas in the rule the form *dā* and *dhā* are mentioned as without being possessed of any *anubandha*.

But NBh says that these doubts are quite baseless since in the said rule by virtue of *ekaśeṣa* all these roots are individually taken into account. So also there is no need for the apprehension that the root *dṛṅ* and *dhṛṅ* which have the form *dā* in instances like *dārayati* and *dhārayati* are contingent to be comprehended as the *anukaraṇa* of these roots cannot entertain *ātva* as they do not end in *ec* and it is the *anukaraṇas* that entertain the substitution by *a* of the final element that are comprehended by the from *dā* and *dhā* which undergoes *ekaśeṣa*. So there is not the contingency of root *dṛṅ* (5th conj) being comprehended by the rule since it does not undergo *ātva* by the rule *"ādeca upadeśe śiti"* (6-1-45). Thus NBh elucidates the idea of Kṭ that by the question *'kim prayojanam?'* it is meant that all the six roots get the designation *ghu* even if the word *Prakṛtayaḥ* is not inserted in the rule and indicates that the insertion is not necessary.

5. *yadapycuyate - iha ca nirglāyāt nirmlāyāt - nirgleyāt nirmleyāti" vānyasya saṃyogādeḥ" ityetvam na prāpnoti-iti aṅgena saṃyogadim viśeṣayiṣyāmaḥ*[34]

In the bhāṣya under the rule *"halonantarāḥ saṃyogaḥ"* (1-1-7), we get a discussion as to whether the term *saṃyoga* relates to each two or to all in instances where there are more are than two contiguous consonants. In the passage *'astu tarhi samudāye saṃjñā'* Pat conceds to the view that the term relates to all contiguous consonants. To the subsequent question reminding of the defects involved in the view, and noted previously, he rectifies one of those six doubts saying "naisa doṣah vakṣyatiyetat. *antyāt pūrvo masjermidanuṣaṅgasaṃyogādilopārtham iti.* After that, he remarks, *'athavāviśeṣeṇa saṃyogasaṃjñā vijñāsyate - dvayorapi, bahūnāmapi tatra dvayor yā saṃyogasaṃjñā tadāśrayo lopo bhaviṣyati'* wherein he admits both the views that the term relates to each two and all when there are more than two contiguous consonants. Now follows the passage cited above. In this passage, the optional operation of the rule, *"vānyasyasaṃyogādeḥ"* (6-4-68) in the instances *nirglāyāt and nirmlāyāt* is achieved by connecting the word *aṅgasya* with the part *saṃyoga* of the compound *saṃyogādeḥ* in the said rule.

Kṭ says that in this passage Pat is rectifying the rest defects, other than that related to the root *masj* (which has already been rectified), pointed out in the view that the term *saṃyoga* relates to all contiguous consonants. He continues that on the strength of the dictum, *'pāṭhakramādarthahramo balīyān'*, this passage is to be interpreted as coming just after the statement, *"naiṣa doṣaḥ vakṣyatyetad antyāt pūrvo masjermidanuṣaṅga saṃyogadilopārtham"* wherein one of the six defects in the view is rectified and this passage does not refer to the statement, just previously made, *"athavā.....bhaviṣyati"* to which the same may relate on the strength of *pāṭhakrama.* He then says, *"vyakhyānantaramatra kliṣṭatvānnoktam.*

As an earnest elucidator, NBh gives the *vyākhyanāntara* of this passage indicated by Kṭ and points out the effort (*kleśa*) involved in it. He informs us that the *vykhyanāntara* has the purpose of adhering to the *pāṭhakrama* by which the cited passage can be interpreted as connected with the just previous passage, *"athavā.....bhaviṣyati"* itself. He points out that the *nipata, 'iti'* coming after the verb *prāpnoti* in the passage is used in the sense of *yasmāt* and is related to the following clause, *'aṅgena saṃyogādim viśeṣyaiṣyāmaḥ'*. The whole sentence is to be supplied with the words *"tadapyasat, yato' viśeṣeṇa saṃyogasaṃjñocyate"*. The passage means, *"yasmāt aṅgena saṃyogādair viśeṣyate tasmāt, "iha ca nirglāyāt nirmlāyāt, nirgleyāt - mirmleyāt "vānyasya saṃyogādeḥ" ityetvam na prapmotīti yadapi, tadapyasat; yato 'viśeṣeṇa saṃyogasaṃjñocyate"*. It is clear that in this interpretation the optional operation of the rule *"vānyasya samyogadeḥ"* in the cited instances is achieved.

NBh adds that the *kleśa* involved in this interpretation is that there is the necessity of supplying many words to arrive at such an interpretation. Moreover the *nipāta, 'iti'* is more appropriately felt to be conveying the idea of the conclusion of the sense of the sentence. Again the assertion of Pat which comes after this passage, *"evam tāvat sarvamāṅgam parihṛtam* does not suit this interpretation. It is quite obvious that by connecting the word *aṅgasya* to the part *saṃyoga* of the compound *saṃyogādeḥ* of the rule, *"vānyasyasaṃyogādeḥ"* the defectes concerning the *aṅga* mentioned in the rules *"ṛtaśca saṃyogādeḥ"* (7-2-43) and *"guṇortisaṃyogīādyoḥ"* (7-4-29) can be explained. All these render the latter interpretation *kliṣta*, says NBh.

REFERENCES

1. Vide *Prdp* p.3.
2. Vide *Udy* p.3.
3. *Mbh* p.21.
4. *Mbh* p.27.
5. *Mbh* p.50.
6. *Mbh* p.131.
7. *Prdp* p.133.
8. *Mbh* p.113.
9. *Phiṭsūtra* 2.5.

10. *Mbh* pp.108-109.
11. Vide *Prdp* p.109.
12. *Mbh* p.109.
13. *Mbh* p.118.
14. *Mbh* p.118. *"athavaikayogaḥ kariṣyate - vṛddhirādaijadeṅguṇaḥ" tataḥ - "ikoguṇavṛddh" iti nacaikayoge' nuvṛthir bhavati"*.
15. *niryāyāt* and *nirvāyāt* are benedictive first person singular forms of the roots *yā* and *vā* each prefied with *nir*.
16. *"naivam vijñāyate - samyoga ādiryasya so'yam samyogādiḥ, samyogāderiti. katham tarhi? smayogāvādī yasya so'yam samyogādiḥ samyogāder iti"* (*Mbh* p.145.)
17. *khatvāyāt* - the benedictive first person singular derived from the nominal root *khatvā* added with *kvip* in the sense of *ācara*.
18. *Mbh* p. 192.
19. *Prdp* p. 63.
20. *Prdp* p. 75.
21. *Mbh* p. 64.
22. *Prdp* p. 136.
23. *Prdp* p. 217.
24. *Mbh* p. 215.
25. *Mbh* p. 217.
26. *Mbh* Vol. II p. 100.
27. *Mbh* p. 8.
28. *Mbh* p. 96.
29. *Mbh* p. 104.
30. *Mbh* p. 6 *"pradhānam ca ṣaṭsvaṅgeṣu vyākaraṇam*
31. *Mbh* Vol. I. Part II pp. 219-220.
32. Here it has to be borne in mind that by this *iṣṭi* of Pat, *sūtras* are treated as alike Veda not only in respect of word formation but also in respect of the fact that the *sūtras* of *Aṣṭ* have *adṛṣṭaprayajana* also. Hence even when Pat who is the supreme authority in grammar refutes a rule of *Pāṇ* or a word in them, the rule is neither removed from the text of *Aṣṭ* nor left unstudied. The refutation (*pratyākhyāna*) made by Pat, simply denotes the fact that the particular rule or the word in them, meant for getting a particular formation is not actually necessary for the same. But his rules are never devoid of the *adṛṣṭaprayojana*. By the refutation of the *sūtras* Pat points out that the particular rule or word which he refutes has only the *adṛṣṭaprayojana* but not the *dṛṣṭaprayojana* of effecting a particular formation. Thus Pat gives to the *sūtras* of *Pāṇ*, the status of Vedas itself, in its full scope.
33. *Mbh* p. 180.
34. *Mbh* p. 148.

Chapter V

Views Cited

NBh has cited a lot of views in his work *Udy*. They are of varied nature and are meant for elucidation and justification of the assertions of Pat and Kṭ. Many are critical in nature. Generally, NBh does not reveal the identity of the persons holding the particular views he cites, the instances where he mentions the name of the authors are very few.[1] From the nature of the commentary, we are able to know that some of the assertions in *Udy* are the views of the author himself. For instance, there is no doubt that the views cited with the statement *'Vastutaḥ bodhyam'* or with the beginning *'vastutastu'* or with the ending *'iti bodhyam'* are those of NBh himself. But many views are cited with other introductory or final expressions and the significance of these is examined here.

The various expressions used to cite different views

NBh uses the expressions *'iti pare,'* *'pare tu āhu'*, *'pare tu....vadanti'*, *'pare tu....icchanti'*, *'ityanye'*, *'anye tu āhuḥ'*, *'ityāhuḥ'*, *'iti kecit'*, *'kecit tu āhuḥ'*, *'iti kaścit'*, *ityeke'*, *'atra vadanti'* and *'ityapare'*. We may notice them class by class.

1. The usage of the word 'pare'

While citing certain views, NBh, uses the word *pare* in the form of *'iti pare'* or *'pare tu.....vadanti'* and such views are generally acknowledged to be representing his individual opinion. Vaidyanātha Pāyaguṇḍe, a disciple of NBh says that NBh would cite with the statement *'pare tu'* the view which he follows wholeheartedly.[2] Thieme also has got the same opinion.[3] Sitārāma Śāstri in his introduction to the edition of *Bṛ. Śab. Śekh* says that NBh uses the word *pare* or *vastutaḥ* to introduce his individual views.[4] the internal evidence in his work also leades one to this conclusion. This is most obvious in *Par. Śekh* where the views, cited in *Udy* and which from the explanatory part of the commentary are undoubtedly understood to be his, are given within the statement *'pare tu....āhuḥ'*in relation to different views on the score. For instance the passage in the bhāṣya under the rule *"dīdhīvevīṭām"* (1-1-6) *"ārdhadhātukasyeḍ valādeḥ ity atra iḍ ityanuvartamāne punaridgrahaṇasya prayojanam ideva yathā syād, yad anyat prāpnoti tan mā bhūd iti. Kiñcānyat prāpnoti? guṇaḥ;* by which he refutes the word *iṭ* in the rule *"dīdhīvevīṭām"* (1-1-6) is established as the assertion of *siddhāntyekadeśin* in the *Udy* and this view is given within the phrase *pare tu* in *Par. Śekh.*[5] In short, instances are many which support the conclusion that the views cited by NBh with the word *pare* are representative of his individual opinion.

The careful examination of his work however, shows that there are also instances to contradict this general conclusion. We are forced to believe that rarely NBh uses the word *pare* to introduce views of others or views which he does not support wholeheartedly. A few examples will suffice to prove this. Under the 'Śivasūtra *"hayavaraṭ"* Pat asks the question why the letter *'h'* alone is mentioned twice, in the *Śivasṭras.*[6] He enquires whether the enunciation of the same, either in the rule *'hayava raṭ'* or in the rule *'hal'* will suffice. His words are *"sarve varṇāḥ sakṛd upadiṣṭāḥ, ayam hakāro dvirupadiśyate. pūrvascaiva paraśca yadi punaḥ pūrva evopadiśyeta para eva vā kaścātra viśeṣah?"*. Here commenting on the portion *"yadi pūrva eva upadiśyeta"* NBh raises an objection.. If as said in this passage, the letter *'h'* is mentioned in the rule *"hayavaraṭ"* alone and not a second time, there is no need of the Śivasūtra *'hal'* and this implies that the *anubandha* in it is also unnecessary. As such how can Pat speak of *tantranirdeśa,* of the rule *"halantyam"* (1-3-3) by which the *'l'* of the rule *'hal'* gets the designation of *it* and thus avoid the defect of interdependence?[7] In answer to this doubt, two different interpretations of the said passage are given at a stretch and then with the expression pare *tu....āhuḥ* an altogether different interpretation of the said passage is given. Here there is no reason to doubt the first two explanations are not of NBh since the question is raised by himself and the answer that follows immediately can in no way be explained as of others without any indication like *'āhuḥ'*, *'kecit'*, *'anye'*, etc. to that effect. Hence the first two assertions in answer to the question being taken to represent the view of NBh, the third explanation given within the expression *'pare tu...āhuḥ'* cannot be his, but only be of others.

Under the rule *"ādyantavadekasmin"* (1-1-20) NBh cites a view explaining the passage in the *Mbh* beginning with the lines *'atrāpyarthena yukto vyadeśaḥ padam nāmarthaḥ yathā tarti....."* and ending with the line *"adyantavaddbhāvaśca śakyo vaktum"*.[8] This view cited with the expression *pare tu āhuḥ* refutes the explanation given by Kṭ to the said passage and can be treated as his individual opinion, since he repeates the same in *Par. Śekh* to refute the view of Kṭ.[9] Then he gives with the statement *vastutastu iti tatvam*, an explanation to the passage *'yathā tarhi......avaktum'* in a particular manner by which the explanation formerly given with the wording *pare tu āhuḥ* is refuted.[10] Hence it can be said that though there are ample instances to draw the conclusion that the views cited with the introductory or final word *pare* represent his opinion, there are also certain rare instances which contradict the above conclusion. In his commentary on *Rasagaṅgādhara* while commenting on the words of Jagannātha, on the distinction between the figure of speech, *pariṇāma* and *rūpaka*, NBh gives with the beginning *vayaṁ tu brūmaḥ* and then gives a slightly different view within the wording *pare tu āhuḥ*. Here it is clear that the word *pare* does not represent his view. However as it is clear that in almost all instances he uses the word *pare* to cite his individual opinion, the views in *Udy* cited as such are treated here to be his own and dealt with in the following chapter since here we are mainly concerned with the views, of others, cited by NBh.

2. *The usage of the word 'anye'*

NBh's usage of the word *anye* in the form *ityanye* or *anye tu āhuḥ* is quite interesting and at the same time confusing. It is said interesting in the sense that the usage of the word *anye* carries a significance. It is baffling in the sense that one cannot arrive at a definite conclussion as to the identity of the author of the view, whether he refers to himself or other. It can be said that he uses the word *'anye'* to cite the views of others. Under the sivasūtra *'laṇ'* dealing with the bhāṣya passage *"evam tarhi sāmarthyāt pūrveṇa na pareṇa"*, NBh raises an objection and answers the same.[11] After that he gives two different views on this point, each with the final wording ityanye. Here there is no doubt that the word *anye* refers to others. Again under the rule *'ṛlk'* NBh indicates his disagreement with the assertion of Kṭ and then cites a view with the expression *ityanye* which supports the view of Kṭ.[12] Besides, while commenting on Kṭ in instances where a view is given in *Prdp* with the statement *anye tu āhuḥ* NBh points out that Kṭ uses the word *anye* to point out that he entertains difference of opinion or disagreement with the view cited as such and NBh makes clear that point of disagreement.[13] Hence the word *anye* used by a person who explains the usage of the word *anye* as expressive of some dissent with the view cited as such can ordinarily be taken in the same sense and hence that view cannot be taken as that of NBh. Again in certain instances he explains Kṭ and then gives a different opinion, with the ending *ityanye.*[14] All these facts lead one to the conclusion that the views cited withe the word *anye* to be not of NBh. But in certain instances NBh uses the word *anye* to cite a *view which it is hardly acceptable* as the view of others. For example in the first *āhnika* of *Mbh,* under the passage *"nanu coktam sūtre vyākakaraṇe ṣaṣṭhyartho 'nu-papanna iti. naiṣa doṣaḥ vyapadeśivadbhāvenāpyetad siddham,"* NBh cites a view with regard to *vyapadesivaddhava* with the wording *ityanye.* The same view is given in *Udy* while explaining the passage *"adyantavadbhāvaśca śakyo vaktum"*, under the rule *"ādyantavadekasmin"* (1-1-20).[15] The noteworthy factor is that here the view is stated as *'vastutaḥ...iti tattavam'* which is characteristic of the citation of the view of NBh himself. Thus the word *anye* used in the first *āhnika,* referred to just previously cannot be treated as that of others. Again in the first *āhnika,* under the passage *"atha gaurityatra kaśśabdaḥ"* a veiw is given in accordance with the *Yogasūtrabhāṣya* of Pat and NBh designates the same as the view of *anye* and then says that he has dealt with this view in another work of his namely *Mañjūṣā* and in that work this view is seen as the one favoured by NBh. Thus it is seen that the usage of the word *anye* by NBh is confusing in the sense that it does not clearly indicate whether views cited are of himself or of others.

It may also be noted that the expression *anye tu āhuḥ* is significant when NBh uses the same in certain instances. He uses this expression to cite views which though not his original, are favoured by him in regard to the view of Kṭ. He uses the expression when he differs with Kṭ and implies by this usage that it cuts both ends. Probably that is why he does not designate such views as that of *pare.* Under the Śivasūtra *'hayavaraṭ'* while discussing the reason for the non-inclusion of anubandhas in pratyāhāras Pat says *'lopaḥ khalvapi tavat bhavati'*. Under this passage, NBh points out as his own view the fact that the vowel *'a'* in the rule *laṇ* is not an *anubandha.*[16] The same view is given with the statement *anye tu āhuḥ* under the passage *'lakārasya lapratvam vakṣyāmi.*[17] Here he points out that as there are arguments to consider that *a* is an *anubandha*, so also there are arguments to negate the same. Again, in the first *āhnika* under the passage *'śakyam cānena śvamāmsādibhirapi kṣut pratihantum'*. NBh refutes the explanation given by Kṭ with regard to the usage *'sakyam kṣut pratihantum'.*[18] He says that the view entertained by Kṭ here is refuted by him in the *Udy*, under the rule *"svādumi ṇamul"* (3-4-26)[19] When we turn our attention to this assertion under the said rule we find that the view is given within the frame *'anye tu āhuḥ'*. Hence it seems that NBh uses the word *'anye'* to cite views which though they are not his original views, are preferred by him to that of Kṭ.

3. *The usage of the expression 'ityāhuḥ'*

According to the traditional interpretation the usage of the word *āhuḥ* after stating a fact or view is treated as indicative of some dissent with the person with regard to the assertion used with the word *āhuḥ*. The usage of the word *āhuh* by NBh also is interpreted as conveying his *aruci*. Commenting on the word *'gonṇikāputraḥ* used by Pat while dealing with the rule *"akathitam ca"* (1-4-51) NBh says, *goṇikāputra bhāṣyakāra ityāhuḥ".*[19(a)]

Yuthiṣṛhira Mimāmsaka says that the usage of *āhuḥ* here by NBh shows that he does not favour that view.[20] Again it can be seen that many views cited as such are expressive of his dissent, which is made clear on the following pages.[21] Hence it can be accepted that the views, cited as such cannot be of NBh's individual opinion, but of others. But it is to be noted that all the views cited with *āhuḥ* are not expressive of his dissent. There we have to find a reason why NBh, uses the word *āhuḥ* there. Probably it is because of the fact that they are not merely his individual view but are accepted by certain others also. Hence the verb *āhuḥ* in such instances can be supplied with the agent *bhāṣyatattvavidaḥ or siddhānlavidaḥ*. Rudradharajhā Śarma supplies these words to *āhuḥ* used by NBh in certain instances.[22] All these are dealt with in the following passages.[23]

4. The usage of the word 'kecit'

Thieme is of opinion that the word *'kecit' used by NBh always refers to certain* scholars whose opinion NBh does not accept because it contains assuptions that are without the support of or even against the *bhāṣya*.[24] The internal examination of *Udy* presents instances to support this view. In the rule *'na dhātulopa ārdhadhātuke'* (1-1-4), under the passage in the bhāṣya *"athāpi kathañcid anavakāśo luk syād. Evam api na doṣaḥ"*, NBh gives a view with the ending *ityāhuḥ* and the same view is elaborated under the rule *"sthānivad ādeśo'nalvidhau"* (1-1-56) by himself with the statement *iti kecit*[25] Here it is clear that *kecit* does not refer to NBh himself. Pāyaguṇḍe notes that there is a difference of opinion with regard to the usage of the word *kecit* by NBh. In his commentary on the *paribhāṣā, sannipātalakṣaṇo vidhir animittam tadvighātasya"* in *Par. Śekh*, Pāyaguṇḍe says that some take the word *kecit* used by NBh while explaining the said maxim, to be of the views of others with which NBh, entertains difference of opinion-while others take the word as amounting to *bhāṣyattatvavidaḥ*[26] But it is noteworthy that the word *kecit* that occurs first in *Par.Śekh* though explained as *bhāṣyatvavidaḥ* by Pāyaguṇḍe, he himself says that NBh indicates his dissent with the view by citing the same with the word *kecit* instead of the word *pare.*[27]

5. The usage of the words 'eke', 'kaścit', 'apare', etc.

There can be no difference of opinion with regard to the usage of the words *eke* and *kaścit* as referring to the views of others and this is made clear in the following pages.[28] The usage of the word *apare* seem to represent the expression *'pare'*. The expression *atra vadanti* can be treated as referring to the view of others.[29]

Views on the Passages in the Bhāṣya

1. "śabdānuśasānam nāma śāstram adhikṛtam veditavyam"

Elucidating the idea of his sentence *'atha śabdānuśāsanam'* Pat says, *śabdānuśāsanam nāma śāstram adhikṛtam veditavyam.* Here NBh finds the necessity for the supply of a word to the part *adhikṛtam* and hence inserts the word *kartavyatvena* in the sentence which thereby means, the science, has been begun. Thus after expressing his opinion he cites another view on the same point as *'vivaraṇakāratvād vyākhyātavyatveneti śeṣa ucita ityanye'*. The word inserted between *'śāstram* and *adhikṛtam* is *vyākhyātavyatvena* meaning to be interpreted. The sentence means, the science by name *śabdānuśāsana* being to be interpreted, has been begun. This seems to be more acceptible since Pat is beginning his work, which is descriptive in nature, with the sentence *'atha śabdānuśāsanam'*. NBh has cited this latter view with the ending *ityanye* and this is clearly indicative of the fact that he makes the usage *ityanye* to cite the views of others.

2. The injunction 'brāhmaṇena niṣkāraṇo dharmo ṣaḍaṅgo vedo'dhyeyo jñeyaśca.

Pat quotes the said vedic passage as the authority ordaining the study of Vyākaraṇa.[30] Kṭ says that this points out the fact that the study of Vyākaraṇa which is the important one among the six Vedāṅgas is a *nityakarman*. NBh says that the study of Vyākaraṇa is a *nityakarman* as well as a *kāmyakarman* since the same involves benefit. Then he cites a view with the ending *iti kascit*. Since there is the word *brāhmaṇena* in this sentence, it is to be understood that to the Kṣtriyas and *Vaiśyas* the study of Vyākaraṇ is only a *kāmyakarman* and it is a *nityakarman* only in regard to Brahmins. Vaidyanātha Pāyaguṇḍe says that this view cited by NBh as *iti kaścit* is that of one Ratnakṛt[31] This person seems to be the author of a commentary or work by name *Ratna.* Rudradharajhā Śarma says that by citing this view with the ending *iti kaścit* NBh exxpresses the fact he does not favour this view.[32] Again in the said passage Veda is spoken of as *dharma* and to this assertion NBh gives an explanation with the ending *ityāhuḥ*. Vedas are the object of a study which, being to be secured by man by means of effort, is treated as *dharma* and hence the word *dharma* is used in a secondary sense to denote the Vedas. This explanation given with ending *ityāhuḥ* shows that NBh uses the word *āhuḥ* to cite views which he favours though they are not his original views.

3. *"Kim punar idam vivṛtasyopaduśyamānasya prayojanam anvākhyāyate āhosvid saṃvṛtasyopadiśyamānasya vivṛtopadeśaḥ codyate".*[33]

Under the Śivasūtra *aiuṇ* there is a vārttika *"akārasya vivṛtopadeśaḥ ākāragrahaṇārthaḥ"*. Pat raises in the above passage a question in regard to the idea of the vārttika. 'Is here mentioned the inclusion of *ā* by *a* as the purpose of the actual utterance of the letter *a* as *vivṛta* or is it here advised the mention of *a* as *vivṛta* instead of the usual *saṃvṛta* which is actually made there (in the rule *aiuṇ*). Elucidating the idea of this passage Kṭ says that the doubt is with regard to whether sūtrakāra has already taught the *a* in the rule as *vivṛta* and Kāṭ is pointing its purpose as the comprehesion of *ā* by *a*, or whether Kāt is stressing the necessity of the *vivṛtopadeśa* of *a* which is taught as *samvṛta* in the rule. Here commenting on the word sūtrakāra used by Kṭ, NBh, says there is a view, which he quotes with the ending *ityāhuḥ* that the word sūtrakāra refers to Śiva or Vedapuruṣa.

At the end of the discussion on the idea of the said vārttika Pat says that it makes no difference in saying that Kāt is stressing the necessity of the *vivṛtopadeśa* of *a*, in the rule, read as *saṃvṛta*, or is pointing out the benefit of the *vivṛtopadeśa* of *a* in *'aiuṇ'* instead of *saṃvṛta*, since in both cases the purpose to be served is the comprehension of *a* by *a*, and the former statement arises out of imprudence. Here NBh remarks with the expression *ityāhuḥ* that of these two views, the view admitting the mention of the purpose of *vivṛtopadeśa* is more favourable and acceptible since to question or order anything in regard to fourteen rules which are treated as non-made by human beings, shows imprudence on one's part. Thus in the said two instances NBh points that there is the view assigning the authorshsip of the fourteen rules to Śiva or Vedapuruṣa. This idea he states with the expression *ityāhuḥ*. However he repeats the same idea without the statement *ityāhuḥ* at the end of the bhāṣya under the Śivasūtra *"laṇ"* Pat says *"tajñāpayatyācāryaḥ bhavatyeṣā paribhāṣā....* Here NBh points out that the word *ācārya* refers to Śiva.[34] In these instances the rules referred to are the fourteen Śivasūtras. Hence it can be seen that NBh uses the word *ityāhuḥ* to cite views which he favours. In such instances it may be pointed out that the full fledged expression of *ityāhuḥ* may be *iti siddhāntavidaḥ āhuḥ*.

4. *"yad ayam kṣubhnādiṣu nṛnamanaśabdam paṭhati*[35]

In this passage in the bhāṣya under the Śivasūtra *"eoṅ"* and *"aiauc"*, Pat says that the grouping of the word *nṛnamana* among those headed by *kṣubhna*, indicates the fact that the letter *n* following *ṛ* will be substituted by *ṇ*. NBh supplies the word *samjñābhūtam* as an adjective to the word *nṛnamanaśabdam* in the sentence. According to him it is the grouping of the *samjñāśabda nṛnamana*, under *kṣubhnādi* that indicates the said fact. It is as follows. The effort to ensure the prohibition of *ṇatva* in the word *nṛnamana* shows the contingency of the same otherwise. That contingency cannot be on the strength of the rule *"aṭkupvāṅnumvyavāye'pi"* (6-4-2) since *nṛnamana* is not a *samānapada* i.e, a word that is not split. Hence to point out the contingency one has to resort to the rule *"pūrvapadātsamjñayām agaḥ"* (8-4-3) which alone prescribes *ṇatva* to *n* in a *sakhaṇḍapada* i.e., split word. However the rule will operate only when the *sakhandaśabda* is a *samjñāśabda*. Hence NBh says that there is the contingency of *ṇatva* by the said rule on the *n* of *nṛnamana* which is a *samjnāśabda*, but for the factor that there is no *nimitta* namely *r* or *ṣ* in it. Even then the effort namely grouping of the *samjñāśabda nṛnamana* under *kṣubhñadi* is made to ensure the prohibition of *ṇatva*. This shows that the letter *ṛ* also is a *nimitta* for *ṇatva*. Hence all other conditions being perfect the rule *"pur-vapadāt samjñāyām agaḥ"* (8-4-3) may change the *n* in *nṛnamana* to *ṇ* and to avoid the same, *nṛnamana* which is a *samjñāśabda* is grouped under *kṣubhnādi*. NBh here cites a views which tries to explain the indication pointed out in the bhāṣya, by saying that there is no contingency of *ṇatva* in *nṛnamana* even by the rule *"cchandasyṛdavagrahāt"* (8-4-26) which enjoins the substitution by *ṇ* of *n* followed by *ṛ*. This is because there is no *avagraha* in the word *nṛnamana* and the rule provides *ṇatva* to *n* followed by *ṛ* only in instances where there is *avagraha*. Thus at a stage when there is no contingency of the substitution by *ṇ* of *n* in *nṛnamana*, the effort of Pāṇ to ensure its prohibition indicates that *n* followed by *ṛ* is substituted by *ṇ*.

It seems however that NBh does not favour this view. The point of disagreement is that the rule *"cchandasyṛdavagrahāt"* (8-4- 260 deals with Vedic words alone and so irrespective of the perfection of other conditions, the rule cannot apply in *nṛnamana* which is a non-vedic word. So an indication with regard to an operation in non- Vedic words on the strength of the non-contingency of a rule which does not bring under its scope non-Vedic words does not appear quite satisfactory. Probably it is to point out his dissent that NBh uses the word *ityāhuḥ* after citing this view.

5. *"Evam tarhi sāmarthyāt pūrveṇa, na pareṇa yadi pareṇa syād aṇgrahaṇam anarthakam syād, uraj rapara ityeva brūyāt"*[36]

Under the Śivasūtra *"laṇ"* Pat discusses the question whether the *pratyāhāra aṇ*, in the rule *"uraṇ raparaḥ"* (1-1-51), which enjoins *raparatva* to *aṇ* that replace *ṛ* is coined with the *ṇ* of the rule *aiuṇ* or with the *ṇ* of the rule *"laṇ"*. After certain queries and answers on the point, Pat concludes in the quoted passage that *aṇ* in the said rule is joined with *ṇ* of the Śivasūtra *"aiuṇ"*. His words are "If so, by *sāmarthya*, it is with the former and not with the latter (*ṇ*). Had it been with the latter, the reading of *aṇ* would be of no avail since he would have read *uraj raparaḥ"*. Pat's argument is that if Pān intended to give *raparatva* to other letters also in addition to *a*, *i* and *u* that replace *ṛ*, he would have read the rule as *uraj raparaḥ*, since vowels alone and not the consonants *y*, *v*, *r* and *l*, additionally comprehended by the *pratyāhāra aṇ* coined with the latter *ṇ*, are to replace *ṛ* or *ḷ* in instance like *mātṛṇām*.

Here NBh cites an instance *gamḷ+ā* and raises the objection that here there is the consonant *l* (comprehended by the *pratyāhāra aṇ*) that replace *ḷ* on the strength of the rule *"iko yaṇaci"* (6-1-77) and how can Pat speak of vowels alone as letters that replace *ṛ* or *ḷ* NBh himself gives the solution that the rule *"uraṇ raparaḥ"* will not operate in the instance *gamḷ+ā*. This is because it can be shown that the *raparatva* ordained to the consonant *r* that replaces *ṛ* has no standing effect. For example in the instance *karthṛ+artham* the consonant *r*, that replaces *ṛ* by the rule *"iko yaṇaci"* (6-1-77) were to become *rapara*, there will develop two *r* sounds as *karthrr artham* and one of them will be elucided, permanently, by the rule *"ro ri"* (8-3-14). Thus the *raparatva* taught to a consonant *r* comprehended by the *pratyāhāra aṇ* formed with the latter *ṇ* being futile the rule does not accord *raparatva* to the consonants *l* that replace *ḷ* which is a *sahacarita* of *ṛ*.

NBh here points out that some others give a different solution to this problem. They opine that even if *ḷ* becomes *lapara* one of them will be dropped by the rule *"ro ri"* (8-3-14) itself since *ṛ* and *ḷ* are having *samānaśruti*. Here it is to be noted that NBh does never accept the *pratyāhāra ra* in which case only *rapara* can be interpreted as *lapara* also. Hence this view cited with the ending *ityanye* is definitely a view held by other scholars.

Again NBh cites a view with the ending *ityanye*, which gives another solution to their problem. On the authority of the bhāṣya that *ac* alone is contingent to replace *ṛ* whereby the rule need be only *"uraj raparaḥ"*; we must accept, the *anabhidhāna* of instance like *gamla* where *ḷ* is substituted by *l* by virtue of the rule *"iko yaṇaci"* (6-1-77).

6. *"tad etad atyantam saṃdigdham vartate ācāryāṇām vibhāṣānuvartate naveti"*[37]

Under the Śivasūtra *"hayavaraṭ"* Pat discusses the question whether the rule *"halo yamām yami lopah"* (8-4-64) that prescribes elision, is optional or uniform. When it is pointed out that the prohibition of doubling by the rule *"śaro' ci"* (8-4-49) is an indication to the fact that there is the *anuvṛtti* of the word *vibhāṣā* in the said rule, Pat explains that it can be equally shown that the prohibition of doubling is an indication that the rules *"halo yamām yami lopaḥ"* (8-4-64) and *"jharo jhari savarṇe"* (8-4-65) enjoin elision uniformly and not optionally. He therefore concludes *"tad etad .... naveti"* meaning, "In short it remains extremely doubtful whether according to the sūtrakāra the word *vibhāṣā* is got by *anuvṛtti* (in the said two rules i.e, 8-4-64 & 65)." Commenting on this Kṭ says that this assertion of Pat shows that the optional operation of the rules by the *anuvṛtti* of the word *vibhāṣā* cannot be accepted on the basis of any indication i.e, *jñāpaka*. But the optional operation of the rules are accepted on the basis of the assertion of *ācārya* Patañjali under the rule *"nājjhalau"* (1-1-10) where he says *"vibhāṣā sa lopaḥ"* which means that elision (enjoined by the rule *"jharo jhari savarṇe"*) is optional.

Here NBh says that a certain scholar *(kaścit)* maintains that the optional function of the said rules is accepted also on the basis of an indication namely the word *aṇ* in the rule *"aṇudit savarṇasya cāpratyayaḥ"* (1-1-69). In the instance of combination of *sam+yantā* the *m* is replaced by nasal *y* which is a cognate form of y, on the strength of the rule *"anusvārasya yayi parasavarṇaḥ"* (8-4-58). In the resultant form *sayyantā* the nasal *y* gets doubling since it is treated as yar considering that it is comprehended by y which is an *aṇ* and to which the power of comprehending cognates is given by the word *aṇ* in the rule *"aṇudit savarṇasya cāpratyayaḥ"* (1-1-69). If the rule *"jharo jhari savarṇe"* enjoins elision uniformly, the doubling of the nasal *y* being treated as yar becomes futile since one of them will be elided and correspondingly the word *aṇ*, in the rule *"aṇudit savarnasya capratyahah"* (1-1-69) which gave the power of comprehending cognates, to *y* by which the nasal *y* is treated as *yar*, becomes superfluous. Hence it is indicated that the rule *"jharo jhari savarṇe"* (8-4-65) enjoins elision optionally and the doubling survives optionally and to achieve the same, the word *aṇ* in the rule *"aṇudit savarṇasya cāpratyayaḥ"* (1-1-69) becomes significant. Thus NBh says that a certain scholar maintains that the word *aṇ* of the rule *"aṇudit savarṇasya cāpratyayaḥ"* (1-1-69) is an indication to the optional function of the rules 8-4-64 & 65.

NBh however adds that Kṭ does not resort to this indication by the word *aṇ* of the rule *"aṇudit savarṇasya cāpratyayaḥ"* (1-1-69) since the word *aṇ* there has been dispensed with by *Kāt*[38].

7. *"yam vidhim pratyupadeśo' narthakaḥ sa vidhir bādhyate yasya tu vidher nimittameva nāsau bādhyate"*[39]

One among the three purposes cited by Kāt of the word *ikaḥ* in the rule *"iko guṇavṛddhī"* (1-1-3) is the prevention of the substitution by *guṇa* of the dipthongs in instances like *glāyati* where the *ai* of the root *glai* is, otherwise, contingent to be replaced by *guṇa* on the strength of the rule *"sārvadhātukārdhadhātukayoḥ"* (7-3-84). Pat refutes this purpose by resorting to the *upadeśasāmarthya* of *ai* in *glai*. If the root *glai* were to become *gle* by the substitution by *guṇa Pāṇ* could have read the root as *gle* itself. The objector resorts that if *upadeśasāmarthya* be resorted to, nothing can replace the *ai* of *glai* on the said score. Hence it would not undergo substitution by *āy* in the instance. To this Pat gives the above reply, "This objection cannot stand, for the *vṛddhi* in respect of which *upadeśa* is of no use, is warded off, and that in respect of which it is only *nimitta*, is not warded off. In respect of *āy* etc. it (the *ai* of glai) is only *nimitta*". Pat means that the substitute *ay* has got *ai* only as its *sthānin*. That is why it replaces the *ai* of the root *glai*. But *guṇa* however can be warded off by the *ekāroccaraṇasāmarthya* in the root *glai*.

Here NBh cites a view (with the ending *ityāhuḥ*) which raises an objection to the assertion of Pat and wards off the same. The objection is thus:- There is the *pātipadika rai*. If this be added with the suffix *kvip* taught in the sense *ācāra*, it will become a root by the rule *"sanādyantā dhatāvaḥ"* (3-1-32). In the instance *rāyati* derived from this root, there is the contingency of the *ai* off root *rai*, being replaced by *guṇa*. Here the *ekāroccāraṇasāmarthya* cannot be resorted to since the *ai* in *rai* has got other purposes to serve, when the same is treated as a base. Hence the word *ikaḥ* is necessary to avoid the dipthong from being substituted by *guṇa*. Thus the objection is as to how can the *ekāroccāraṇasāmarthya* be resorted to. The answer is that though the argument is correct, Pat's statement stands unrefuted. This is because on the authority of the statement that *iggrahaṇa* is not necessary to ward off the substitution by *guṇa* of dipthongs, and the *aikāropadeśa* is of no use with regard to *glai* if the dipthong were to be substituted by *guṇa*, the usages of forms derived by the addition of *kvip* taught in the sense of *ācāra* to bases ending in dipthongs are not to be accepted on the score namely *anabhidhāna*. And in the absence of an instance like *rāyati* the word *ikaḥ* is not necessary in the rule *"iko guṇavṛddhī"* to ward off *guṇa* replacing *ai* in *rai*. This view given with the ending *ityāhuḥ* cannot be interpreted as showing any dissent from the point of view of NBh since NBh himself in many instance resorts to *anabhidhāna* to justify Pat. Hence it seems that this *āhuḥ* may be supplied with the agent *bhāṣyatattvavidaḥ*.

8. *"kṣiprakṣudrayor api nyaṇādiparam guṇa itīyatā siddham so'yam evam siddhe yat pūrvagrahaṇam karoti tasyaitad prayojanam, iko yathā syād aniko mā bhūditi"*[40]

Under the rule *"iko guṇavṛddhī"* (1-1-3) Pat discusses the question whether this rule and the rule *"alo'ntyasya"* (1-1-52) have the relationship of *śeṣaśeṣitva*. In this case, *guṇa* and *vṛddhi* shall replace only the final letter of the *aṅga* and *Kāt* says that there is the necessity of the insertion of the word *ikaḥ* in six rules among which the rule *"sthūladūrayuvahrasvakṣipraksudrāṇām yaṇādiparam pūrvasya ca guṇaḥ"* (6-4- 156) is the one so that the base *kṣipra* and *kṣudra* shall be beneffitted by way of the nonfinal *i* and *u* in them being substituted by *guṇa*.[41] In the above quoted passage Pat says that there is no necessity of the insertion of the word *ikaḥ* here. He says that in regard to *kṣipra* and *kṣudra,* since though the desired object is won by reading the word *guṇah* after the word *yaṇādiparam* (i.e, *sthūla...ṅām yaṅādiparam guṇaḥ*), Pāṇ reads the word *pūrva,* it has the *prayojana* that *guṇa* replaces *ik* and does not replace *anik*. The argument is that if only the final letter i.e, *p* is to be replaced by *guṇa,* Pāṇ could have read the rule as *"sthūla...nām yaṇādiparam guṇaḥ"* so that the part *ra* (in *kṣipra* and *kṣudra*) which is *yaṇādi* can get elided and *guṇa* can replace the final letters *p* and *d* of that parts *kṣip* and *kṣud* that survives. Here NBh cites a view with the ending *ityāhuḥ* that there is no room to doubt that if the rule is read as pointed out above, in regard to the base *hrasva* mentioned in the rule, the part *rasva* which is *yaṇādi* is contingent to be elided. This is because in regard to the bases *sthūla dūra* etc. along with which *hrasva* is also mentioned, *yaṇ* denotes the penultimate letter and hence in the base *brasva* also, we take by the word *yaṇ* the penultimate *v* and so *va* alone being treated as *yaṇādi*, gets elided. Thus this view supports the assertion of Pat that the word *pūrvasya* is unnecessary and hence results in bringing about the purpose of *yaṇādiparam* being treated as a *pañcamītatpuruṣa* compound where the part *yaṇādi* treated as a *bahuvrīhi* compound denotes *p* and *d* so that the part beginning with the same gets alided and the *i* and *u* previous to them gets substitution by *guṇa*. It seems that NBh has here used the statement *āhuḥ* in the sense *'bhāṣyatattvavidaḥ āhuḥ'*.

9. The scope of the maxim "yadāgamāstadguṇībhutāstadgrahaṇena gṛhyante"

Pat speaks, first, of the maxim *'yadāgamāstadguṇībhutāstadgrahaṇena gṛhyante'* under the rule *"dādhāghvadāp"* (1-1-20). NBh points out that this maxim cannot be applied universally.[42] In certain circumstances, this maxim does not apply. This is because by prescribing the augment *m* (*muk*) to the letter *a*, the component of the *aṅga*, by the rule *"āne muk"* (7-2-82), *Pāṇ* shows that the *m* augmented with *a* shall not be treated as *a* on the basis of the maxim as otherwise the prescription of the argument *m* to *a* will be of no avail since the same taken along with *a* wil be coalesced into *ā* on account of being followed by the suffix *āna*. Thus it can be seen that the application of maxim is not universal. Hence, NBh says, we get the form *didīye*.[43] There the maxim does not apply so that there is no contingency of *ye* (the augment *y* the suffix *e*) being treated as *e* which is an *ac*, and thereby causing *yaṇ* to replace the previous *i* by the rule *"iko yaṇaci"* (6-1-77).

NBh says that there is a view according to which, the fact that the maxim does not apply in all instances where letters are taken into consideration, is implied by the word *arthavad* used by Pat while citing the maxim, *arthavata āgamāstadguṇībhūto'rthavad grahaṇena gṛhyate*. This view cited by NBh with the remark *ityhuḥ* is expressive of his dissent with the same. It may be pointed out here that NBh does not admit the fact that the maxim does not apply in all instances where letters are taken into consideration.[44] He accepts this much that on the basis of the prescription of the argument *muk* to *a*, the maxim need be only universally non-applicable i.e, *anitya*. Hence the above view is cited by NBh with the statement *āhuḥ* which shows his dissent with the same.

10. *"tadviśeṣebhyastarhi prāpnoti"*[45].

Under the rule *"bahugaṇavatuḍati saṃkhyā"* (1-1- 23) Pat speaks of the maxim *kṛtrimākṛtrimayoḥ kṛtrime kāryasampratyayaḥ*. He points out that if this maxim be accepted and thereby rules operate on *ktrima* alone among *kṛtrima* and *akṛtrima*, the rule *"nadīpaurṇamāsyāgrahāyaṇībhyaḥ"* (5-4-110) will operate on *kṛtrima nadī* which is described in the rule *"yūstrākhyau nadī"* (1-4- 3) and not on the word *nadī* which means a river. When it is answered that it does not happen since the word *nadī* is read along with the words *Paurṇamāsī* and *āgrahāyaṇī* it is pointed out *"tadviśeṣebhyas tarhi prāpnoti"*. The idea is that if the operation of the maxim *kṛtrimākrtrimayoḥ kṛtrime kāryasampra tyayaḥ* be not accepted, the word *nadī* may refer to the individual rivers like *Gaṅgā* etc. and not to the word *nadī*. Here with the ending *ityāhuḥ* NBh says that the instances referred to by the word *"tadviśeṣebhyaḥ"* in the passage, are *parigaṅgam* and *pariyamunam* which are *avyayībhāva* compounds. Here the *samāsānta* suffix *ṭac* optionally operates on the strength of the rule *"nadīpaurṇamāsyagrahāyaṇībhyaḥ"* (5-4-110) and those forms become *antodātta* by virtue of the suffix *ṭac*. In the absence of the operation of the suffix *ṭac* these forms are endowed with *prvapadaprakṛtisvara* by the rule *"paripratyupāpā varjyam-ānāhoratrāvayaveṣu"* (6-2-33). NBh does not seem to enertain any diffference of opinion with this view and hence this *āhuḥ* may be supplied the word *bhṣyataitvavidaḥ*.

11. *"lrāntasya ityatra vakāropi nirdiśyate kim vakāro na śrūyate? luptanirdiṣto vakāraḥ"*[46]

Under the rule *"iko guṇavṛddhi"* (1-1-3) the *siddhāntyekadeśin* says that in the process of formation of the word *alāvit* during the stage *a+lū+is+īt*, the *guṇa* by the rule *"sārvad-hātukārdhadhātukayoḥ" shall operate on the u.*[47] The rule *"sici vṛddhiḥ parasmaipadeṣu"* (1-2-1) shall not substitute *u* by *vṛddhi* since *guṇa* that depends on *sic* alone is *antaraṅga* whereas *vṛddhi* depending on *sic* and the *parasmaipada* termination is *bahiraṅga* and that *antaraṅga* rules prevail over *bahiraṅga* rules. As a result of the substitution of *u* by *guṇa* the form becomes *a+lo+is+it* wherein *o* undergoes substitution by *av* and in the resultant stage *a+lav+is+īt*, the rule *"ato lrantasya"* (7-2-2) will provide substitution by *vṛddhi* i.e, *ā* of *a*. This is because he says that in the rule *"ato lrntasya"* (7-2-2), *v* is added before *l* and it is not heard owing to its elision caused by rule *"lopo vyor vali"* (6-1-66). Thus he is of opinion that the rule *"ato lrntasya"* (7-2-2) provides the substitution by *vṛddhi* to *aṅgas* ending in *l*, *r* and *v*.

NBh here introduces a doubt. The rule *"ato lrāntasya"* by the addition of the letter *v* to it, shall teach that the *aṅgas* ending in *r* or *l* or *v* that are in the vicinity of *a* is substituted by *vṛddhi*. In this case in the root *śav* also, during the process of formation of the aorist form *aśavīt* from it, i.e, in the stage *a+śav+is+īt* the vowel *a* of the roots *'sav'* is liable to undergo substitution by *vṛddhi* permanently whereas the optional substitution by vṛddhi on the strength of the rule *"ato halāder laghoḥ"* (7-2- 7) is desirable on *a*.

Here an answer to this doubt is given by MBh with the ending *ityāhuḥ*. The assertion that the rule *"sici vṛddhiḥ parasmaipadeṣu"* (7-2-1) doe snot operate first as it is *bahiraṅga* whereas *guṇa* is *antaraṅga* is that of *ekadeśin*. Hence the statement of *vakārapraśleṣa* in the rule *"ato lrāntasya"* coming from his mouth, can be treated as one that does not pay heed to the root *śav*.

NBh continues that others (*anye*) give a different answer to this question. On the authroity of the *bhāṣya* passage which speaks of *vakārapraśleṣa* in the rule, it is to be accepted that the root *śav* originally possessed the form *śap*. Since *p* and *v* are having *samānaśruti* the root is being heard as *śav* in its usages. The root, hence, can be seen as not ending in *v* and so there is no problem of substitution by *vṛddhi* in the view that there is the *vakārapraśleṣa* in the rule *"ato lrntasya"*.

12. *"Naiva sandhyakṣaram antyam asti"*[48]

Under the rule *"iko guṇavṛddh"* (1-1-3) Pat says that, though the rule *"sici vṛddhiḥ parasmaipadeṣu"* (7-2-1) in the absence of the supply of the word *ikaḥ* by the rule *"iko guṇavṛddh"*, enjoin *vṛddhi* as the substitute of any letter located at the end of an *aṅga* followed by *sic*, a dipthong is never contingent to be replaced by *vṛddhi* since there is no instance having a dipthong at the end of the *aṅga*, (*"naiva sandhyakṣaram antyam asti"*). Kṭ cites an instance *agavīt* the aorist first person singular of the root *'go'* and anticipates the contingency of the diphthong *o* being substituted by *vṛddhi*. The *prātipadika 'go'* when added with the suffix *kvip* in the sense of *ācāra* on the strength of the vārttika *'sarvaprātipadikebhyaḥ kvib vā vaktavyaḥ'* becomes a root by the rule *"sanādyantā dhātavah"* (3-1-32). During the process of formation of the aorist third person singular form from this root, we arrive at a stage *a+go+is+īt* and here the *aṅga a+go* can be seen as ending in the dipthong *o* being followed by *sic* and that diphthong is contingent to be replaced by *vṛddhi*.[49] In answer to this doubt, Kṭ says that this contingency can be warded off by the *anuvṛtti* of the word *dhatoḥ* in the rule *"sici vṛddhiḥ parasmaipadeṣu"* (7-2-1). In the rule the word *dhātoḥ* can already be got by means of the suffix which can be added to a root alone. And so, the *anuvṛtti* of the same in this rule, from the rule *"ṛta id dhātoḥ"* (7-1-100) serves the purpose of conveying the idea that *sic* is to be followed by an *aṅga* which is an original root and not a nominal root (like *go* which being originally a base attain the status of root by the rule *"sanādyantā dhātavaḥ"* (3-1-32). At the stage *a+go+is+it*, go being thus not an *aupadeśikadhātu* the dipthong *o* at its end is not liable to undergo *vṛddhi*. So also in the aorist first person singualr of the root *kavi* arrived at by the addition of *kvip* to the base *kavi* the rule *"sici vṛddhiḥ parasmaipadeṣu"* (7-2-1) does not operate on *i* in the stage *a+kavi+is+* and so the resultant form is *akavīt* and not *akāvīt*.

NBh here cites the view of Mādhava. Here he is of opinion that in the rule *"sici vṛddhiḥ parasmaipadeṣu"* there is the *anuvṛtti* of the word *bahulam* and by virtue of the same it can be said that the rule enjoins *vṛddhi* to the last letter of all the roots eccept the nominal roots ending in diphthongs. Thus according to him, the nominal root *kavi*, as it does not end in a dipthong can well undergo the substitution by *vṛddhi* in the aorist form and the first person singular form is *akāvīt*. However when *kvip* is added to bases like *go, se* etc., these nominal roots, when followed by *sic* shall not undergo the *vṛddhi* enjoined by the rule *"sic vṛddhiḥ parasmai padeṣu"* (7-1-1).

Refuting these views of kṭ and Mādhava, NBh cites a view with the ending *ityāhuḥ*. As Pat gives stress on the fact, that there is no dipthong which is the final of an *aṅga* and at the same time is liable to undergo *vṛddhi* by the rule *"sici vrddhiḥ parasmaipadeṣu"* (7-2-1), by virtue of using the word *eva* in the statement *"naiva sandhyakṣaram antyam asti"*, it is better to accept the *anabhidhāna* of the addition of *kvip*, in the sense of *ācāra*, to bases ending with dipthongs whereby the assertion of Pat becomes alright. Here it is to be noted that though Kṭ and Mādhava invent devices to point out that *vṛddhi* won't operate on a diphthong at the end of a root, they do not negate the existence of a root, ending with diphthong and is followed by *sic*. What Pat says is *"naiva sandhyakṣaram antyam asti"*. It seems that though NBh cites the last view with the ending *ityāhuḥ* he prefers the same to the view of Kṭ and Mādhava. More over the non-addition of *kvip* in the sense of *ācāra* to bases ending with diphthongs, is favoured by him on the authority of Pat.[50].

Views on Certain Expressions

1. *The word 'mantra'*

While elucidating the verse *'duṣṭaḥ śabdaḥs avarato varṇato vā..."* quoted by Pat Kṭ narrates the story of Indra killing *Vṛtra*.[51] In order to procure a son who would kill Indra, the father of Vṛtra perfrormed a sacrifice and Kṭ says that the priests coined a *mantra* in the form of *"Indraśatrur vardhasva"*. NBh points out that since the inferred words (*ūhita*) cannot be called *mantra*, the word *mantra* used by Kṭ in apposition with *'Indraśatrur vardhasva'* is to be understood in the sense of *bodhaka*. NBh quotes the sūtra of Jaimini, namely *"anāmnateṣvamantratvam"* to support the fact that construed (*ūhita*) words cannot be called *mantra*.[52] Kṭ says that the expression *'Indraśatrur vardhasva'* did not convey the desired sense on account of the *ādyudātta* accent erroneously used in the place of *antodātta* accent. He says that however in the said expression there is no contingency of *ekaśruti* by the rule *"yajṅakarmaṇyajapanyuṅ khasāmasu"* (1-2-34) as the expression is not originally a *mantra* but an inferred one.

NBh raises a doubt that if an inferred expression (*ūhitaśabda*) cannot be called *mantra*, how can a sacrifice in which *laukika* śabdas are used can be fruitful and then gives the answer with the ending *ityāhuḥ*. On the strength of the statement *'prakṛtivad vikṛtiḥ kartavyā*, which sanctions *ūha* in mantras, *sūryāya tvā juṣṭam nirvapāmis* is inferred on the model of the *mantra, agnaye tvā juṣṭam nirvapāmi'* and the sacrifice performed with the utterance of this having the *laukika śabda sūryāya* in it is considered as bringing the desired effect. Hence though *ūhitaśabda* are not mantras, yet they are fruitful on the strength of the very sanction of *ūha* in mantras.

2. The verse by name bhrāja mentioned by Pat

While dealing with the accessory benefits accrued from the study of grammer Pat refers to a certain verse, by name bhrāja which deprecate the value of the soma sacrifice.[53] NBh points out that there is a view ascribing the authority of this verse to *Kāt*. He cites this view with the ending *ityāhuḥ*. Yudhiṣṭhira Mīmamsaka says that from this *āhuḥ*, it is understood that NBh does not favour this view.[54]

3. The expression 'ayamaham vadet' iṇ the verse "avidvāmsaḥ....vadet"

While dealing with the accessory benefits of the study of grammer, Pat quotes a stanza beginning with the word *avidvāmsaḥ*.[55] In that verse it is stated that a person who is ignorant of using the protraction of the vowel in the name of the pupil to whose salute he responds, is to be saluted by the pupil saying *'ayamaham'* as in the case of saluting women. Here with the ending *ityāhuḥ* NBh gives a view with regard to the absence of *samāsa* in the expression *'ayamaham vadet'*. There is a rule *"anukaraṇam cānitiparam"* (1-4-62) which provides the designation *gati* to an *anukaraṇa* when it is semantically connected with a *kriyā* and not followed by the word *iti*. Here the part *ayamaham* is the *anukaraṇa* of the actual salutation in regard to women. Though not followed by *itiśabda* it does not get the *gati samjñā* since the same is not connected with a *kriyā*. The part *ayamaham* is semantically connected with the verb *vadet*, but it cannot be compounded with *vadet* since *vadet* is a *tiṅanta* and the rule *"kugatiprādayaḥ"* (2-2-18) prescribes the *samāsa* of a *gati* with a semantically connected *śabda* which however must not be a *tiṅanta*.

4. The word akṣara in the Vedic passage 'yo vā imām..'

While dealing with the accessory benefits of the study of *Vyākaraṇa* Pat refers to the Vedic passage *"yo va imām padaśaḥj svaraśaḥ akṣaraśaśca vcam vidadhāti sa ārtvijīno bhavati.*[56] Here commenting on the word *akṣaraśaḥ* Kṭ says that the word *akṣara* means a vowel along with consonants. Thus the expression *yeyajāmahe* can be described as possessed of five *akṣaras.* NBh says that in the opinion of others *akṣara* denotes a single letter. The basis of this view is that in the vārttika *'varṇam vāhuḥ pūrvasūtre'* quoted by Pat at the end of the second *āhnika* it is stated that according to the grammatical rules of ancients, *akṣara* means a *varṇa* i.e, a letter.

5. The expression ūcchrityānucchritya in the bhṣya śakyam cānena yatkiñcideva kāṣṭham ucchrityānucchritya vā paśuranubandhum"[57]

NBh gives the meaning of these two words as 'after chopping or without chopping'. He then says that according to certain others (*anye*), the said expression means after making it upright (in the earth) or otherwise. Of these two views, Amarnath favours the latter and establishes the same by giving quotations from Ṛg Veda, *Rāmāyaṇa* and Śrautasūtra.[58] P.S. Sastry also favours the latter view.[59] But K.V. Abhyankar resorts to the former.[60]

6. The expression dharmaniyamaḥ in the vārttika "siddhe śabdārthasambandhe..."

The compound word *dharmaniyamaḥ* occurs in the first *vārttika 'siddhe śabdarthasambandhe lokato'rthaprayukte śabdaprayoge śāstreṇa dharmaniyamah kriyate yathā laukikavaidikeṣu'* It is given three explanations by Pat as *dharmāya niyamaḥ dharmaniyamaḥ, dharmārtho vā niyamah dharmaniyamaḥ,* and *dharmaprayojano vā niyamaḥ dharmaniyamaḥ.*[61] After elucidating the explanation of Kṭ to this *bhāṣya,* NBh cites a different explanation given by certain schlars (*Kecit....āhuḥ*). According to them, the word *dharma* in the first explanation *dharmāya niyamaḥ,* denotes *pratyavāyaparihārarūpadharma.* The *niyama* or restriction that meaning is to be denoted by corect words alone, wards off *pratyavya* that may occur otherwise i.e, when ideas are denoted by incorrect words. Thus *dharmāya niyamaḥ* means the said *niyama* is for *dharma* which is in the form of the removal of *pratyavya.* In the second explanation *dharmārtho va niyamaḥ dharmaniyamaḥ, dharma* means *yajña.* The said *niyama* is necessary for the performance of a *yāga* since an incorrect word used in the sense of the correct word can be designated as *anṛta* and the same has been prohibited in a *yāga* by the Vedic passage *'nānṛtam vadet'*. In the third explanation *dharmaprayojano va niyamaḥ dharmaniyamaḥ*, the word *dharma* means *adṛṣta*. This is because in the Vedic passage *'ekaḥ śabdaḥ samyak jñātaḥ ṣuṣṭhu prayuktaḥ svarge lke kāmadhuk bhavati'*, it is pointed out that the usage of correct words bring forth merit. Therefore the interpretation *dharmaprayojano vā niyamaḥ dhar maniyamaḥ* shows that the said *niyama* results in merit. Kṭ however takes the word *dharma* to denote *adṛṣta* in the three interpretations uniformly.[62]

7. The word 'eka' in the bhāṣya etadekam ācāryasya maṅgalārtham mṛṣyatm".[63]

While discussing the criteria by which the *samjā* and *samjñin* in a *sūtra* can be specified, Pat says, *"athavā purvoccāritaḥ samjñī paroccaritā samjñā* which means 'Or else that which is mentioned formerly is *samjñin*, the one mentioned subsequently (to the *samjñin*) is the *samjñā*. The rules *"aden guṇaḥ"* (1-1-2), *halonantaraḥ samyogaḥ* (1-1-7) exemplify this assertion. But in the rule *"vṛddhirādaie*, the *samjñin* namely *ādaic* is not given the former mention, but is mentioned in the contrary, as subsequent to the *samjñā*. Therefore there arises the question *"katham vṛddhirādaic?"* and Pat answers *'etad ekam ācāryasya maṅgalārtham mṛṣyatām'* and concludes that *"sarvatra vyākaraṇe purvoccaritaḥ samjñiparoccaritā samjñā"*. Pat means that the former mention of the *samjñā* namely *vṛddhi* in the rule instead of its mention subsequently to the *samjñin*, serves the purpose of *maṅgalā-cāraṇa* for his work. In all the other *samjñāsūtras*, samjñin is the one mentioned formerly.

With the ending *ityāhuḥ* NBh cites a view with regard to the significance of the word *ekam* in the said passage. The word *ekam* means first. Therefore the idea is this: The exception or change that we find for the first time in the rule *"vṛddhirādaic"* in regard to the usual order of the mention of *samjñā* and *samjñin* is to bring the benefit of *maṅgalācaraṇa*. This implies that in other *samjñāsūtras* too if there be any change of usual order of the *samjñā* and *samjñin* it must have some purpose. For example in the rule *"ārdhadhātukam śeṣaḥ"* (3-4-114) which is a rule defining the *samjñā ārdhadhatuka*, the order of the mention of *samjñā* and *samjñin* is reverted and this change of order has got a purpose to serve.

Acording to the usual conception, to secure the connection of two ideas as *uddeśya* and *vidheya* (subject and predicate) in a sentence, the word denoting *uddeśya* ought to be mentioned formerly and the word denoting the *vidheya* deserves to be mentioned latter. It is in order to point out the fact that, to secure the *anvaya* in *uddeśyavidheyabhāva* one need not necessarily mention the *uddeśya* formely and the *vidheya* later, that *Pāṇ* has changed the order of *samjñā* and *samjñin* in rules like *"ardhadhātukam śeṣaḥ"* (3-4-114) and *apṛkta ekāl pratyayaḥ"* (1-2-41). In these rules the *uddeśya* namely *śeṣaḥ* and *ekāl pratyayaḥ* are deliberately mentioned later to point out the above fact. However in the *śābdabodha* derived from these, śeṣaḥ and *ekālpratyayaḥ* are *uddeśya*. These rules mean *śeṣaḥ ārdhādhatukam* and *ekāl pratyayaḥ apṛktam*.

It is noteworthy here that to explain the exception to the usual order of *samjñā* and *samjin* Kṭ resorts to treating the rule *"apṛkta ekāl pratyayaḥ"* (1-2-41) as a paribhāṣāsūtra. He does not say anything with regard to the rule *"ārdhadhātukam śeṣaḥ"*. NBh however refutes this view of Kṭ and points out that this discrepancy cannot be accounted for by what has been stated by Kṭ [64]. The view cited above, however explains the change of order in the said two sūtras and so this view, cited by NBh with the ending *āhuḥ* seems to be favourd by NBh. Most probably what NBh, means by *āhuḥ* may be *siddhāntavidaḥ āhuḥ*.

8. The form '(he) picavya' doubted by Kṭ as being contingent to undergo substitution by guṇa in regard to the i that follows p in it[65].

Kāt says that if the rule *"iko guṇavṛddhī"* (1-1-3) enjoins *guṇa* to all the *ik* whether it be the final element of the *aṅga* or not, the *guṇa* enjoined by the rules *"Jusi ca"* (7-3-85) *"sārvadhātukārdhadhātukayoḥ"* (7-3-84) *"hrasvasya guṇaḥ"* (7-3-108) *"jasi ca "* (7-3-109) *"ṛto ṅisarvanāmasthānayoḥ"* (7-3-110) *"gherṅiti"* (7-3-111) and *"orguṇaḥ"* (6-4-146) ought to be prohibited from replacing the *ik* that is not final. Pat points out that though by resorting to *niyama* in a two-fold manneer i.e, 'pugantalaghūpadhasyaiva sārvadhātukārdhadhātukayoḥ guṇaḥ; sārvadhātukārdhadhātukayor eva pugantalaghūpadhasya guṇaḥ, the contigency of *guṇa* by the rules *"sārvadhātu-kārdhadh.tukayoḥ"*, *"hrasvasya guṇaḥ"*, etc., can be averted from replacing the *ik* that is not final, the *guṇa* by the rule *"jusi ca'* is contingent to replace the non-final *ik* in instances like *anenijuḥ paryaveviṣuḥ*[66]. Here Kṭ adds that there is the contigency of *guṇa* in spite of the two-fold *niyama* also in instances like (he) *picavya buddhe and buddhayaḥ* where the rules *"orguṇaḥ",' 'harasvasya guṇaḥ", "jasi ca "* 7-3-109) that enjoin *guṇa,* may operate on the non-final *ik* in the bases *picu* and *buddhi*. The *niyama* relating to *laghūpadha aṅgas* in both ways cannot restrict *guṇa here since picu and buddhi* are non-laghupadha *aṇgas.* NBh explains this statement of Kṭ. *(he) picavya* is the vocative case of the base *picavya* which is derived by the addition of the suffix *yat* dto the stem *picu* by the rule *"ugavādibhyo yat"* (5-1-2). Here the contigency of *guṇa* pointed out by Kṭ can be explained only when the rule is treated as enjoining *guṇa* to the *ik* which is a component of the *aṅga* ending with *u*. After thus elucidating the view of Kṭ, NBh points out that there is a view (ityāhuḥ) which doubts the contingency of the operation of the rule *"orguṇaḥ"*.(6-6- 146) narrated by Kṭ in the instance (he)*picavya.* Before speaking of the *niyama* Pat has stated that *"orguṇaḥ"* (6-4-146) is contigent on the non final *ik* in the instance *sauśrutaḥ*. Here it may be noted that the *aṅga* in sauśruta*ḥ* is *sauśrut* that ends in *t* and not in *u* and since Pat stated that there is the contigency of the operation of the rule *orguṇaḥ"* here, the rule cannot be inerpreted as enjoining *guṇa* to the *ik* namely *u* of the *aṅga.* As such, there is no contigency of *guṇa* on the *i* of the instance *picavya*. The statement of Kṭ in regard to *picavya,* therefore requires reconsideration.

Nbh however rescues Kṭ, pointing out that in certain copies of Kṭ's work, the instance (he) picavya is not mentioned and so Kṭ has not not made this assertion.

9. The word pradhānāni used by Kṭ in the sentence "pradhānāni ātmasamskārāya sannidhiyamānāni guṇabhaedam prayuñjate[67]*.*

Under the rule *'kṅiti ca'* (1-1-5) Pat offers many *suggestions to refute the view* that the word *nimitta* is to be inserted in the rule so as to bring the penultimate *ik* under the prohibition of *guṇā* prescribed by the rule. One among them is *"athavā yad etasmin yoge kṅidgrahaṇam kriyate tad anavakā'sam. Tasyānava-*

kāsatvād guṇo na bhaviṣyati. Kṭ says that this passage offers a solution to bring the penultimate *ik* under the prohibition of *guṇa,* in accordance with the maxim *yathodesam samjñāparibhāṣam* and points out *yathoddeśe pradhānāni ātmasamskārāya Sannidhīyamānānāni guṇabhedam prayuñjate.* Here Nbh says that there is a view *(ityāhuḥ)* that by using here the word *pradhāna* to refer to the vidhisūtras, Kṭ is implying the reason to account the fact that the rule enjoining prohibition get attached to each and every *vidhisūtra* that enjoin *guṇa*[68].

10. The forms (he) asuka and asukā derived from the base adas

Under the rule *"adaso māt"* (1-1- 12) Pat refutes the view that the rule is framed to procure the single benefit namely the prohibition of nasalaization of *i* and *u* in the instance *amī* and *amu* by means of providing the same with the designation *pragṛhya* and establishes that the rule has more purposes to serve.[69] He says *"naikam prayojanam yogārambham prayojayati. Yadyetāvad prayojanam syāt tatraivāyam brūyāt aṇopragṛhyasyānunāsikodaso na"* which means "a sūtra is not read with reference to only one benefit. Had the sūtrakāra meant that this sūtra operates only with reference to the sūtra *"aṇopragṛhyasyānunāsikaḥ* he would have read this sūtra after it, thus, *adaso na".*

Kṭ here points out that in this reading *'adso na* after *aṇo pragṛhyāsyānunasikaḥ* there is no necessity of the insertion of the words *idūt* and *māt* which are in the existing rule adaaso *māt*. There is no room for the doubt that in case of the absence of these words in the reading *adaso na,* the *au e* and *a* in the forms *asau amuke* and *amukābhyam* respectively, derived from the base *adas,* shall be prohibited nasalization. Thus is because Kṭ says even in the existence of the rule "adaso māt" these do not get nasalization since *au* and *e* in *asau* and *amuke,* are not comprehended by the word *aṇ* of the rule *"aṇo pragṛhyasyāsikaḥ",* which is coined with the *ṇ* of the rule *aiuṇ*. The *a* in *amukābhyām* also does not become nasalised since it is not the final element.

Here NBh says that there is a view which takes into consideration the forms *"(he)asuka* and *asukā* in this connection. *(he) asuka* is the vocative case of the base *adas* added with the suffix *akac* and *asukā* is the nominative case of the feminine **base** derived from *akas* added with the suffix *akac*. The final vowel in these undergo nazalization, since they are not provided with the term *pragṛhya*. Hence in the wording *adaso na* the part *adasaḥ* is interpreted in such a way as to avoid the contigency of the prohibition of nazalization to vowels in these derived from *adas* caused by the rule 'adaso na. The part *adaso* is repeated. One of them is derived in the following manner. *"na vidyate dasya sthāne saḥ yasya tasya"* meaning that which does not have the letter *d* being replaced by *s* and the other one conveys the usual sense *"of the word adas"*. Thus the idea that nasalization is prohibited to the *adas* that does not have the *d* in it being replaced by *s* and hence in the instance *asuka* and *asukā* the final vowels do not come under the scope of the prohibition of nasalization since the *d* of *adas*, there, is being replaced by *s*, and so they get nasaization.

After giving this view, NBh points out that others *(anye)* hold a different opinion. According to this latter view the forms *(he) asuka* and *asukā* are not to be accepted on the basis of *anabhidhāna*, This is because in the existence of such forms, it comes out that the rule *"adaso mat"* has two purposes, namely, the prohibition of nasalization of *i* and *u* in the instance *amī* and *amu* by giving them the designation *pragṛhya* and thereby endowing the *a* and *ā* in *asuka* and *asukā* with nasalization. This contradicts Pat's assertion that the rule serves a single purpose of the prohibition of nasalization and to procure such a benefit a rule in the form *'adaso māt'* need not be framed, (*"naikam prayojanam .... na"*).

Hence the former view cited with ending *āhuḥ* is expressive of NBh's dissent with the view. There is no valid authority for the repetition of the word *adasaḥ* and the peculiar derivation accepted in the word *adasaḥ* and also it involves comprousness. It seems that NBh favours the latter view cited with the ending *'ityanye'*.

Refutation of Cited Views

In addition to citing views, that are elucidative, justificatory or critical in nature, on the assertions of Pat and *Kṭ*, NBh has introduced in his work certain other views for purpose of refuting the same. He shows clearly that those views entertained by other scholars are erroneous. He elucidates the text of *Mbh* and *Prdp* in such a way that critical views on them are related and the assertion of Pat and Kṭ are established. However, he does not generally reveal the identity of the personality whose view he is refuting. We many examine such views.

1. Criticism on Kṭ who resorts to the vārttika "hrgṛhor bhaśchandasi hasyeti vaktavyam" to explain the substitution of h by bh in Vedic Words.

To point out change of letters, seen exclusively in Vedas, *Kṭ* cites two instances *udgrābham* and *nigrābham* and says that these words are derived from the root *grah* prefixed with the *upasarga ud* and *ni*, respectively, by the addition of the suffix *ghañ.*[70] The suffix *ghañ* here is not enjoined to the said roots by any rule, but is understood to be so by the *nipātana* of these words in the *vārttika udgrābhanigrābhau ca cchandasi srugudyamananipātanayoḥ"* Kṭ says that this vārttika allows the usage of the words like *uddgrābha* and nigrābha derived by the addition of the suffix *ghañ* and in the sense of *srugudyamana* and *srugnipātana. Kṭ* continues that the substitution of *h* by *bh* in these instance is sanctioned by the vārttika *'hṛgrahor bhaśchandasi hasyeti vaktavyam'*. Here some express a disagreement. They point out that the former vārttika is however necessary as an authority for the addition of the suffix *ghañ* to the root *ghah* and that vārttika itself can be resorted to explain the replacement of *h* by *bh*. Therefore there is no necessity of the vārttika, cited secondly to explain the substitution by *bh* of *h* and they are of opinion that Kṭ has in vain resorted to the second vārttika. Refuting this assertion, NBh makes the position of Kṭ unquestionable. He points out that there is another usage *grabhṇāmi* in the Veda. This form is derived from the root *grah*. Here there is the substitution of *h* by the letter *bh* and the vārttika is necessary for explaining the substitution of *h* by *bh* here, so also the same in the form *jagrābha* derived from the root *grah*. The vārttika cited fromerly does not enjoin the substitution by *bḥ* because it simply allows the usage of the word *udgrābha* and *nigrābha* in a particular sense. Therefore, NBh points out, Kṭ has quite correctly resorted to the second vārttika as an authority for the change of *h* into *bh* in the root *grah*.

2. The optional correctness of the word ḷtake

In the vārttika *ḷkaropadeśa yadṛcchāśaktijānukaraṇaplutyādyarthaḥ*, it is pointed that one among the purposes served by the enunciation off the letter in the sivasutras is to procure vowel-operation on ḷ that is seen in yadṛcchāśabdas like *ḷtka* (words coined at random)[71]. Pat refutes this saying that there are only three kinds of standard śabdas and no fourth variety formed by yadṛcchāsabdas. Hence words like *ḷtaka* being an incorrect word, *ḷkāropadesa* is not necessary for its sake[72]. To this the objector remarks that this kind of argumentation iṣ not fair. He argues that as the utility of the mention of *ḷ* in the Śivasūtras is given by admitting the existence off yadṛcchāśabdas, the negation of the same on the strength of the view that there are no yadṛcchaśabdas, is not logical gives the reply *"naiṣa doṣaḥ. Pakṣāntarairapi parihārā bhavanti"*, which means 'The difficulty pointed out does not arise. Refutations are made even on the basis of different views". NBh points out that there is an erroneous interpretation of this passage in the following manner[73]. This bhāṣya treats the word *ḷtaka* as correct in the view that there are four divisions of standard words and as an incorrect one in the view that there are only three groups of standard sounds and it is in this latter view that the utility of the mention of the letter ḷ is refuted. Hence it comes out that words like *itaka* like the words *ṭi, ghu* etc. coined by Pāṇ are fit for grammatical operations in the view that there are four groups of sounds among which one group is that of yadṛcchāśabdas. NBh strongly argues against this interpretation. The foremost point of objection is this. The acceptence of the fact that a particular word can treated as correct and incorrect on the basis of two different views is contradictory to the statement of Pat in the rule *"naveti vibhāṣā"* (1-1-44). There the fact that a word becomes correct only partially, is pointed out as a defect[74]. Hence words like *ḷtaka* are ever unfit for grammatical operations. They are unlike the words *ṭi ghu* etc, since the latter are cointed by siṣṭas, like Pāṇ. There is no such authentic usage by siṣṭas, in regard to the words like *ḷtaka*. Hence they are unfit for grammatical operations. Moreover if we accept these as partially correct words and fit for grammatical operation partially, it will be contradictory to the reference made by Pat to this science of grammar as *sādhvanusasana*. Besides, there is a doubt as to whether these words like *ḷtaka* are to be accepted as whether fit for grammatical operation or even if fit for grammatical operations, are not correct words. Hence it is wise to accept that *ḷtaka* as incorrect word and the idea of the passage is that, the utility of the mention of *ḷ* aditting the existence of yadṛcchāśbdas is refuted since Pat favours the view that there are only three groups of standard sounds.

3. Śabdaparavipratiṣedha.

Under the Sivasūtras *"eoṅ"* and *"aiauc"* NBh points out that *vivarannakāra* is of opinion that the letters *ai* and *au* get *i* and *u* as the *hrasva* substitutes on the basis of *śabdapravipratiṣedha (vipratiṣedha* based on the position of the letters in a sound). The dipthong *ai* is constituted of *a* and *i* whereas *au* is constituted of *a* and *u*. When *hrasva* is enjoined as a substitute to *ai* and *au* for instance in words like *rai, sudyau* and as these letters do not have the *(hrasva)* short variety there is the contingency of *ai* being subustituted either by *a* or *i* since both these are *antaratama* to *a* and *i* that are the components of the letter *ai*. Thus there results a *vipratiṣedha* between the substitutes *a* and *i* and *i* will substitute, on the strength of the *"vipratiṣedhe param kāryam"* (1-4-2) since it is *antaratama* to *i* which is *para* among the cocmponents *a* and *i* when looked at from the point of view of sound position. Similarly *u* will substitute *au* which has the components *a* and *u*.

NBh does not agree to this view. He points out that in the circumstance narrated by *vivaraṅkāra* the probablity is the substitution by *a* of *ai* and *au* on the basis of *antaraṅgatva* which is given prominence over *bahiraṅga* by the maxim *'asidhaṃ bahiraṅgam antaraṅge'*. This is because *a* is *antaraṅga* since it is concerned with the *pūrva* viz. *a* whereas *i* and *u* are concerned with the *para* viz. *i* and *u* in *ai* and *au*. This is quite clear, NBh says, from the bhāṣya under the rule *"acaḥ parasmin pūrvavidhau"* (1-1-57) where in the instance *kartr+ī+ā* the *yaṇādesa* caused by *i* which is *pūrva* to *a*, supersedes the *yaṇādeśa* caused by *a* which is *para* to *i*, on the basis of antaraṅgatva.[76] Thus looking from the point of view of sound position the *kārya* concerning the *pūrva* has been given prominence. But Pat says *'asiddham bahiraṅgalaksaṇam antaraṅgalakṣaṇe ityanena siddhyati'* Here Pat makes clear that the rule *"vipratisedhe param kāryam"*

(1-4-2) does not operate where one of the operation is *para*, simply from the point of view of sound position.

4. Acceptance of Lakṣaṇā in the sentence "pañcapañcanakhā bhakṣyāḥ".

To the question as to how the exposition of śabdas has to be given whether by expounding all correct words or by expounding all incorrect words or in both ways, the answer given by Pat is that the exposition of science is to be achieved by either of the two methods i.e, by the exposition of correct words alone or by the exposition of incorrect words alone. Pat then illustrates his assertion *"tad yathā bhakṣyaniyamenābhakṣya-pratiṣendho gamyate. pañca pancanakha bhakṣyāḥ ityukte gamyata etadato nye bhakṣyā iti"*.[77] NBh here points out that there is a view that the assertion *pañca pañcanakhā bhakṣyāḥ* denotes the idea that those other than the five five-nailed animals are not to be eaten. This idea is derived by accepting *lakṣaṇā* by which the word *pañca* denote those other than the five and the word *bhakṣya* indicate *abhakṣya*.

Nbh refutes this view totally. The first point of objection is that the acceptance of *lakṣanā* in these words involve ambiguity. NBh cites many a reason to refute the above view. The most important one among them is the statement of Pat himself *"bhakṣyaniyamenābhakṣyapratiṣedho gamyate"* wherein it is made clear that the restriction in this statement of a few as edible implies the prohibition of others as non-edibles. If the sentence stands for abhakshyaniyama, how can Pat speak of *bhakṣyaniyama*? Again it cannot be agreed to that on the strength of the word *bhaksyaniyamabodhakena* and by virtue of *lakṣaṇā* in the part *niyama* in it, the sentence can be stated as prohibiting one from tasting the flesh of others other than the stipulated five. This is because there lurks the defect of ambiguity if *lakṣaṇā* is accepted.

Thus this view cannot be accepted when one takes into consideration the words of Pat. Kṭ too has stated that *'niyamyamānam lakṣaṇam sāmarthyād anyebhyo nivartate,* and that too will be contradicted. Again the subject of this illustration is *śabdopadeśaḥ* i.e., *upadeśa* of śabdas like *gauḥ* whereby others like *gāvī goṇī* are understood as incorrect ones. Hence this example so as to be coherent with the subject of illustration ought to be treated as conveying the idea of the specification of those that are edible by which other than these can be understood as non-edibles. Moreover learned men have stated that an assertion which comes under the group of *parisamkhyāvidhi* only implies the avoidance of others and never directly states the same. Since according to Mīmāmsakas this is a *parisamkhyāvidhi* which is here treated as *niyama* by Pat, this must therefore directly mean the injunction of those which are edible. The sentence directly means "eat the five five-clawed animals". Since even without this injuction the posssibility of the consumption of those five animals is natural, the statement points out that the consumption must be restricted to these five animals alone. The sentence therefore never means by *lakṣaṇā* the fact that those other than the five five-nailed animals are not to be eaten, but only results, by means of the restriction of above mentioned, in the prohibition of the tasting of the flesh of others which involves *prāyaścitta.*

5. A view with regard to the meaning of the rule vrddhirādaic in the kāryakalapakṣa.

Under the rule *vṛddhirādic*" (1-1-1) NBh cites a view according to which the meaning of the rule in the *kāryakālapakṣa* is "where there be *vṛddhi* there the word *ādaic* presents itself and the rule has the status of a *samjñāsūtra* simply on the basis of the fact that in *sūtras like mṛjervṛddhiḥ* the word *vṛddhi* which attracts the word *ādaic* denotes *ā ai* and *au,* just as only in the śruti *'jyotiṣṭomena yajeta'* enjoining *jyotisṭmayaga* the word *jyotiṣṭoma* is understood as a *samjñā* since it is *samānādhikaraṇa* with *yāga.*[78]

NHb refutes this view. He points out that if the rule were to mean in *kāryakālpakṣa* the idea that, where there be the word *vṛddhi,* there the word *ādaic* presents itself, Pat's statement under the rule *"synaḥ samprasāraṇam putrapatyoḥ"* (6-1-13) 'kāryakālam samjñāparibhāṣam bhasyetyupasthitam idam bhavati yaci bham iti' and another statement under the rule *'īdūdeddvicanam pragṛhyam* (6-1-11) 'kāryakālam samjñāparibhāṣam. Pragṛhyaḥ prakṛtyetyupasthitam idam bhavati idūdet dvivacanam pragrvham iti" cannot be coherent. He ought to have asserted as *'kāryakālam samjñāparibhāsam upasthitam idam bhavati yaciti.* Since he does not state like that the above view is not tenable. Again the fact that even in *kāryakālapaksa* it is an independant *samjñāsūtra* is clear by the arguments of vārttikakāra for the formation of an *adhikāra sūtra* like *atha samjñā* before the rule *vṛddhirādaic*. Pat rerutes this attempt pointing out that in spite of the absence of an *adhikarasūtra* it can be understood as a *samjñāsūtra.*

There are also other defects involved in this view. The *paribhāṣāūtra, "iko guṇavṛddhī"* presents the word *ikaḥ* to the rule *"mṛjervṛddhiḥ"* since the rule enjoins *a ai* and *au* by the term *vṛddhi*. If it is accepted that the word *ādaic* presents itself where there be the word *vṛddhi*, the rule *"mṛjervṛddhiḥ"* (7-2-114) directly enjoins *ādaic* and so *ā, ai* and *au* won't have the status of being prescribed by the term *vṛddhi* and hence there is the difficulty, that the rule *"iko guṇavṛddhī"* (1-1-3) will never present the word *ikaḥ* to that rule. Though however the word *vṛddhi* will have relation with the rule *mṛjervṛddhiḥ* since they relate to *ādaic* enjoined by the rule it can never have the status of a *samjña*. But with regard to the rule *"jyotiṣṭomena yajeta"* the word *jyotiṣṭoma* is treated as a *nāmadheya* since here the case is different. In this *sruti* the idea of *yāga* is denoted by the part *yaj* of *yajeta* and hence *jyotiṣṭoma* can but be a *nāmadheya* on account of its being *samānādhikaraṇa* with *yīga*. Moreover there will arise a doubt as to whether the rule *vṛddhirādaic* is to be treated as a paribhāsā sūtra since the word *vṛddhi* in the rule attracts the word *ādaic*, or *samjñā sutra* since it expresses *ādaic* attracted by it. Above all it is difficult to accept that a word attracts another word by the expressive power of 'sabdas known as *vṛtti*. Last of all, NBh points out that in the sense of the rule as suggested the rule is contingent to present the word *ādaic* only where there be the word *vṛddhi* as *vidheya*.

But Pat has accepted the function of the rule *vṛddirādaic* even in sūtras like *"vṛddhir yasyācām ādis tad vṛddham"* (1-1-74) where *vṛddhi* is *anuvadya*. All the above arguments completely disprove the idea delineated in the view. According to NBh in the *kāryakālapakṣa*, the rule *vṛddhirādaic* becomes a sub clause of the rule *mṛjervṛddhiḥ* and from that sub clause it is understood that *vṛddhi* is the term for *a, ai* and *au* and it is that *vṛddhi* which is enjoined by the main clause *mṛjeṛvrddiḥ*.

6. The treatment of samjñasūtrās as niyamasūtras.

Haradatta is of opinion that the rule *"vṛddhirādaic* is a *niyamasūtra.*[79] *The word vṛddhi* is derived from the root *vṛdh* by the addition of the suffix *ktin* taught in the sense of *bhāva* and hence means increment. The letters *a, ai* and *au* are possessed of increment itself and hence by *abhedopacāra* they can be treated as increment itself i.e, *vṛdāhi*. Thus the word *vṛddhi*, can even in the absence of a rule like *"vṛddhirādaic"* can denote by *lakṣaṇa ā, ai* and *au* and so the rule *vṛddhirādaic* pointing out the same is restricting the term *vṛddhi* to *a, ai* and *au* alone and thereby prevents the term from being applied to the prolate *a* the lengthened *i* etc. which also possess increment. Haradatta thus opines that samjñāsūtras are niyama sūtras. NBh refutees this view pointing out that this kind of explanation cannot be given to the rule *"aden guṇaḥ* (1-1-2) which enjoins the term *guṇa* to letters *a, e* and *o* and this view is quite negligible.

7. The maxim 'samjñāpūrvako vidhiranityaḥ'

Bhaṭṭojidiksita is of opinion that there is a maxim that a rule is not universally valid, when, that which is taught in it, is denoted by a technical term. He says that the rule *"uto varddhir luki hali"* (7-3-89) that enjoins *au* as the substitute of *u* therefore functions optionally alone i.e, it does not function in certain instances. Otherwise Pāṇ would have read the rule as *'uta au luki hali'*. Therefore the contigency of the substitution by *vṛddhi*, on the strength of this rule, of the *u* in *stuyāt* and the like is avoided , NBh refutes this, pointing out that such a maxim is nowhere mentioned or indicated by Pat.[80] Moreover he says that if such a maxim were to exist, Pat won't have resorted to the indication of a maxim *'angavṛtte punaṛvṛttavavidhiḥ* by virtue of lengthening in the subtitute *jā* taught in the rule *"jñājanor jā"* (7-3-79). In this rule the substitute *jā* is enjoined to the roots *jñā* and *jan* whereby forms like *jānāti* and *jāyate* are arrived at. During the process of formation of the word *jānāti* at the stage *jñā+nā+ti*, if the substitute be *hrasva* i.e, *ja* the resultant form will be *janāti* and the *a* in *ja* cannot be lengthened by the rule *"ato dīrgho yañi"* (7-3-101) since it enjoins lengthening by using the term *dīrghaḥ* and hence does not operate universally. Therefore in order to arrive at a form, when there is the maxim *'samjñāpurvako vidhir anityaḥ'* the mention of the substitute as being lengthened i.e, *jā* is quite necessary and being satisfied for the same, it cannot indicate a maxim *'angavṛtte.........."*. Since Pat indicates the above maxim by virtue of the lengthened substitute of this rule, one cannot accept the maxim *"samjñāpūrvako vidhir anityaḥ"* which makes this indication impossible. So also the contingency of the substitution by *vṛddhi* by the rule "*uto vṛddhir luki hali*" (7-3-89) on the *u* of *stuyāt* cannot be warded off on the basis of this maxim. It is to avoid this *vṛddhi* that Pat. accepts the formula *pit ṅinna bhavati ṅit ca pinna bhavati*. This idea is arrived at by splitting the rule "*sārvadhātkamapit*" (1-2-4) as *sārvadhātukam* and *apit*. The split rule by virtue of the *nañ* in the sense of *prasajyapratiṣedha* and the *anuvṛtti* of the word *ṅit* means '*pit ninna bhavati*'. Therefore in the instance *stuyāt*, the *yāsuṭ* being *ṅit* (*yāsuṭ parasmaipades"datto ṅicca*) 3-4-103) cannot be treated as *pit* even though the substitute *ti* to which it is the augment, is *pit* and in the absence of precedance of a non-pit suffix, *vṛddhi* enjoined on the precedence of a *pit* suffix by the rule "*uto vrddhir luki hali*" (1-3-89) cannot substitute the *u* of *stu* which is immediately followed by *yāsut* which is *ṅit*. Thus the view held by Bhaṭṭojidīksīta is refuted by NBh.

REFERENCES

1. Vide Supra, p. 21. Ref. 19.
2. Vide *Par Sekh* with the commentary '*Gadā*' p. 9 - "ata evaitavadamsasya duṣtatvena tatrārucisūcanāya kecit ityuktam. Anyathaitadanyasya granthasya siddhāntatvena paretvitu vaktumucitam."
3. Vide *S.K. Belvalker felicitation Volume*, p. 127 - "His final view, his siddhānta he would introduce by 'pare tu', others (who are correct), which amounts with him, to bhāṣyatattvavidas, those who know the true meaning of the bhāṣya."
4. Vide *Bṛ. Sąb. Sekh* p. 7.
5. Vide *Par. Sekh* p. 33.
6. *Mbh* p. 86.
7. Vide *Mbh* Vol. II p. 28.
8. *Mbh* pp. 127-128.
9. Vide *Par. Sekh* p. 52.
10. *Mbh* p. 128.
11. Vide *Udy* p. 99 and Infra pp. 112-113.
12. Vide *Udy* p. 72.
13. Vide *Udy* p. 109 and Supra p. 85.
14. *Udy* pp. 5 & 19.
15. *Udy* p. 189.
16. *Udy* p. 95.
17. *Udy* p. 159.
18. Vide *Udy* p. 31.

19. Vide *Mbh* Vol. II. p. 253.
19(a). Vide *Mbh* Vol. I Part II, pp. 272-273.
20. op.cit, p. 165.
21. Vide Infra p. 109--136.
22. Vide *Mbh* (with the commentary Tattvāloka) pp. 23-24 & 256.
23. Vide Infra pp. 109-136.
24. Vide *S.K. Belvalkar felicitation volume,* p. 127.
25. Udy pp. 135 & 291.
26. Vide *Par.Śekh* with the commentary gadā' p. 179.
27. Vide *Par Śekh* with the commentary *'gadā,* pp. 4 & 9.
28. Vide Infra pp. 109-136.
29. The expressions *'na ca ....vācyam'* 'namu ......iti cenn' etc. used by NBh for anticipating objections on the assertions of Pat and Kt is taken by some scholars to indicate the citation of the view of others. For instance T. Chandraśekharan in his introduction to the *Mbh* edited with the commentary *Mahabhāṣyapradipoddyotana* of Annambharra points out that in the statement in *Udy* (p. 13) *'na ca vanamiti samoohābhiprāyam tat'* NBh is referring to the view of Annambharra which he refutes subsequently.
30. *Mbh* p. 16.
31. Vide *Chāyā* p. 18.
32. Vide *Mbh* with *Tattovāloka* p. 15.
33. *Mbh* pp. 63-64.
34. *Udy* p. 100.
35. *Mbh* p. 85.
36. *Mbh* p. 99.
37. *Mbh* p. 97.
38. *Mbh* p. 373.
39. *Mbh* p. 117.
40. *Mbh* p. 124.
41. *Mbh* p. 120:- "vṛddhigunāvalontyasyeti cet midimṛjipugantalaghūpadharcchidṛśikṣprakṣudreṣviggrahaṇam"
42. *Udy* p. 183.
43. *didiye* - Perfect first person singular of the root *dīn* with *ātmanepada* termnination.
44. Vide *Par Sekh* pp. 23-26.
45. *Mbh* p. 193.
46. *Mbh* p. 128.
47. alāvit - Aorist third person singular of the root lū. a+lū+is+īt: *a = adāgama, lū* = the root, *is* = *sic* prefixed with *idāgama, īt* = the *parasmipada* termination with *īḍāgama.*
48. *Mbh* p. 126.
49. *a+go+is+īt* : *a = adāgama, go* = the root, *is* = *sic* perfixed with

iḍāgama, it = the *parasmaipāda* termaination *t* prefixed with *īḍāgama*.

50. Vide Infra p. 167, *Mbh*. p. 98.
51. *Prdp* p. 23.
52. *Udy* p. 24.
53. *Mbh* p. 27.
54. op. cit, p. 302.
55. *Mbh* p. 28.
56. *Mbh* p. 30.
57. *Mbh* p. 50
58. Vide *Vishvesvarananda Indological Journal, Hoshiarpur*, 1963, Vol. I, Part I, p. 170.
59. Vide *Lectures on the Mahabhasya of Patanjali*, Vol. I, p. 51.
60. Vide *The Mahabhasya of Patanjali*, edited by K.V. Abhyankar, Fasciculus I, p. 33.
61. Mbh p. 51.
62. *Prdp* p. 51.
63. *Mbh* p. 110.
64. *Udy* p. 110.
65. *Prdp* p. 122.
66. Vide *Mbh* p. 122. *"evamapayam jusi guṇo'niyataḥ so 'nantyasyāpi prāpnoti"*.
67. *Prdp* p. 138.
68. *Udy* p. 139.
69. *Mbh* p. 168.
70. *Prdp* p. 15.
71. *Mbh* p. 72.
72. *Mbh* p. 73.
73. *Udy* p. 74.
74. *Mbh* p. 141. sādhvanusāsane'smin s'āstre yasya vibhāṣā kriyate sa vibhaṣā sadhuḥ syāt".
75. *Udy* p. 79.
76. *Udy* p. 79.
77. *Mbh* p. 41.
78. *Udy* pp. 114-115.
79. *Mbh* p. 103.
80. *Udy* p. 141 and *Mbh* with the commentary *Tattvāloka*. p. 183.

Chapter VI

Criticism of the Pradīpa
I Difference of Opinion

NBh's gloss on *Prdp* can be characterised as a critical study of the observations of Kṭ. Though as a commentator he has elaborated *Prdp* by way of elucidations and justification of the statements found in it, he has subjected the work to his criticism also. His observations in *Udy* show his difference of opinion with Kṭ on many points. In many instances he expresses his disagreement with the view of Kṭ. He points out that several assertions of Kṭ require reconsideration.

Interpretation of Passages

1. *Keṣām śabdānām? laukikānām vaidikānām ca*[1]

After stating the fact that the science by name *śabdānuśāsana* has been begun, Pat employs the above question and answer, "Of which śabdas? Of these current in the world and the Vedas". Kṭ and Nbh differ in their opinion in regard to the purpose of this question and answer. The former is of opinion that since the word *śabda* denotes not only words of human speech but also the sounds produced by birds, animals, etc. Pat wishes to inform the readers clearly that it denotes only words of human speech here. NBh on the other hand feels that since the word *'sabdānuśāsana* is a significant name for grammar, it goes without saying that incorrect expressions and sounds produced by animals or birds are not to be dealt with in this science. Hence, the possibility is that one may entertain a doubt as to whether the science, just like the *Śākaṭāyana Vyākaraṇa* deals with words of the spoken language alone or just like the treatises like the *prātiśākhya* deals with words of vedic literature alone and hence the question, *'keṣām śābdānām (anuśasanam)?*[1] The answer tells the reader that Pāṇ deals with both of them in his work.

2. *Kim punar idam vyākaraṇam evādhijigāmsamānebhyaḥ prayojanamucyate na punar anyad api kiñcid - "om ityuktyvā vṛttāntaśah śam ityevamādin śabhān paṭhanti?*[2]

To the question *'kāni punaḥ śabdānuśasanasya prayojanāni'?*, Pat enumerates the main benefits and subsidiary benefits accruing from the study of grammar. This is followed by the above question which means "why the benefits accrued from the study of grammar alone are enumerated and not those of Vedas also?" Kṭ feels an inconsistency in this question raised by one who has just before enquired about the benefits of the study of grammar and got the answer for it. He therefore takes this question to imply that Pat is about to specify the need of the enumeration of benefits, to be only in the case of the study of subjects other than the Vedas. But, with the conclusory remark *ityanye* NBh removes this inconsistency in another way. The question is taken to be raised by a third person different from those two who enquired about and enumerated respectively, the benefits of the study of grammar.

3. *astyanyad gargādibidādipāṭhe prayojanam kim? samudāyānām sādhutvam yathā syād iti*[3]

In the first *āhnika* of the *Mbh* to the question concerning the purpose to be derived from the fourteen Sivasūtras, the *ekadeśin* replies that the said sūtras are for the understanding of correct pronounciation and in this case, the necessity of uttering correct vowels like those that are grave, acute, etc., no longer arises, as there is the authoritative utterance of their general forms i.e., *ākṛtyupadeśa* in the Śivasūtras. Now an objection is raised that if *ākrtyupadeśa* be accepted there arises the necessity of prhibition of such letters that are possessed of the faults such as *samvṛta, kala* and the like. To the answer that the vowels possessed of faults will not be included on account of their faultless pronounciation by Sūtrakāra himself in words which are put in groups beginning with *garga bida* and the like, an objection is again raised in the above quoted passage which means: "There is another purpose served by reading of the collection of words headed by *garga and bida*. What? so that the *samudāya* may be taken to be correct. According to Kṭ the word *śamudāyānām* in the said passage refers to words like *garga, bida*, etc. The reason for putting groups of words headed by *garga and bida* is that the whole words like *garga* etc. (which are a collection (*samudāya*) of certain letters in a particular order) may be taken as correct. NBh on the other hand, refers by the word *samudāyānām* to the words like *gārgya, baida*, etc. (which are the collection (*samudāya*) of the base *garga* and the like and suffix *yañ añ* and the like. The reason for grouping words headed by *garga* etc. is that words like *gārgya* etc. could be looked upon as correct ones. NBh says that this interpretation is more befitting when one considers the further assertion of the *siddhantin* *'ubhyayam anena kriyate, pāṭhaścaiva viśeṣyate, kalādayaśca nivartyante'*. Here the part *pāṭhaścaiva viśeṣyate* means "by the groups like *gargādhi* words like *garga* are instructed to be possessed of the suffix *yañ* enjoined by the rule *"gargādibhyoyañ"* (1-1-105) It may be pointed out here that Kṭ does not say anything of this assertion of Pat.

4. *'na hi dyayor ākṣarasamāmnayikayor yugapat samavasthānamasti'*[4]

Under the Śivasūtra *'aiuṇ'* Kāt says that the vowel *a* which is *saṃvṛta* in roots bases etc. is to be mentioned as *vivṛta* so that it may be comprehended by the *a* in the Śivasūtra *'aiuṇ'* where it is mentioned as *vivṛta*, otherwise the *a* in roots bases etc. shall not be comprehended by the *a* of the rule *'aiuṇ'*. Pat says that this difficulty does not arise since the comprehension of *a* by *a* is indicated by Pāṇ through the word *akaḥ* in the rule *"akaḥ savarṇe dīrghaḥ"* (6-1-101). His words are "ācāryapravṛttir jñāpayati - bhavatyākṣarasamāmnāyikena dhātvādisthasya grahaṇam iti-yadayam akaḥ savarne dīrghaḥ iti pratyāhāre'kograhaṇam karoti katham kṛtvā jñāpakam? na hi dvayor ākṣarasamamnāyikayor yugapat samavasthānam asti". The idea is that in the absence of the comprehension of the vowel *a* that is in the roots bases etc. at no places can the letter *a* (*vivṛta*) belonging to the list of alphabet be found together with another letter *a* of the same kind so as to be coalesced into *ā* by the rule *"akaḥ savarṇe dīrghaḥ"* (6-1-101). Hence the word *akaḥ* in the rule serves no purpose with regard to the vowel *a* and therefore could be taken to indicate the inclusion of its cognate *a* occurring in roots bases etc. by the *vivṛta* a of *aiuṇ* although the cognate *a* be *saṃvṛta*.

Here commenting on the word *dvayoḥ* in the passage Kṭ points out that the vowel *a* which is *vivṛta* is found in the Śivasūtras alone and in other instances one can never find even a sigle *a* which is *vivṛta*. Yet Pat has made the remark that at no places can two *ākṣarasamānāyika (vivṛta) a* vowels can be seen. This assertion of Pat, is therefore, to be understood in the sense that, as the *savarṇadīrgha* enjoined by the rule *"akaḥ savarṇe dīrghah"* is an *ekādeśa* i.e., substitute of two *sthānin* viz. *pūrva and para, the sthānin* viz. *vivṛta a* is mentioned here in dual number in the expression *dvayoḥ* says Kṭ.

NBh on the other hand gives a different opinion as the view of other scholars. He says that in the sentence *'devadatta ajasti'* the initial *a* in the word *ac (ac+asti = ajasti)* can be understood as *vivṛta* since from the *pratyāhāra aç* wherein it occurs, one can understood that it belongs to the Śivasūtra *'aiuṇ'*. Thus in this instance viz. *ac* it is possible to find a *vivṛta a* along with a *samvṛta a* which is at the end of the word *devadatta*, to be coalesced into *ā*. Therefore the presence of one *vivṛta a* being feasible and there being the absence of two *vivṛta a* vowels, Pat has rightly said, *"na hi dvayor ākṣarasamamnāyikayor yugapot samvasthānam asti"*.

5. *Dīrghaplutau punar naiva loke na ca vede samvṛtau staḥ*[5]

Under the Śivasūtra *'aiuṇ'* Pat says that there are no *ā* and prolate *a* that are *samvṛta*. Kṭ opines that their non-existence is due to the fact that it is not possible to utter the *ā* and prolate *a* as *saṃvṛta*. NBh points out that there is a different opinion held hy certain scholars with regard to the reason for the non-existence of *saṃvṛta dīrgha* and *pluta*. The *vivṛta dīrgha* and *vivṛte pluta* are admitted by śiṣṭas i.e., by the learned. That is why they are treated as existant. But, the *saṃvṛta dīrgha* and **pluta** are treated as non-existant since they are **not** acknowledged by śiṣṭas.

6. *"na cāpaśabdaḥ prakṛtiḥ na hyapaśabdā upadiśyante na cānupadiṣṭā prakṛtirasti"*[6]

Pat says that words like *ḷtaka*, mispronounced due to the disability to utter properly as *ṛtaka* are apaśabdas but the imitatory words like *ḷtaka* as in the sentence *'brāhmaṇī ḷtaka ityāha'* are not apaśabdas. He says that one cannot superimpose *apaśabdatva* on a correct word i.e., *sādhuśabda*, even on the basis of the maxim *'prakṛtivad anukaraṇam'*. This is because *apaśabda* can not be charaterised as the *prakṛti* mentioned in this maxim, since *prakṛti* is that which is enunciated and apaśabdas are never enunciated. Hence they being non-enunciated cannot be called *prakṛti*. His words are *"na cāpaśabdaḥ prakṛtiḥ na hyapaśabdā upadiśyante nacānupadiṣṭā prakṛtir asti"*. Kṭ says that the maxim allows the superimposition of only technical factors and operations. *Apaśabda* is not a technical factor. Moreover, he adds, it is not reasonable to superimpose *asādhutva* on *sādhuśabda*. Hence NBh points out that a certain scholar feels that this assertion of Kṭ requires reconsideration. *Apaśabdatva* can well be superimposed on a *sādhuśabda*, just as *abrāhmaṇatva* can be superimposed on a brahmin. Any attribute can be superimposed on another. There is no question of being reasonable or not, in it. The reason for Pat's assertion, that the imitatory word *ḷtaka* of the mispronounced word *ḷtaka* due to disability, cannot be treated as *apaśabda* by the maxim *"prakṛtivad anukaraṇam"* is that *apaśabda* being not enunciated is not a *prakṛti*, the quality of which alone can be superimposed on its *anukaraṇa* by the said maxim.

7. *Saṃghātasyaikatvam arthaḥ tena varṇāt subutpattir na bhaviṣyati*[7]

To establish the fact that letters are possessed of sense individually, several arguments are advanced under the Śivasūtra *'hayavaraṭ'*. To this the objector points out that if letters are accepted as individually possessed of sense, there shall be the contingency of case-suffix after each letter in bases like *dhana vana*, etc. This difficulty is warded off by Pat in this passage *'Saṃghātasyaikatvam.....bhaviṣyati"*.

Kṭ takes the sentence *saṁghātasyaikatvaṁ arthaḥ* to mean *saṁghātasyāpi ekatvam arthaḥ*. (The *samudāya* too has got the sense of oneness). This takes for granted that the components have got the sense of oneness. Kṭ says that just as many people see a particular object with the help of a single lamp, a single case suffix namely, *su* is enough to convey the sense of oneness of the components and the whole. It will come as latter (*para*) to the whole (*samudāya*) so that it can be 'para' to the component letters as well as the *samudāya*. Kṭ says that this is just like *samudāyadvirvacana* by which the components as well as the *samudāya* gets republicated. However, the *samudāya* alone will be designated as *pada*, since the same alone can be treated as *subanta* to which the rule "*suptiṅantam padam*" (1-4-14), wherein there is the *anuvṛtti* of the part "*yasmāt pratyayavidhiḥ*", prescribes *padasaṁjñā*.

NBh, here offers a different interpretation of the Bhāṣya, maintained by certain scholars (*Kecit tu .... āhuḥ*). They say that *saṁghātasyaikatvam arthaḥ* means oneness is the sense of *samudāya*. This is because the transposition or disappearance of letters in the base does not cause any corresponding effect in the sense of number. Hence the sense of number conveyed by the suffix is to be treated as relating to the base or *samudāya* as a whole and not to the components individually. Thus the sense of number being related to the *samudāya* there is no contingency of case suffix that indicates the sense of number, from each component letter. However one may doubt that there is the contingency of the case suffix from each letter since the case suffix is added to the avyayas in the sense of which there is no distinction involving the sense of number. Hence the case suffix *su* being a general suffix that can be added to any base having a sense irrespective of whether this sense is distinguished by number or not is contingent to be added after each letter in a word. NBh continues that such a doubt is not correct. It is because even though there is the addition of case suffix after *avyayas* which denote a sense distinguished by number the addition of case suffixes to the letters in a base(*samudāya*) wherein the sense distinguished by number is conveyed by the *samudāya* is not justifiable. Therefore case-suffix can be added to the *samudāya* and not to the component letters. Strictly speaking the letters in *vṛkṣa* are not even *prakṛti* and so they do not fall under the scope of the statement *"na kevalā prakṛtiḥ prayoktavyā nāpi pratyayaḥ"*. Thus it is pointed out that letters being not the base for a suffix there is no contingency of case suffix after each letter in the base like *dhanam, vanam,* etc.

8. "Aśnute ityakṣaram"[8]

While discussing the denotation of the word *akṣara* Pat quotes the vārttika *'aśnotervā saro'kṣaram'* and says *aśnute ityakṣaram*. Kṭ explains it saying that *artham aśnute vyāpnoti iti akṣaram padam vākyam vā* i.e., that which involves a sense is *akṣara* and it is *pada* or *vākya*. NBh does not favour this interpretation. The disagreement lies in the point that the word *akṣara* cannot in this interpretation of Kṭ refer to a letter as there are letters having no sense. He then cites a view, of others (*anye*) according to which *akṣara* means that which pervades. Since *sphoṭa* is exhibited in different places at one time, the same can be described as one that pervades and hence it is quite apt to refer to it by the term *akṣara*. This view seems to be more acceptable. Since *sphoṭa* is exhibited by *varṇa pada* or *vākya, akṣara* can well refer to *varṇa* also that exhibits *sphoṭa*.

9. "athāpi kathañcid anavakāśo luk syād evam api na doṣaḥ"[9]

Under the rule *"na dhātulopa ārdhadhātuke"* (1-1-4) Kṭ says that this rule which prohibits *guṇa* can be dispensed with if in the formation of words like *loluvaḥ* and *popuvaḥ* derived by the addition of the suffix *yañ* to roots *lū* and *pū*, the elision caused by the rule *"ato lopaḥ"* (6-4-48) operates on the strength of *paratva* on the *a* of the suffix *ya* as a whole. In this case there is the benefit that the elision caused by *lopa* can enjoin *sthānivadbhāva* so as to prohibit *guṇa* to the vowel *u* in *loluvaḥ*.

Supporting this view of Kāt it is stated in the bhāṣya that the rule *"ato lopaḥ"* (6-4-74) shall operate first since *"yañoci ca"* (2-4-74) is satisfied (i.e., *sāvakāśa*) by bringing the elision of the remaining part *y* of the suffix *yañ*. Though the rule *"yañoci ca"* prescribes the elision of the suffix *yañ*, it can very well operate on the part *y* since the same can be treated as *yañ* on the strength of the maxim *ekadeśavikṛtamananyavad*. Pat then proceeds to give an alternative suggestion to bring about the former operation of the rule *"ato lopaḥ"* with the introductory remark quoted above. It means "if it is said that somehow *luk* will have no room to operate, there is no harm". This statement does not seem to be harmonious with the statement, just previously made, that *luk* is *sāvakāśa.*[10]

To avoid this discrepancy, Kṭ interprets the idea of this as follows. The rule *"yañoci ca"* prescribes *luk* to that which is designated as *yañ*. The designation of *y* that remains after the elision of *a* in *ya,* on the strength of the maxim *'ekadeśavikṛtam ananyavad'* is only secondary and such a secondary designation does not help in any way for the operation to be brought about by the principal designation (*mukhyavyapadeśa*). The rule *"yañoci ca"* that prescribed *luk* to *yañ* cannot therefore operate on *y*. Thus if it be *"ato lopaḥ"* that operates formerly, *luk* will have no room to operate and so cannot be superseded by the rule *"ato lopaḥ"* on the strength of *paratva*. Hence Pat gives another suggestion to bring the operation of *"ato lopaḥ"* with the said remark, says Kṭ.

NBh does never admit the fact that the designation attained by atideśas like *'ekadeśavikṛtam ananyavad', sthānivad ādeśonalvidhau'*, etc. are secondary. If it were so, the super-imposition itself is prone to be effete since the designations thus arrived at fail to serve any purpose. The assumption of *y* as *yañ* is therefore quite correct. The discrepancy caused by the reference to the rule *"yañoci ca"* as *anavakāśa* just after the illustration of the fact that it is *sāvakāśa* (having a scope for operation) is explained by NBh as follows. A rule, can supersede another even when the scope of their operation is different. For instance in regard to the formation of the imperative form *vivyātha* of the root *vyath* the rule *"vyatho liṭi"* (7-4-68) that enjoin *samprasāraṇa* and can well have the letter *v* of the root as the scope of operation operates on the letter *y* of the root superseding the rule *"halādiśśeṣaḥ"* (7-4-60) that enjoin elision and has the part beginning with *y* of the root as its scope of operation. Pat too states that unlike other suffixes, the suffix *śnam* does not precede the root to which it is enjoined, since the rule *"mid acontyāat paraḥ"* (1-1-47) which has *mit* as its scope of operation supersede the rule *"paraśca"* (4-1-2) which has suffixes as its scope of operation. Similarly here also Pat points out that though the rule *"yañoci ca"* becomes *sāvakāsa* by the operation on the part *y* which remains after the lopa of *a* in *ya,* caused by the rule *"ato lopaḥ"*, it can be considered *anavakāśa,* since its operation on *ya* is prohibited by the rule *"ato lopaḥ"* on the strength of *paratva.*

10. evam hi kañcid kaścid pṛcchati anantare ete brāhmaṇakule iti sa āha nānantare, vṛṣalakulam anayor antarā iti[11]

Under the rule *"halo 'nantaraḥ samyogaḥ"* (1-1-7) Pat points out that by virtue of the word *'anantarāḥ'* in the rule, consonants intercepted by vowel will never be designated as samyoga. When it is argued that the wrod *anantara* is also used with reference to objects which are intervened by dissimilar ones as for example two villages that are intercepted by dissimilar objects like rivers and mountains, are referred to as *anantarāvimau grāmau,* Pat asserts that unlike ones always form an interception between similar ones. To illustrate the same, he makes the assertion quoted above. It means "Someone asks another. Are these two Brahman houses adjoining (*anantara* without having any *antara* - interception)? He replies, "No They are not adjoining, a house of *śūdra* is between them".

Here Kṭ makes the remark that a brahman house can be treated as intercepting them and the house of *śūdra* is stated to intervene the Brahman houses, with a view to refute the argument that dissimilar ones are not interceptory to similar ones. Thus Kṭ upholds the view that interception of objects can be by a dissimilar or similar one.

NBh on the other hand maintains that interception of two objects cannot be formed by a similar ones. This is, according to him, implied by this statement itself wherein he uses the genitive case of *idam* (*"vṛṣalakulam anayor antarā"*). The usage of the genitive case here in spite of the proximity of the word *antarā* that brings about accusative case by the rule *"antarāntharena yukte"* (3-3-4) shows that the two brahman houses are not exactly the limit (*niyatāvadhi*) relating to the interception. By the usage of the genitive case, Pat points out that two Brahman houses are not taken individually for the enquiry whether there is any interception. The interception enquired is with reference to two brahman houses that are situated along with other brahman houses and Pat suggests that a brahmin house is not an interception between brahman houses. Therefore interceiption cannot be by a similar one in the opinion of NBh.

11. *"ubhayato niyamo vijñāsyate kṣijyorevaicaḥ tayośca śakyārtha eveti"*[12]

Under the rule *"sthānentaratamaḥ"* (1-1-50) Pat, resorts to a two-fold *niyama* in the *sūtra "kṣayyajayyau śakyārthe"* (6-1-81) so as to avoid the substitution by *ay*, contingent in case of the non-utterance of the word *vāntaḥ* in the rule *"vānto yi pratyaye"*, (6-1-79) of letter *e* in the instance *ceyam* and in instances like *kṣeyam* and *jeyam* where the suffix *yat* is in the sense of *'yogyam'* (*kṣetum yogyam and jetum yogyam*). The two fold *niyama* drawn from the rule *"kṣayyajayyau śakyārthe"* which gives the forms *kṣayya* and *jayya* in the sense *kṣetum śakyam* and *jetum śakyam* is that the change of *e* and *ay* is only with reference to the roots *kṣi* and *ji* and that too only in *śakyārtha*.

Here Kṭ says that this *niyama* in both ways is got by the splitting up of the rule *"kṣayyajayyau śakyārthe"* into two rules one as *kṣayyajayyau* and the other as *śakyārthe*. Here NBh gives a different opinion as that of others *'anye'*.[13] He says that in the rule *"brahmabhrūṇavṛtreṣu kvip"* (3-2-87) a two-fold *niyama* is accepted and there it is not stated by Pat that the same is got by the splitting up of the rule. Similarly too, there being no decisive proof for the splitting up of the rule, it is better to accept the *niyama* in two ways since it is told by Pat.

12. *"yadi punar 'alantyasya' ityucyeta tatrāyamapyarthaḥ anekālśit sarvasya ityetanna vaktavyam bhavati idam niyamārtham bhaviṣyati alevāntyasya bhavati nānya iti"*[14]

Under the rule *"alontyasya"* (1-1-52) Pat discusses the question whether the word *alaḥ* as the genitive singular of the word *al*, be treated as an adjunct to the word *antyasya*, or as the nominative plural be treated as an adjunct to the substitute. in regard to the latter view he makes the above assertion. There he refers to the rule as *alantyasya* so as to make it clear that the word *alaḥ* is to qualify the word *ādeśaḥ*. He points out that in the latter view there is no necessity of the rule *"anekālśit sarvasya"* (1-1-53) since the rule means that the substitute which are *al* replace the final letter of the *sthānin* whereby it comes out that a substitute that is not *al* replace the *sthānin* wholly. Thus the rule results in a *niyama* that only the substitute that are *al* replace the final element whereby other substitutes get the status of *sarvādeśa.*

Here Kṭ points out a defect in this view. The rule *'arurmanśca-kṣuścetorahorajasām lopaśca"* (5-4-51) enjoins the elision as a substitute to bases like *arus,* etc. This substitute is desired to replace the final element of the bases like *arus, manas, cakśus, cetas, rahas and rajas.* But in the said view according to which only the substitutes that are *al* can replace the final element, the substitute elision which is not *al* can hardly replace the final element of *arus manas,* etc. and so forms like *arūkaroti, virahīkaroti virajīkaroti,* etc. cannot be arrived at.

With the ending *"ityanye"* NBh cites a view according to which there is never the said defect pointed out by Kṭ. The word *alaḥ* in the rule when treated as an adjunct to the *ādeśa,* is said to effect a *niyama* that only substitutes that are *al* replace the final element, whereby the substitutes other than *al* becomes *sarvādeśa.* Here the substitutes other than *al* can be taken as the substitues that are *anekāl* and not the substitute which is in the form of elision and such a substitute replaces the final element alone. There is an indication to this effect. The rule *"lug vā duhadihalihaguhām ātmanepade dantye"* (7-3-73) enjoins *luk* as the substitute of the suffix *ksa.* When the word *lopaḥ* can be got by *anuvṛtti* sicne both the words *luk* and *lopa* ultimately denote the *adarśana,* Pāṇ. could have avoided the mention of the word *luk* in the rule. The mention of the word *luk* which denotes the *adarśana* of a suffix, can therefore be treated as serving the purpose of the elision of the suffix as a whole. If *lopa* also were to bring the elision of *ksa* wholly the mention of the word *luk* becomes superfluous. Hence it indicates that *lopa* shall replace the final element of the *sthānin* and lest the final element should be substituted by elision, Pāṇ mentions the word *luk* in the rule. Thus the mention of the word *luk* in the said rule indicates that *lopa* substitutes the final alone and so there is no defect of *lopa* substituting the whole base like *arus* and the like.

13. *"sthānivad analvidhau itiyatyucyamāne ka idānīm sthānivat syāt"*[15]

Under the rule *"sthānivad ādeśo'nalvidhau"* (1-1-56) Pat discusses the purpose of the mention of the word *ādeśa* in the rule. To the question *'athādeśagrahaṇam kimartham?"* a counter-question quoted above is raised. "If the sūtra is read *'sthānivad analvidhau' without the word ādeśa,* which will act like *sthānin?"* Kṭ gives an explanation to this counterquestion to which NBh cites a different explanation as the view of certain scholars. Kṭ is of opinion that as there are two varieties of substitutes one *pratyakṣa* and the other *ānumānika,* i.e., direct and indirect, the rule without the word *ādeśa* can comprehend only the substitutes like *i* that are directly mentioned in the rule like *"eruḥ"* (3-4-86) and so the inferred substitutes like *tu* seldom act like *sthānin.* NBh on the other hand says that according to certain scholars, the question does not have this motive behind it. It is simply a question raised by one who is ignorant of the idea of the previous question *athādeśagrahaṇam kimartham?* which means that even in the absence of the word *ādeśa,* it shall be comprehended in the rule since, the only one word related to *sthānin* i.e., *sambandhiśabda,* is the same. The answer to this counter-question is *"yaḥ sthāne bhavati"* and this comes from the person who knows the fact that the word *ādeśa* is the *sambandhiśabda* of the word *sthānin.*

This is followed by the question and answer *"kaśca sthāne bhavati? ādeśaḥ".* Now follows the passage *"idam tarhi prayojanam ādesamātram sthānivad yathā syāt ekadeśavikṛtasyopasamkhyānam codayiṣyati tanna vaktavyam bhavati"* which means all the substitutes both direct and indirect are to act that *sthānin.* NBh says that the answer *"yaḥ sthāne bhavati kaśca sthāne bhavati? ādeśaḥ"* is to be treated as given by a person who is ignorant of the context, so as to suit the explanation given by Kṭ to the last passage.

Here it may be pointed out that the idea pointed as the view held by certain scholars and the latter idea cited with the ending *ityāhuḥ* are held by the same group of scholars whom he designated as *kecit* which RudradharaJhā Śarma takes to amount to *bhāṣyatattvavidaḥ.*

14. *"tasilādayaḥ prāk pāśapaḥ, śasprabhṛtayaḥ prāk samāsāntebhyaḥ, mānteḥ, tasivatī, kṛtvo'rthaḥ nānāñau iti"*[16]

Under the vārttika *'siddham tu pāṭhāt'* in the rule *"taddhitaścāsarvavibhaktiḥ"* (1-1-38) Pat enumerates the suffixes that are to be designated as *avyaya*. They are the suffixes beginning with *tasil* upto the suffix enjoined just before the rule that enjoin the suffix *pāśap*, the suffixes beginning with *śas* upto the suffix enjoined just before the rule enjoining *samāsānta* suffixes, the two suffixes *tasi* and *vati* the suffix ending in *m* the suffix having the meaning of the suffix *kṛtvasuc* and the two suffixes *nā* and *ñañ*. Here Kṭ says that the *tasi* referred to in the passage as *tasivatī* is the suffixes enjoined by the rule *"pratiyoge pañcamyāstasiḥ"* (5-4-44) and the rule *"tasiśca"* (4-3-113).

NBh maintains that the part *tasi* in *tasivatī* points out the suffix *tasi* enjoined by the rule *tasiśca* alone and not the same enjoined byt the rule *"pratiyoge pañcamyāstasiḥ"* (5-4-14) the reason being the fact that the suffixes referred to as *śasprabhṛtayaḥ prāk samāsāntebhyaḥ* include the *tasi* enjoined by the rule *"pratiyoge pañcamyāstasiḥ"*. NBh therefore opines that the assertion of Kṭ requires reconsideration.

Neverthless, NBh cites a view in support of Kṭ. Others maintain that Kṭ has merely illustrated the rules that enjoin the suffix *tasi*.

15. *"atha dvitiyam pratyayagrahaṇam kimartham? pratyayalakṣaṇam yathā syād varṇalaksaṇam mā bhūd iti. gave hitam gohitam rāyaḥ kulam raikulam"*[17]

After discussing the purpose seved by the part *pratyaya* in the expression *pratyayalope* of the rule *"pratyayalopa pratyaya-lakṣaṇam"* (1-1-62) Pat puts forward the question what for is, then, the *pratyayagrahaṇa* a second time and answers the same, that the *kārya* depending upon *pratyaya* may set in and not that depending upon a letter.

Kṭ and NBh differ in the interpretation of the idea of this question. According to Kṭ the question means that the part *pratyaya* in the word *pratyayalakṣaṇam* is superfluous since it can be referred to by a pronoun *tad* considering that *pratyaya* is already mentioned in the rule in the expression *pratyayalope pratyayalakṣaṇam* instead of *pratyayalope tallakṣaṇam*. The answer is that if the pronoun is used instead of the word *pratyaya*, the pronoun is liable to refer to the *pratyaya* as well as the letters in it, since pronouns refer to the object and not to any particular characteristic of the object unless otherwise mentioned. To avert this, Pāṇ uses the word *pratyaya* itself and thereby disallows *pratyayalakṣaṇa* in instances where an affix by virtue of the letter comprised in it arranges the gound for an operation.

NBh points out that according to some scholars, the question expresses the superfluous nature of the mention of the whole expression *pratyayalakṣaṇa* whereby the word *pratyaya* occurs a second time in the rule *"pratyayalope pratyayalakṣaṇa"*. The question does not imply the enquiry of the purpose of the mention of the word *pratyaya* alone instead of using the pronoun *tad*. This is because in the said rule the usage of *tad* or *pratyaya* in the part *pratyayalakṣaṇam* makes no difference as they are synonymous in the said context. The question therefore implies the fact that the rule need only be as *pratyayalope api* which can well convey the idea that an operation that occurs at the time of the existence of a *pratyaya*, may take place even when the *pratyaya* has elided. Or a rule with the wording as *pratyayalope* which can by virtue of the *anuvṛtti* of the word *sthānivad* from the previous rule, can convey the idea that a *pratyaya* obtains *stānivadbhāva*, when the elision of the same take place. To the question with this idea is given the answer *'pratyayalakṣaṇam yathā syād varṇalakṣaṇam mā bhūditi'*. This is the interpretation given by certain scholars to the question quoted, says NBh.

Interpretation of Sūtras

1. Absence of euphonic combination in the Śivasūtras

In the rules *'aiuṇ'*, *'ṛḷk'*, *'eoṇ' and 'aiauc'* we do not find the euphonic combination of vowels which can occur on the strength of the rules *"ādguṇaḥ"* (6-1-87) *"eco'yavāyāvaḥ"* (6-1-78) and *"iko yaṇaci"* (6-1-77). Kṭ's justification for the same is that technical terms like *ac ik* etc. which are the basis for the operation of the said rules have not come into being at the time of the recital of the alphabets in the form of Śivasūtras and euphonic combination does not occur here.[18]

NBh points out that this reasoning is not logical. The rules like *"iko yaṇaci"* (6-1-77) which come into being after the accomplishment of the Śivasūtras, technical terms like *it* and the subsequent formation of pratyāhāras, can well operate in the Śivasūtras just as they operate in instances like *suddhyupāsyaḥ* since *a, i, u,* etc. are the ones comprehended by the word *ac, ik,* etc. Otherwise, we can't justify the euphonic combination namely cognate lengthening in the body of the rule *"tulyāsyaprayatnam savarṇam"* (1-1-9) (*tulya+āsyaprayatnam = tulyāsyaprayatnam*). Since there also it can be argued that only after the accomplishment of this sūtra, the term *savarṇa* is understood and so in the body of the said rule the operation namely *savarṇadīrgha* effected by the term *savarṇa* would become questionable. Hence NBh disagrees with the reason pointed out by Kṭ to account for the absence of euphonic combination in the Śivasūtras. According to him the same may be treated as *sautra* i.e., peculiarity relating to sūtras alone. Or it can be said that *samhitā* which is the basic factor for the combination is not intended here. It may be noted that here NBh agrees with Bhaṭṭojidīkṣita.

2. The remodelling of the rule "gururanṛto'nantyasyāpyekaikasya prācām"

In the bhāṣya under the rule *"ṛḷk"* Pat speaks of the remodelling of the rule *"guroranṛto'nantyasyāpyekaikasya prācām"* (8-2-86).[19] The rule with the word *anṛtaḥ* prohibits the prolation of the letter *ṛ* and here there arises the difficulty of the prohibition of prolation of *ḷ* in the instance *kḷptaśikhaḥ* since on the strength of the maxim *'ekadeśavikṛtam ananyavad bhavati'*, the *ḷ* which is a changed form of *ṛ* by the rule *"kṛpo ro laḥ"* (7-2-18) can be regarded as *ṛ*. By the change of the word *anṛtaḥ* to *aravataḥ* the letter possessing *r* sound is forbidden from being prolated. Thereby, the letter *ṛ* which is *ravat* i.e., possessed of the *r* sound gets the prohibition and *ḷ* being not possessed of the *r* sound is not forbidden from being prolated.

Here Kṭ says that the suffix *matup* in the word *ravat* is to be understood in the sense 'permanently possessed 'of' and not merely 'possessed of'. This is because in the word *vartaka* the letter *a* that follows *v* is possessed of the sound *r* as adjacent to it and hence *a* here being *ravat,* its prolation will also be prohibited. If the *matup* is understood in the sense of permanently possessed of, the *a* here cannot be pointed as *ravat.* Since a is not possessed of *r* wherever it occures in words, the *a* in *vartaka* will be not prohibited from being prolated.

According to NBh it is in vain to resort to the sense, 'permanently possessed of' instead of 'possessed of'. The sense 'possessed of' assigned to the suffix *matup* by the rule "*tad asyāstyasminniti matup*" (5-2-94) relates to the possession of something as an organ and not as an adjacent one. The letter *a* in *vartaka* does not possess the sound *r* as an organ of it but possesses the same only as an adjacent one. Hence it can never be treated as *ravat* i.e., possessed of *r* as a part. Thus even without resorting to the sense of permanent possession of the sound *r*, the purpose is achieved here and hence he differs with Kṭ here.

3. The rule "arthavad adhāturapratyayaḥ prātipadikam" (1-2-45) as the basis for the existence of non-derivative stems coined at random.

Kṭ observes that the rule "*arthavad adhaturapratyayaḥ prātipadikam*" (1-2-45) presumes the existence of stems which are not derived from roots with addition of some suffix.[20] If all stems are formed from roots, they can well be grouped as *kṛdanta* i.e., those having a *kṛt* suffix at their end and they will get the designation *prātipadika* by the rule "*kṛttadhitasamāsāśca*' *(1-2-46) itself, which entitles kṛdanta* stems to the title of *prātipadika*. Hence in the absence of non-derivative stems the rule "*arthavad adhāturapratyayaḥ prātipadikam*" (1-2-45) will become reduntant and hence it implies the existence of the said stems, to endow which with the designation, the rule becomes necessary.

NBh does not agree with Kṭ here. He cites stems like *bahupaṭu* where the *taddhita* suffix *bahuc* is added before the word *paṭu* by the rule "*vibhāṣā supo bahuc purastāt tu*" (5-3-65). These words are *taddhitapūrva* and hence the rule "*kṛttaddhitasamāsāśca*" cannot provide them with the said designation and to serve that purpose the rule "*arthavad adhāturapratyayaḥ prātipadikam*" (1-2-45) is necessary and hence is no longer reduntant to indicate the existence of non-derivative stems.

NBh however cites a view in support of Kṭ's presumption. Others hold that the part *taddhita* in the rule "*kṛttaddhitasamāsāśca*" (1-2-46) is to be understood not as *taddhitānta* but as *taddhitaviśiṣṭa* i.e., having *taddhita* suffix (either in the beginning middle or end). Hence instances like *bahupaṭu* which has a *taddhita* suffix at the beginning can be designated as *prātipadika* by the rule *"kṛttaddhitasamāsāśca"* (1-2-46). The rule therefore is reduntant and that is why Kṭ says that the rule implies the existence of the non-derivative stems. There is no scope for the doubt, that the rule *"arthavad adhāturapratyayaḥ prātipadikam"* (1-2-45) may endow *prātipadikasamjñā* to the word *pacataki* which is *tiñanta* and possessed of *taddhita* suffix *akac*, since it is *arthavat*. This is because the part *apratyayaḥ* of the rule shall bring the prohibition of *prātipadikasamjñā* to *pacataki* which has got the *tiñ* suffix at the end. So also there is no need for another doubt that if the rule *"kṛttaddhitasamāsāśca"* (1-2-46) endows to a *śabda*, possessed of a *taddhita* suffix, the *prātipadikasamjñā*, there is the contingency of the *samjñā* on the *śabda bahupaṭavastiṣṭhanti*. This is because the *taddhita* suffix can ever be possessed by *subanta* words like *paṭu* alone and not by *tiñanta* words like *tiṣṭhanti* and so *bahupaṭu* alone will be designated as *prātipadika*. Thus others justify the view of Kṭ.

4. *The śābdabodha of the rule "vṛddhirādaic".*

Pat establishes that the rule *"vṛddhirādaic"* (1-1-1) is a *samjñāsūtra* defining the technical term *vṛddhi* since there is *sāmānādhikaraṇya* and *ekavibhaktikatva* in the said rule.[21] Kṭ here says that *'tattu sāmānādhikaraṇyam śabdārthayor eva kecit icchanti, dvābhyam śabdābhyām bhinnapravṛthinimittābhyām ekasya adkhikaraṇasya abhidheyasya pratipādanāt'*. According to this view of Kṭ, the *śabdabodha* derived from the rule is given by NBh. In a *samjñābodhakaśabda* the *pravṛttinimitta* is that *śabda* itself whereas in a *samjñibodhakaśabda* the *pravṛttinimitta* is the quality that rests in the *samjñin*. Accordingly the *pravṛttinimitta* of *vṛddhiḥ* is *vṛddhiśabda* itself and that of *ādaic* is *ādaictva*. The *śabdadodha* of the rule therefore is as follows. That which has got *vṛddhiśabda* as the motive force of denotation is identical with *ā, ai and au* (*vṛddhisabdavadabhinnāḥ ādaicaḥ*). The contention of Kṭ is that in this way only the *sāmānadhikaraṇya* of the word *vṛddhiḥ* and *ādaic* can be explained. NBh now cites a view of certain scholars in which the *śabdabodha* of the rule is pointed out in a different manner. According to them, the word *vṛddhiḥ* denotes *vṛddhiśabda* itself and not *vṛddhiśabdavat* that which has got *vṛddhiśabda* as the *pravṛttinimitta* i.e., the motive force of denotation. Accordingly the *śābdabodha* derived from the rule is *vṛddhisabdābhinnāḥ ādaicaḥ* i.e. *vṛddhiśabda* is identical with *ā ai* and *au*. The verse of Bhar is quoted here by NBh.

vṛddhyādayo yathā śabdāḥ svarūpopanibandhanāḥ
ādaicpratyayitaiśśabdaissambandham yānti samjñibhiḥ"

NBh says that the holders of this view maintain that *sāmānadhikaraṇya* of two words is the denotation of ideas within which one shall be the principal element in regard to the other. They find no necessity of considering *pravṛttinimitta* as a determining factor of *sāmānādhikaraṇya.*

5. The word 'taparaḥ' in the rule "taparastatkālasya" (1-1- 76).

Under the *Śivasūtra "econ & aiauc"* Pat observes that the compound word *taparaḥ* in the rule *"taparastatkālasya"* (1-1-70) denotes both viz. that which has *t* as its predecessor and that which precedes *t*.[22] How can the single expression *taparaḥ* convey these two ideas? *Kṭ's* explanation is that *taparaḥ* is an expression by *tantra* and NBh agrees to it. Kṭ then gives an alternative explanation that *taparaḥ* is an expression by *ekaśeṣa*. Among the two similar words *taparaḥ* (one in the sense of the *bahuvrīhi* compound and the other in the sense of the *tatpuruṣa* compound) one alone is retained by the rule *"sarūpāṇām ekaśeṣa ekavibhaktau"* (1-2- 64) and thereby the expression *taparaḥ* which conveys the sense of both, is accomplished.

NBh does not give his consent to this explanation. He says that if it were *ekaśeṣa,* the retained word ought to have the dual number as *taparau*. If we accept *taparaḥ* to be a *samāhāra dvandva* compound the singular number in it can be explained, yet there is the difficulty of the non-achievement of *ekaśeṣa,* since *ekaśeṣa* is not enjoined in *samāhāradvandva*. NBh therefore finds the view of Kṭ here to be defective.

6. The significance of the technical term 'sāmyoga' defined by the rule "halo'nantarāḥ sāmyogaḥ".

Kṭ considers the term *sāmyoga* defined by the rule *"halo'-nantarāḥ sāmyogaḥ"* (1-1-6) to be significant one.[23] The term, in accordance with its derivative sense (*samyujyante asmin varṇā iti samudāyaḥ samyogaḥ*) the term relates to the continguous consonants as a whole and not to each of them individually. Hence, he says that, there is no need of the insertion of the word *saha* in the body of the rule so that the term may relate to the whole alone.

NBh does not support this view of Kṭ. He points out that the derivative sense of the word is over-extensible since a word like *vṛkṣaḥ* or a sentence like *rāmaḥ gacchati* is contingent to get this *saṁjñā,* in as much as both of them are equally samudāyas in which contiguous letters viz.*ks and cch* are combined. The presence of other letters in them do not contradict this status. NBh, therefore, does not favour the acceptance of the application of the derivative sense of the term in regard to those that are designated by the term.

7. The purpose served by the word 'eka' of the compound ekāc in the rule "nipāta ekājanāṅ" (1-1-14).

Under the rule *"nipata ekajanāṅ"* (1-1-14) Pat says that the part *eka* of the compound *ekāc* in the rule indicates the maxim *varṇagrahaṇe jātigrahaṇam.*[24] NBh does not agree with the explanation given by Kṭ as to how the word *eka* indicates the paribhāṣā. Kṭ observes that the expression *ekāc* in the rule being a *tatpuruṣa* compound means a single vowel and this idea can be obtained even if the expression be *ac*. He gives the reason. It is the term *pragṛhya* that is predicated here and hence is the important (*pradhāna*) one in the rule. *Ac* is the *samjñin* and since it helps the *samjñā*, is *guṇa* i.e., subordinate to the *samjña* *Kṭ* maintains that the number in the word denoting the *apradhāna* can be intended. He cites the vedic injunction *'paśunā yajati'* wherein the singular number in the word *paśunā* which denotes the animal is intented considering that *paśu* is unimportant in as much the animal is meant for sacrifice and not vice-versa. Hence even if the rule need be *"ac nipātaḥ"*, a single vowel is provided with the term and the part *eka* becomes superfluous to indicate the maxim.

NBh on the other hand, points out that in fact it is the *samjñā* that exists for the *samjñin*. Hence *samjñin* cannot be treated as *apradhāna* but is *anuvādya* since a *samjñā* is predicted in regard to it. The sense of *ekatva* standing as adjacent to the *samjñin* by virtue of the singular number in the word *ac* cannot be intended.

NBh quotes the dictum of Mīmāmsakas, *'vidheyaviśeṣaṇam vivakṣitam anuvādyaviseṣaṇam avivakṣitam'*. Hence *ac* cannot be taken to convey the idea of a single vowel in the manner described by Kṭ. According to NBh the word *eka* becomes superfluous in the following manner. The word ac denotes that which is possessed of the quality *'actva'* and a group consisting of more than one vowel cannot be treated as possessed of the quality *actva* just as there is not the quality namely *svāñgatva,* in *svāñgasamudāya* (a group of organs). Hence by the expression as *ac* in the said rule, the term shall relate only to a single vowel (that which is possessed of *actva*) and not to the *acsamudāya* which is not possessed of *actva*. Hence the word *eka* in the rule becomes superfluous. Hence NBh differs with Kṭ here.

After pointing out that the word *eka* in *ekāc* is superfluous, Kṭ and NBh agree in pointing out that the same indicates the maxim *varṇagrahaṇe jātigrahaṇam* meaning *"Genus* is referred to in instances when letters are referred to". In the existence of such a maxim if the wording of the rule be as *nipāta ajanāṅ*, the term *pragṛhya* may shoot to the group of the vowels in each of which there is the genus *actva*, otherwise the reference to genus cannot be effective since even without reference to genus a single vowel can be referred to. Thus the word *eka* is used here to avoid the group of vowels being designated as *pragṛhya*.

8. The technical term 'samprasāraṇa ' defined by the rule "ig yaṇaḥ samprasāraṇam" (1-1-45).

While interpreting the rule *"ig yaṇaḥ samprasāraṇam"* (1-1-45) Pat says that the term *'samprasāraṇa'* is applicable to both i.e., to the letter namely the *ik* that replaces *yaṇ* and to the sentence *'yaṇah ig bhavati'* that conveys the sense that *yaṇ* replaces *ik*.

Kṭ here points out that the rule can provide the term to the above mentioned two in case the *sūtra* is repeated twice as *igyaṇaḥ samprasāraṇam* and *igyaṇaḥ samprasāraṇam*. This can be secured by treating the rule as *"tantranirdeśa āvṛttinirdeśa* or *ekaśeṣanirdeśa"*.[25]

NBh on the other hand does not feel the necessity of repetition here. A sentence is to be repeated in the case the predication made, by the sentences that are got by repetition are different. In the context, in both the sentences got by repetition, the predication made is of the same namely the term *samprasāraṇa* and hence it is quite possible to predicate in one sentence a single *samjñā* though it relates to more than one. The basis of NBh's view seems to be *'vidheyabhedād vākyabhedaḥ'*. Again Kṭ maintains that in the view that the term relates to the letter *ik* that substitutes *yaṇ*, there shall be accepted the influence of the rule *"yathāsaṅkhyam anudeśaḥ samānām"* (1-3-10) so that the term may relate to *i u ṛ* and *ḷ* that replace *y, v, r* and *l* respectively. Otherwise the term may relate to *i u ṛ* and *ḷ* that replace *y v r* and *l* and as such there is the contingency of this designation to each one of *ik* that replaces one among *yaṅ*. Thereby the letter *i* which replaces *l* in the formation of the word *aduhi* (Aorist First person singular of the rood *duh*) is contingent to derive this designation and it may result in the undesirable lengthening of *i* by the rule *"halaḥ"* (6-4-2).

Here also NBh disagrees with Kṭ. He points out that if the respective order be accepted in relation of *ik* and *yaṇ, ik* has to comprehend the four letters in the order *i, u, r and l* and to secure this order the enunciation of *l* after *r* in the Śivasūtras is essential. Otherwise the *pratyāhāra ik* shall comprehend only the three letter *i,u and ṛ*. The substitutes being four in number, it can be seen that the respective replacement of three by four is improbable. Thus the enunciation of the letter *ḷ* in the rule can be treated as serving the purpose i.e., the term *samprasāraṇa* relates to *i, u, r and l* only when they replaçe *y, v, ṛ and ḷ* respectively. Thus the enunciation of *ḷ* in the Śivasūtras being purposeful the questioning of the same by Pat is contradicted.[26] NBh therefore does not favour the adoption of the rule *"yathāsaṅghyamanudeśaḥ samānām"* (1-3-10). The purpose he says can be achieved by taking recourse to the *tadbhāvitapakṣa* in words like *samprasāraṇasya* in rules like *"halaḥ"* (6-4-2).

9. The number of letters comprehended by the pratyāhāras ik and yaṇ and the substitution by l of the vowel ḷ.

Under the rule *"sthānantaratamaḥ"* (1-1-50) Pat discusses the instances which form the scope for the operation of the rule *"sthānentaramaḥ"*.[27] In the passage *"iko yaṇacidadhyatra madhvatra tālusthānasya tālusthānaḥ, oṣṭhāsthānasya oṣṭhasthānaḥ yathā syād iti"* it is pointed out that the rule *"sthānentaramaḥ"* (1-1-50) has its play in the function of the rule *"iko yaṇ aci"* (6-1-77) so that the palatal *i* among *ik* get the palatal *y* among *yaṇ* and the labial *u* gets the labial *v* among *yaṇ* as substitutes, and *dadhyatra* and *madhvatra* form the instances for the same. Here Kṭ makes the remark that the criterion, for determining the substitutes and their *sthanin,* cannot be the rule *"yathāsaṅkhyam anudeśaḥ samānām"* (1-3-10) since the number of the *sthānin* and the substitutes are not equal. The letters *i, u, ṛ and ḷ* denoted by the word *ik* comprehends totally sixty six varieties of letters i.e., 18 varieties of each of the vowels, *i, u and ṛ* and 12 varieties of *ḷ* which is devoid of the six varieties of *dīrgha. Yaṇ* comprehends seven letters namely r and the nasalised and non-nasalised varieties of *y, u and l.* Thus *sthānin* number sixty six and substitutes amount to seven.

NBh maintains that though theoretically it can be said that *ṛ* possesses eighteen varieties and *ḷ* twelve it is to be remembered that the nasalised varieties of lengthened *ṛ* and those of prolate *ṛ and ḷ* are nowhere seen in usages and so the statement of Kṭ that *ik* comprehends 66 varieties, requires reconsideration. The same is the case with the statement that *yaṇ* comprehends seven letters. The nasalized varieties and non-nasalized varieties of *y, v and l* are not identical, and are cognates and cannot be comprehended by *yaṇ* which on the strength of the negation *apratyayaḥ* made in the rule *"aṇudit-savarnasya cāpratyayaḥ"* (1-1-69) denotes only *y, v, r and l* and does not comprehend the nasalized varieties which are cognates.

In the following passage *"naited asti samkhyātānudeśenāpyetad siddham"*, Pat establishes that the criterion for determining the respective *sthānin* and substitutes is the rule *"yathasaṅk-hyamanudeśaḥ samānām"* (1-3-10). Here Kṭ says that the letters denoted by the pratyāhāras *ik* and *yaṇ,* being four, are equal though the number of letters comprehended by these four i.e., *i, u, ṛ and ḷ* which form *ik* and *y, v, r and l* that form *yaṇ* vary. Kṭ then anticipates a doubt. Is there an instance where the *ḷ* is found substituted by *l*? And in the absence of such an instance how can one resort to the rule *"yathāsaṅkhyamanudeśaḥ samānām"* (1-3-10), for determining the *sthānin* of *yaṇ*. He feels answered by citing an instance like *ghaslādeśaḥ* where *ḷ* has been substituted by *l* considering that there is the precedance by *ac* for *ḷ*.

NBh points out that a doubt as such is quite out of place. The rule *"yathāsaṅkhyamanudeśaḥ samānām"* (1-3-20) depends, for its operation, on the equality of number of the denotary words, of two groups connected to each other in a rule. The rule does not care for the number of those comprehended by these denotary words. This fact has been made clear by Pat in the *pratyāhārāhnika.*[28] Hence without paying heed to the existence or non-existence of an instance where *ḷ* is found substituted by *l* the rule *"yathāsankhyamanudeśaḥ samānām"* (1-3-10) can operate here since the denotary words of the *sthānin* and ādeśas are four in number. NBh therefore feels that the doubt entertained by Kṭ and the consequent justification given by him is quite unnecessary.

10. The nature of the nimitta of dhātulopa in the function of the rule "na dhātulopa ārthadhātuke" (1-1-4)

Under the rule *"pratyayalope pratyayalakṣaṇam"* (1-1-62) Pat clarifies that the rule operates in cases of the elision of suffixes which are the *nimitta* of an operation, for its nature as suffix and not by virtue of a letter compraised in it. This specific function of the rule is brought about by the mention of the word *pratyaya* a second time in the said rule.[29]

Here Kṭ makes the remark that the function of the rule *"na dhātulopa ārdhadhātuke"* (1-1-4) which disallows *guṇa* and *vṛddhi* to *ik* when, the *ārdhadhātuka* suffix that stands as the *nimitta* of *guṇa* or *vṛddhi* is the cause of the elision of the part of the root, is also likewise. The *ārdhadhātuka* suffix brings about the prohibition of *guṇa* and *vṛddhi* only when the said suffix brings the elision of the part of the roots on the basis of its nature as an *ārdhadhātuke* suffix. As a result, forms like *sudheḥ* and *sukeḥ* the nominative singular of the bases *sudhin* and *sukṛn* are obtained. These bases are derived by the addition of the suffix vic. respectively to the roots *dhinv* and *kṛnv* prefixed with *su*. In the resultant stage *sudhinv+vic* and *su+kṛṇv+vic,* the letter v of the root elides depending on the letter *v* of the suffix *vic* in accordance with the rule *"lopovyorvali"* (6-1-66). Thus it can be seen that suffix *vic* does not bring the elision on the basis of its nature as *ārdhadhatuka* suffix and so *vic* does not bring the prohibition of *guṇa* in the nominative singular form. The forms like *suddēḥ* and *sukēḥ* wherein *guṇa* has been prohibited are thus avoided. NBh expresses his strong disagreement in regard to the function of the rule *"na dhātulopa ārdhadhātuke"* (1-1-4) in a way similar to the operation of the rule *"pratyayalope pratyaya-lakṣaṇam"* (1-1-62). He points out that it is by virtue of the second *pratyayagrahaṇa* that the function of the rule *'pratyayalope pratyayalakṣaṇam'* in the specified manner is accepted. The second *pratyayagrahaṇa* is an excess so long as there is the word *pratyaya* in the expression *pratyayalope pratyayalakṣaṇam.* But in regard to the rule *"na dhātulopa ārdhadhatuke"* the state of affairs is different. There is no guiding factor in the rule, so as to accept the function of the rule in the said manner. NBh establishes his standpoint by pointing out that the word *ārdhadhātuke* in the rule cannot achieve this purpose. Kṭ himself has stated that the word *ārdhadhātuke* is necessary for arriving at forms like *totorti.* Pat has stated that the word *ārdhadhātuke* in the rule is necessary to arrive at the form *roravīti* where otherwise the *guṇa* shall operate. Hence to resort to the idea that by the word *ārdhadhātuka,* the suffix is to be *nimitta* of *dhātulopa* for its nature as an *ārdhadhātuka,* cannot be in harmony with the said assertion of Pat in the rule *'kṅiti ca'* (1-1-5). Again, there is no authority too for the acceptance of the repetition of the word *ārdhadhātuke* so as to comprehend the purpose of arriving at the form *roravīti* and of making *ārdhadhātuka,* the *nimitta* of *dhātulopa* for its nature as an *ārdhadhātuka* suffix. All the more, the function of the rule as told by Kṭ does not agree with the part *valopa* of the vārttika *'na yaṅyakkyavalope'* in the present sūtra and the Patṣ illustration of the same by citing the instance *jīradānuḥ.* Kāt and Pat unanimously opine that in the instance *jīradānuḥ, guṇa* contingent by the *ārdhadhātuka* suffix *radānu* is prohibited since there is elision of the part *v* of the root *jīv* caused by the letter *r* of the suffix *radānu* by the rule *"lopo vyog vali"* (6-1-66). If the prohibition of *guṇa* functions only when the *ārdhadhātuka* is the cause of elision for its nature as *ārdhadhātuka,* the prohibition cannot apply here since the elision of *v* does not depent upon the suffix *radānu* for its nature as an *ārdhadhātuka* suffix but depends only on a letter comprised in it. Therefore NBh cannot but disagree with Kṭ here.

Explanation of Certain Words

1. The meaning of the word āmrabuddhyā in the sentence 'sa tatrāmrabuddhyā nyagrodhabuddhim pratipadyate'.

Under the rule *"sthānivad ādeso'nalvidhau'd* (1-1-56) while explaining the idea behind *sthānivadbhāva* in relation to the conception of sounds as eternal Pat makes use of a sentence *'sa tatrāmrabuddhyā nyagrodhabuddhim pratipadyate.*[30] Kṭ gives the meaning of the word *āmrabuddhyaḥ* of this sentence as *"tasyāḥ anantaram"*. Thus according to him the sentence means, 'In that case, after the cognition of them as mangotrees, he has the cognition of them as *nyagrodha* trees'. Here NBh offers a different sense to this word pointed out by certain scholars. They take the word to mean *"āmrabuddhim vihāya"*, according to which the sentence means 'In that case, discarding the cognition of them as mango trees, he cognizes them to be *nyagrodha* trees'.

2. Jaṅgamaḥ

At the end of his gloss on the bhāṣya unde the rule *"na dhātulopa ārdhadhātuke"* (1-1-4) Kṭ deals with the above word.[31] According to him the formation of the word is as follows. The root *gam* takes the suffix *yaṅ* after and gets itself republicated. From the resultant form *gam+gam+ya* wherein all operations pertaining to *abhyāsa* take effect, a stage like *jaṅgam+ya* is arrived at. This *yaṅata* root takes the suffix *ac* after it and leads to the stage *jangam+ya+a*. Here Kṭ says that the letter *a* of the suffix *yaṇ* is dropped on the strength of the rule *"yasya halaḥ"* (6-4-49). They *y* is dropped by the function of the rule *"yaṅoci ca"* (2-4-74) and thereby the complete from *jaṅgamaḥ* by the addition of the nominative singular suffix.

Assuming the formation of the word as pointed out above, Kṭ raises an objection here and gives the solution to which NBh disagrees totally. He doubts that there is the contingency of the elision of the letter *a* of *yaṅ* whereby there is the threat of the elision of the *upadhā* i.e., *a* of *jaṅgam* by the rule *"gamahana janakhanaghasām lopaḥ kṅityanaṅi"* (6-4-98). He clears the doubt giving the solution that *a* of *yaṅ* can be treated as *aṅ* whereby the prohibition of *upadhālopa* is brought by the part *anaṅi* of the said rule. Here an objection may be raised. The *aṅ* in *yaṅ* is meaningless whereas there is the suffix *aṅ* (substitute of the suffix *cli*) which is meaningful and therefore the *aṅ* mentioned in the rule cannot refer to the meaningless *aṅ* of the suffix *yaṅ* and so how can the elision of the penultimate be prohibited by the part *anaṅi*? Kt's retort to this argument is that the rule *"gamahana..."* (6-4- 98) enjoin the elision of the penultimate when *gam* is followed by a suffix beginning with a vowel and the *a* of *yaṅ* cannot be treated as a suffix since it is meaningless considering that suffix referred to is possessed of meaning. So it cannot bring the elision of the penultimate and so the previous doubt regarding the contingency of the elision of the penultimate is baseless.

NBh does not agree with the view that *a* of *yaṅ* cannot be treated as an *ajādipratyaya*. He points out that the acceptance of the same as such is necessitated by the part *vare* in the rule *"na padāntadvirvacanavareyalopa.."* (1-1-58). This rule prohibits the *sthānivadbhāva* of the substitutes of a vowel, when the *nimitta* of the substitute for replacing the vowel be the suffix *vara(c)* which the *yaṅata* roots take after them. With reference to the formation of words like *yāyāvaraḥ* formed by the addition of the suffix *vara(c)* to the *yaṅanta* root *yāyāya,* the substitute namely elision of the vowel *ā* in the suffix *yaṅ* can be treated as a suffix by virtue of *sthānivadhāva*. Fearing the *sthānivadbhāva* of elision in which case there is the contingency of the elision of the vowel *ā* at the end of *yāyā* by the rule *"āto lopa iti ca"* (6-4-64) which enjoin the fact that the vowel *ā* elides when followed by an *ajādi suffix;* the rule *"na padānta dvirvacna"* (1-1-58) prohibits the same. Here it is to be noted that if the vowel *a* of *yaṅ* can no longer be treated as an *ajādi* suffix, its substitute namely elision, too cannot be the same by *sthānivadbhāva* in which case only the *ā* is contingent to be dropped. Hence the prohibition of *sthānivadbhāva* to that effect implies that congtingency of the elision of *ā* here which confirms that the *sthānivadbhāva* brings an *ajādi* suffix and thus in turn points out that the *sthānin* i.e., *a* of *yaṅ* is an *ajādi* suffix.

Again forms like *yātiḥ* can be obtained only if *a* of *yaṅ* is treated as an *ajādi* suffix. The *yaṅanta* root, i.e., *yāyāya* takes the suffix *ktic* after it. In the resultant form *yāyā+ya+ti* the *a* of *yaṅ* is dropped by the rule *"ato lopaḥ"* (6-4-48) and *y* is dropped by the rule *"lope vyor vali"* (6-1-66). Now the *ā* at the end of *yāyā* has to be dropped by the rule *"āto lopa iṭi ca"* (6-4-64). It is possible only if the elision is treated as an *ajādi* suffix by *sthāni vadbhāva* which necessitates the acceptance of *a* as an *ajādipratyaya* and when the preceding *y* of *a* is also dropped, the form *yātiḥ* is arrived.

Thus NBh establishes the fact that *a* of *yaṅ* has to be treated as *ajādi suffix*. Therefore there always lurks the contingency of the elision of penultimate of *gam* in *jaṅgamaḥ* by means of *sthānivadbhava* of the elision of the *a* of *yaṅ*. To prevent this contingency NBh suggests the process of formation of the word in a manner different from the one described by Kṭ. During the stage *jangam+ya+ac* wherein the *yaṅanta* root is followed by the suffix *ac*, the suffix *ya(ṅ)* is dropped wholly by the rule *"yaṅoci ca"* (2-4-74). The result is that the elision of *yaṅ* is never an *ajādeśa* since it has replace *a* and *y* and so here there is no contingency of *sthānivadbhāva* which is enjoined to the substitute of a vowel alone by the rule *"acaḥ parasmin pūrvavidhau"* (1-1-57).

3. *The expression 'anyathājatēyaka' in the bhāṣya passage "anyathājātēyakena nirdeśaḥ kriyate, anyathājātēyaka udāhriyate"*[32]

Under the rule *"tasminniti nirdiṣṭe pūrvasya"* (1-1-66) Pat uses the base *anyathājātiyaka* with two different case-endings in the sentence *"anyathājātīyakena nirdeśaḥ kriyate, anyathājātīyaka udāhriyate"*. The base *anyathājātīyaka* is formed by the addition one by one of the two *taddhita suffixes thāl* and *jātīyar* to the word *anya*. These suffixes are ordained by the rules *"prakāravacane thāl"* (5-3-23) and *"prakāravacane jātīyar"* (5-3-69), from which it is clear that they convey the same idea. Since the addition to a base of two suffixes denoting the same meaning may appear to be in vain, such usages require explanation.

With the above view in mind Kṭ makes a distinction in the sense conveyed by these two suffixes. Though both these are enjoined in the same sense *"prakāravacana"* there is a natural distinction in their sense. The suffix *thāl* denotes *prakāra* alone whereas the suffix *jātīyar* denotes *prakāravat*. *Anyathā* shall accordingly means *anyasādṛśyam* and *anyajātīyaḥ* may mean *anyasadṛśāḥ*. In the context if the suffix *thāl* alone is added to the base, the expression *anyathā* shall convey the idea *anyaprakāreṇa* and with a view to convey the idea *anyaprakāravat* there is the addition of the suffix *jātīyar* to *anyathā* and thereby the expression *anyathājatiyakena*. Kṭ continues that in fact *jātīyar* alone is capable of conveying the sense of *anyaprakāravat* and the suffix *thāl* is here superfluous. He remarks that hence the usage of the same in addition to *jātīyar* is to show that with regard to usages in language (*lankikaprayoga*) as opposed to that in grammar brevity or parsimony in expression need not be much cared for.

NBh is quite in conformity with Kṭ in regard to the above implication. But he does not feel the necessity of a distinction, in the sense, conveyed by these suffixes enjoined with the same wording *prakāravacane*, to indicate the above fact. His contention is that this implication is possible even when these two suffixes are treated as conveying the sense *prakāravat*. It is quite correct to say that the usage of the two suffixes conveying the one and the same idea, imply that one need not pay heed to brevity in regard to the usages in language. Again both rules have the same wording *prakāravacane* and therefore one cannot contradict the denotation of the idea of *prakāravat* by the suffix *thāl* when the suffix *jātiyar* conveys the idea of *prakāravat*. Moreover Pat has used the suffix *ka* also here and the same, being a *svārthika* suffix that which does not convey a sense in addtion to that conveyed by the base to which it is added, can also indicate the above fact. Thus NBh points out that a distinction in the sense of these two suffixes is hardly justifiable for the implication of the above fact.

4. *The expression 'taparopadeśaḥ' in the bhāṣya "sandhyaksareṣu taparopadeśaścet taparoccāraṇam kartavyam"*[33]

Under the Śivasūtra *hayavaraṭ* Pat discusses the question whether the dipthongs are to be enumerated in Śivasūtras just as they are read, or along with *t* as *"et otṅ"* and *"ait autc"*. He inaugurates the discussion saying that *"sandhyakṣareṣu taparopadeśaścet taparoccāraṇam kartavyam"*. In this sentence if the expression *taparopadeśaḥ* means the utterance of *t* as para, the sentence may convey a non-sensical idea "If there is the utterance *t* as para to the dipthongs, the utterance of *t* is to be effected". Hence Kṭ opines that the part *upadeśaḥ* in the said expression should mean the purpose of utterance. What Kṭ means is that, NBh says, the suffix *ghañ* in the part *upadeśa* is in the sense of *sampradāna*. The sentence can now be shown as conveying logically correct idea i.e, if there is any purpose served by the utterance of *t* as para to dipthongs, the utterance of the same (*t*) is to be made.

NBh points out that others hold a different opinion. The suffix *ghañ* in *upadeśa* in the said expression is in the sense of *karaṇa* i.e., instrument of an action. The purpose of an action can be treated as the *karaṇa* of that action. Hence the word *upadeśa* by virtue of the suffix *ghañ* being in the sense of *karaṇa*, means the *karaṇa* of utterance in other words the purpose of the action. Hence the sentence *"sandhyakṣareṣu taparopadeśaścet.."* signifies that 'if there is the instrument namely the purpose of utterance, of *t* as para to the dipthongs, the utterance of the same as a para, is to be made'.

5. *The process of formation of the word 'vṛkṣav'*

According to Kṭ the form *vṛkṣav* is to be formed from the root *vṛṣkavṛśc* by the addition of the *kṛt* suffix *vic* and not by that of *kvip*.[34] The original root *vraśc* takes *kvip* after that, when there is the *upadada* namely *vṛkṣa*. The resultant form with *samprasārana vṛkṣavṛśc+kvip* is a *prātipadika* by the rule *"kṛttad-hitasamāsāśca"* (1-2-44). When on the strength of the vārttika *'prātipadikād dhātvarthe bahulam iṣṭhavacca'* the suffix *ṇic* is added to it the same becomes *vṛkṣavṛśc+i* and the part *ṛśc* which is the *ṭi*, is substituted by *lopa* on the strength of the said vārttika. The subsequent form *vṛkṣav* is now a root by the rule *"sanādyantā dhātavaḥ"* (3-1-32). This root takes the suffix *vic* after it. *Lopa* replaces *i* by the rule *"ṇeraniṭi"* (6-4-51) and then follows the elision of *vic* by the rule *"veraprktasya"* (6-1-67). Thus the form *vṛkṣav* is arrived it.

Kṭ argues that if the termination added to the root *vṛkṣav* be *kvip*, a stage like *vṛkṣav* may be arrived at, but the process of formation may not end with it. By the application of the maxim *"ekadeśavikṛtam ananyavad bhavati"*, the *v* in *vṛkṣav* can be treated as *vṛśc* in spite of the lopa of *ṛśc* and hence the same is prone to *samprasāraṇa* enjoined to *vṛśc* by the rule *"grahijyāvay-*

ivyathivaṣṭivicativṛścati..." (6-1-16). The accomplished form will therefore never be *vṛkṣav* and hence the necessity of the eddition of *vic* alone to the root.

NBh deems that this view of Kṭ requires reconsideration. The *v* in *vṛkṣav* cannot be regarded as *vṛśc* by the maxim *'ekadeśavikṛtam ananyavad bhavati'*. There are two reasons for the same. The one is that the *sthānin* of *ṭilopa* is the *prātipadika vṛkṣavṛśc* and not *vṛśc*. Hence there being no change of *ṛśc* in the status as the *ṭi* of *vṛśc v* is the *ekadeśavikṛta* of *vṛkṣavṛśc,* and not of *vṛśc* alone in which case the same have been considered as *vṛśc* by the said maxim. Even if *ṭilopa* be however treated as connected with *vṛśc,* one cannot apply the maxim on *v* because the major portion of *vṛśc* has undergone change and in instances where half or more than half of the portion of a *śabda* has undergone a change, the maxim cannot be applied there. This is the second reason.

NBh adds that if *vṛśc* is taken as the *sthānin* of *ṭilopa,* the same being an *ekāc* there is the contingency of the operation of *prakṛtibhāva* to *vṛśc* by the sūtra *"prakṛtyaikāc"* (6-4-163) and that will supersede the *ṭilopa*. Therefore the *sthānin* of *ṭilopa* need necessarily be the *prātipadika vṛksavṛśc* so that it may not to be superseded by *prakṛtibhāva*. Thus *v* can in no way be considered as *vṛśc* and hence there is no contingency on *v* of the *samprasāraṇa* originally enjoined to the root *vṛśc*. NBh thus points out that the assertion of Kṭ that in case of the addition of *kvip* to the root *vṛkṣavṛśc* the form *vṛkṣav* cannot be arrived at, requires reconsideration.

REFERENCES

1. *Mbh* p.8.

1a. Yudhiṣṭhira Mēmāṃsaka says that NBh has gone wrong in considering that Sākaṭāyana Vyākaraṇa is concerned with words of spoken language alone and points that the same is concerned with Vedic words also. Op.cit., p.112.

2. *Mbh* p.39.
3. *Mbh* p.61.
4. *Mbh* p.65.
5. *Mbh* p.67.
6. *Mbh* p.76.

7. *Mbh* p.93.
8. *Mbh* p.101.
9. *Mbh* p.135.
10. *Mbh* p.135. *"Sāvakāśo luk ko'vakāśaḥ? avaśiṣṭaḥ"*.
11. *Mbh* p.149.
12. *Mbh* p.279.
13. Rudradharajhā śarma says that this is the view held by the author of the word *"Ratna"* Vide *Mbh* edited with the commentary *'Tattavāloka'* p.375.
14. *Mbh* p.285.
15. *Mbh* p.289.
16. *Mbh* p.223.
17. *Mbh* p.340.
18. *Prdp* p.62.
19. *Mbh* p.77.
20. *Prdp* p.72.
21. *Mbh* p.109.
22. *Mbh* p.80.
23. *Prdp* p.145.
24. Vide *Mbh* p.174.
    "yadi tatpuruṣo'yam samānādhikaraṇo nārtha ekagrahaṇena-evam tarhi siddhe sati yadajgrahaṇe kriyamāṇe ekagrahaṇam karoti tajñāpayācāryaḥ anyatra varṇagrahaṇe jātigrahaṇam bhavati iti".
25. *Prdp* p.252.
26. *Mbh* pp.72-77.
27. *Mbh* p.166.
28. *Udy* p.101.
29. Vide *Mbh* p.340. "atha dvitēyam pratyayagrahaṇam kimartham? pratyayalakṣaṇam yathā syād varṇalakṣaṇam mā bhūd iti".
30. *Mbh* p.297.
31. *Prdp* p.136.
32. *Mbh* p.359.
33. *Mbh* p.78.
34. *Prdp* p.98.

Chapter VII

Criticism of the Pradīpa (Contd.)

II Refutations

The criticism of the *Prdp* by NBh is not the mere expression of his disagreement with the assertions of Kṭ. With precise and decisive arguments he refutes certain assertions of Kṭ in regard to the interpretations of sūtras and vārttikas and the explanation of the expressions and passages in the bhāṣya.

Interpretation of Sūtras

1. The necessity of enunciation of letter ḷ in the Śivasūtras.

The letter *ḷ* is looked upon as an *ac* as it is anunciated in the sūtra *ṛḷk*. Kṭ brings to our attention the vārttika *ṛḷvarṇayoḥ mithaḥ sāvarṇyam vācyam* and says that this vārttika is competent to serve the above purpose. The letter *r* is an *ac*. The letter *ḷ* also which according to this vārttika is a cognate of *ṛ*, can be looked upon as an *ac* on the basis of the fact itself that it is comprehended by an *ac* namely *ṛ*. Kṭ points out that one is thus naturally prone to doubt the necessity of the enumeration of the letter *ḷ*. But he says that the fact is that Pan does not pay heed to the said varttika. Form the point of view of Pāṇ, *ḷ* is never a cognate of *ṛ* so as to comprehend *ḷ* whereby *ḷ* will be designated as an *ac*. Therefore the enunciation of *ḷ* in the Śivasūtras. Refuting this view of Kṭ NBh points out that if *ḷ* were not taught as one among the letters enunciated in the form of the fourteen Śivasūtras, the authenticity of *ḷ* itself will be doubted. At this juncture, the assertion too, of cognateness between *ṛ* and *ḷ* cannot be sustained. As a matter of fact, it is the enunciation of *ḷ* that facilitated the assertion of cognateness by Kāt. The justification of the enunciation of *ḷ* in the Śivasūtras cannot therefore be made on the basis of the fact that Pāṇ is negligent or ignorant of the vārttika.

NBh's refutation of the view of Kṭ becomes all the more effective when he quotes the words of Pat at the end of the bhāṣya under the Śivasūtras *"eoṅ and aiauc" "Anupadiṣṭam sat katham śakyam vijñātum?* which means "How can one accept the existence of a letter that is not enumerated".[1] Pat makes this assertion to show that the existence of a consonant having one *mātra* cannot be accepted. This passage supports the view that in the absence of the enunciation of *ḷ* even the existence of the same cannot be accepted and so the assertion too of cognateness of *ḷ* with *ṛ* is not feasible. The existence of the letters like *ā* etc. can be accepted in spite of the absence of their enumeration. This is because, NBh says that they are comprehended by the letters *a i* etc. that are emumerated in the sūtras. But with regard to the letter *ḷ*, the guiding principle of cognateness, namely the rule *"tulyāsyaprayatnam savarṇam"* (1-1- 9) cannot apply on *ṛ* and *ḷ* as they are not *"tulyāsyaprayatna"* with each other. *ḷ* will not therefore be comprehended by *ṛ* and that is why *ḷ* is enumerated in the Śivasūtras.

2. *The meaning of word 'sthāna' in the sūtra "ṣaṣṭhī sthāneyogā" (1-1-49).*

Pat points out that in the sūtras of Pāṇ ādeśas are enjoined to those that are uttered in the sūtras with the sixth case at the ending. Since there is no *ṣaṣṭhīnirdeśa* in the *sūtra* in *vṛddhirādaic* (1-1-1), he refutes the view that the sūtra prescribes *ādaic* as the substitutes of the word *vṛddhi.*[2] However in contrary to the said assertion it is found that sūtras like *"nābhi nabham ca"* and *"parastrī paraśu ca"* teach the substitutes *nabha* and *paraśu* in the place of the *sthānin* namely *nābhi* and *paraśtrī* which are not *ṣaṣṭhīairdiṣṭa* in the said rule.[3] In order to justify this *sthānyadeśabhāva* in spite of the absence of *ṣaṣṭhīnirdeśa* of the *sthānin,* Kṭ resorts to the double meaning, *prasaṅga* and *artha,* conveyed by the word *sthāna* in the sūtra *"ṣaṣṭhīsthāneyogā"* (1-1-49). The word *sthāna* there, is a *tantranirdeśa.* The rule is interpreted to be conveying two ideas. One is that in grammar the sixth case denotes the sense of scope (i.e. *prasaṅga*). The idea got by taking the word *sthāna* to mean *artha* is that the *sthānin* gets as its substitute the one which is competent to denote the sense of the original. Accordingly, the rule points out *ṣaṣṭhīnirdeśa* and *arthasadbhāva* as the deciding factors of *sthānyadesabhāva*. It is owing to the presence of the same *artha* that *nabha* is understood as the substitute of *nābhi* and *parasu* as the substitute of *parastrī*. This is why, Kṭ says that there is no *ṣasṭhīnirdeśa* in the rules *'nabhi nabham ca'* and *'parastrī paraśu ca'*.

According to NBh it is in vain to take the word *sthāna* to mean *artha*. The word conveys the idea of *prasaṅga* alone. The *prasaṅga* of a *śabda* itself means the same of the *śabda* possessed of *artha*, since one employs a *śabda* to convey an *artha*. Thus the sense namely *prasaṅga* conveyed by *ṣaṣṭhīnirdeśa* in a rule points out that the connection of *sthānin* and *ādeśa* is brought about by *artha*. Thus it comes out that the *sthānin* gets as its substitute the one which conveys the sense of the *sthānin*. Thus in sūtras like *"nābhi nabham ca"*, *nabha* is understood as the substitute of *nābhi* in spite of the absence of *ṣaṣṭhīnirdeśa* in the rule and thus NBh refutes Kṭ's interpretation of the word *sthāna*, in the rule *"ṣaṣṭīsthāneyogā"* to mean *artha* also in addition to *prasaṅga*.

3. The necessity of the insertion of the word nimitta in the rule "kṅiti ca"

In the vārttika *"kṅitipratiṣedhe tannimittagrahaṇam"*, it is pointed out that the rule *"kṅiti ca"* (1-1-5) ought to be read as *"kṅinnimitte ca"*.[4] Kṭ says that in the said rule, the word *ikaḥ* and *guṇavṛddhī* are got by *anuvṛtti* and *tannimittagrahaṇa* is necessary only if in the interpretation of the rule, the word *kṅiti* is taken to be the *viśeṣaṇa* of *ikaḥ* and not that of *guṇavṛddhī*. The prohibition of *guṇavṛddhī* by this rule is desired on the last (as in *citam*) as well as on the penultimate of the *aṅga* in the instances of *bhinnam* and *chinnam* respectively.[5] By the application of the *paribhāṣā* rule *"tasminnitinirdiṣṭe pūrvasya"* (1-1-66) on the word *kṅiti*, the rule shall mean that the *ik* which is adjunctly previous to the *kṅit* suffix shall get the prohibition. Though the *ik* which is the last element of the *aṅga* in *citam stutam* etc. get the prohibition thereby, the penultimate in *bhinnam* and *chinnam* cannot be benefitted as the same cannot be adjunctly previous to the *kṅit* suffix. The insertion of the word *nimitta,* thereby becomes a necessity. Kṭ says that if the word *kṅiti* relates to *guṇavṛddhi,* the *paribhāṣā* rule *"tasminniti nirdiṣṭe pūrvasya* won't apply on the word *kṅiti*. One can achieve the probibition of anything which is yet to take effect and not that of an operation which has already taken effect. The *guṇa* and *vṛddhi,* being not taken effect if to be probibited, cannot be designated as previous or subsequent to a suffix. Hence the absence of the influence of the rule *"tasminniti nirdiṣṭe pūrvasya"* on the word *kṅiti*. The locative case in *kṅiti* can only be in the sense of *nimitta* by the rule *"yasya ca bhāvena bhāvalakṣaṇam"* (2-3-37) in which case there is no need of the insertion of the word *nimitta* in the rule.

The arguments advanced by NBh completely upset the standpoint of Kṭ. NBh establishes that the word *kṅiti* is necessarily to be treated as an adjunct to the word *guṇavṛddhī* and the insertion of the wrod *nimitta* is indispensible in this case. He points out that during the discussion of the topic, Kāt and Pat have nowhere mentioned the *anuvṛtti* of the word *ikaḥ*. NBh continues that even if the *anuvrtti* of the wrod *ikaḥ* be accepted, it is to be treated as *'sabdādhikāra* i.e., *anuvṛtti* of the word *ikaḥ* devoid of the meaning denoted by it in the previous rule and the word *kṅiti* cannot relate to the *'sabdasvarūpa ikaḥ* pointed out by the word *ikaḥ*. Among the other words *guṇavṛddhī na bhavataḥ,* the word *'kṅiti'* cannot relate to *na* or *bhavataḥ* since *bhavatikriyā* or absence cannot be followed or preceded by a suffix since they have got no form. The word *kṅiti* cannot therefore but be the *viśeṣaṇa* of *guṇavṛddhī*. The locative case in *'kṅiti'* makes the word liable to the influence of the rule *"tasminniti nirdiṣṭe pūrvasya"* (1-1- 66). Though there is *nimittasaptamiī* enjoined by the rule *"yasya ca bhāvena bhava-lakṣaṇam"* 2-3-37) the *parasaptamī* will supersede it on the aut-hority of the statement *'upapadavibhakteḥ kārakavibhaktir balīyasī'*. Nor can one doubt it again to be *nimittasaptamī* by the *sid-dhasādhyasamabhihāranyāya,* as a rule possesses greater force than a nyāya. Besides the application of the *paribhāṣā* cannot be doubted by the maxim *'viddhau paribhāṣopatiṣṭhate nānuvade'* since such a statement is seen nowhere in the *Mbh*. Even in case of its acceptance, it has been established that this maxim relates to the two rules *"iko guṇavṛddhiī"* and *"acaśca"* (1-2-28).

Thus by the operation of the *paribhāṣā Tasminniti nirdiṣṭe pūrvasya* the rule means *'kṅiti pare pūrvasya avyavahitasya guṇavṛddhī* na bhavataḥ'. The rule therefore shall accord the prohibition to those *guṇavṛddhī* alone that substitute an *ik* which is adjunctly previous to the *kṅit* suffix. This necessitates the *tannimittagrahaṇa* in the rule. NBh says that the application of the rule *"tasminniti nirdiṣṭe pūrvasya"* (1-1-66) on the word *ikaḥ* is sanctioned by Pat when he states *'yatra kṅityanantaro guṇabhavyasti tatra syād'*.[6] In this statement the absence of the word *ikaḥ* has got a significant bearing to the argument of NBh. The fact is again borne out by the citation of the instance *hataḥ* by Pat as the *prayojana* of the insertion of word *nimitta*. If, as according to Kṭ, the word *ikaḥ* is got by *anuvṛtti,* the instance *hataḥ* can never be the exclusive benefit of *tannimittagrahaṇa* as the absence itself of *ik* in the word can bring the prohibition of *guṇa* feared to operate there.

4. The technical term samyoga prescribed by the rule "halo'natarāḥ samyogaḥ" (1-1-7).

Kāt considers that the word *saha* is to be added to the rule *"halo'nantarāh samyogaḥ"* (1-1-7) so that the designation *samyoga* shall relate to contiguous consonants collectively and not to each of them individually.[7] Pat considers the same to be unnecessary. This is because there are instances where the predicate relates to the subject individually as in *'devadattayajña-dattaviṣṇumitrā bhojyantām* and where the predicate relates to the subject collectively as in *Gargāḥ śatam daṇḍyantām*. In the former sentence the word *pratyekam* is not found, nor is the word *saha* found in the latter. Since Pāṇ has followed the practice current in the world in not using the word *pratyekam* in the sūtra *"vṛddhirādaic"* (1-1-1) and *"adeṅ guṇaḥ"* (1-1-2) he does not mention the word *saha* in this sūtra and it is quite correct says Pat.

Here Kṭ opines that the word *samyoga* is a technical term functioning in accordance with its derivative sense. He says *samyujyante varṇāḥ asmin iti samudāyaḥ samyogaḥ*. In accordance with its derivative sense, "wherein letters are combined" the term shall relate to contiguous consonants as a whole and not individually. Hence there is no need of the insertion of the word *saha* in the rule.

NBh refutes this view of Kṭ. However before attacking his view he makes the point of view of Kt clear. Kṭ's opinion is that though there are instances of the predicate relating to the subject in a sentence individually, that process does not apply in this sūtra, since it contradicts the action of the term according to its derivative sense. Moreover to accept the term as relating to contiguous consonants individually, results in treating the word *anantarāḥ* as *upalakṣaṇa* whereas when the term relates to the consonants collectively the word has the function of *viśeṣaṇa* i.e. adjective in the sense and it is always preferable to the former. Again favourites of the view that the term relates individually seeks to explain rules like *"vānyasya saṃyogādeḥ"* (6.4-68) by resorting to the splitting of the word *saṃyogādeḥ as saṃyogauādī* yasya tasya, so as to avoid the over- applicability of the rule in instance like *niryāyāt*. These people may have to face this objection that *saṃyogādeḥ* may be split as *saṃyogāḥ ādayaḥ yasya,* as there is no guiding factor as to the number of the components used while splitting a compound and this will prevent the function of the rule in instances like *gleyāt*. Thus after explaining Kṭ's standpoint NBh adds the word *āhuḥ* communicating that he does not favour this view.

To refute the view of Kṭ NBh points out that the derivative sense of the term is misleading as it may lead the designation to a word or to a sentence wherein also letters are combined. Just as in a statement *ghaṭapaṭau saṃyujyante yatra* we conceive of a thing which is different from *ghaṭa* and *paṭa* and wherein there is the *saṃyoga* of these two, so also a word or a sentence too, wherein we get contiguous letters, shall also be prone to the designation *saṃyoga*. Therefore the designation *saṃyoga* need not be accepted as *anvarthasaṃjñā*, though the same be a *mahāsaṃjñā*. Perhaps Pan used the term not for its derivative sense, but in accordance with his ancestors who used this term. This is evident from another point, also says NBh. Pat while refuting the view that the word *saha* need by added to the rule, resorts to the instance *'gargāḥ śatam daṇḍyantām'* wherein even in the absence of the word *saha* the predicate relates to the subject collectively.[8] Pat does never resort to the *anvarthatā* of the term. With this strong support at his command NBh refutes the view of Kṭ.

5. The expression 'halaḥ' in the rule "halo'nantarāḥ saṃyogaḥ" (1-1- 7).

Under the rule *"halo'nantarāḥ saṃyogaḥ"* (1-1-7) Pat discusses the question that where there are more than two contiguous consonants, every two gets the designation or the whole alone. In this context, Kṭ makes an observation that the plural number in the expression *halaḥ* in the rule is according to the rule *"jātyakhyāyāmekasmin bahuvacanam anyatarasyām"* (1-2-58). Thereby the word *halaḥ* denotes the genus *haltva* and not three or more consonants. Therefore, Kṭ says that, the term *samyoga* shall relate to two contiguous consonants also, as there is the genus *haltva* in those two.

Refuting this assertion of Kṭ, NBh says that the word *halaḥ* is an expression by *ekaśeṣa* of the words *halau* and *halaḥ*. *Halau ca halaśca* become *halaḥ*. This is because under the rule *"svaritāt samhitāyam anudāttānām"* (1-2-39), Pat in answer to the problem that the word *anudāttanām* in the plural number fails to comprehend single and double *anudātta* letters, says that *anudāttānām* is an expression by *ekaśeṣa* of the words *'anudāttasya cānudāttayoścānudāttanām*. There Pat does not say that *anudāttānām* is an expression in plural number according to the said rule *"jātyākhyym ekasmin bahuvacanam anyatarasym"* (1-2-58)[9].

6. The splitting (1) of the compound expression samyogādeḥ in the rule "vānyasya samygādeḥ and (2) of the compound expressions kumāryagāram and vadhvagāram as kumāryor agāram and vadhvor agāram.

Under the rule *"halonantarāḥ samyogaḥ"* (1-1-7) Kt argues for the addition of the word *saha* to the rules so that contiguous consonants shall get the term collectively and not individually. It is pointed that if each of them gets the term individually there is the contingency of the over-applicability of the rule *"vānyasya samyogādeḥ"* (6-4-68) in instances like *niryāyāt* where *r* of the prefix *nir* and *y* of the root *yā*, being contiguous consonants are liable to be designated as *samyoga* whereby the root being *samyogadi*, the optional substitution by *e* of *a* of the root *yā* is liable to take place. To refute this contingency it is said in the bhāṣya *"naiṣa deṣaḥ yat tāvad ucyate iha tāvanniryā yāt, nirvāyāt vānyasya samyogādeḥ ity etvam prasajyeteti. Naivam vijñāyate-samyoga ādir yasya so'yam samyogādiḥ, somyogāder iti"*.[10] The idea is that the aforesaid contingency can be avoided by splitting the compounds into components of dual number so that the root, in order to get the optional substitution by *e* ought to have at its beginning two consonants which are termed as *samyoga* and the root *ya* being devoid of the same there is no contingency as suspected before.

Here Kṭ raises an objection; how can the compound *samyogādeḥ* be split with components in dual number? His doubt relates to the fact as to how the sense of duality in the idea conveyed by the components in a *vṛtti* (like *samāsa* and so on) can be understood. Kṭ himself clears the doubt saying that it is the presence of the word *ādi* that helps in splitting the compound with components in the dual number. The idea derived by splitting the compound *samyogādi* with components in singular number i.e., *samyogaḥ ādiḥ yasya* can be got even without the word *ādi*. The rule need only be *vānyasya samyogāt*. By the help of the maxim *"tasmād ityuttarasya"* (1-1-67) which operate on the word *samyogāt*, the letter which follows a *samyogā* and is at the beginning of the root shall get the optional substitution by *e* and hence the *a* of the root *yā* in *niryāyāt* shall get the substitution by *e* and the presence of the word *ādi* is of no avail. Hence its presence makes the compound to be split up by the components in dual number and hence no contingency of substitution by e of *ā*. Thus the word *ādi* of the compounds helps to have the idea of duality in the sense conveyed by the compound *samyogādeh*.

Here it is interesting to note that NBh refutes the manner in which the doubt is raised here. He points out that the term *samyoga* of course implies the sense of union of more than one but it does not indicate the union of two specifically. Therefore the doubt here ought to be "how the idea of more than one can be conveyed in the sense of the components of a compound"? Pat has never denied that the idea of more than one in the sense of the components of a compound can be expressed. What Pat has stated is that the idea of a specific number is not conveyed in the sense of the components of a *vṛtti* like compounds. NBh therefore argues that the question, to be more correct, ought to be as how the sense of more than one as expressed in the splitting *samyogau ādi yasya* be conveyed from the *vṛtti, samyogādeḥ*. NBh however agrees with the solution as giving the circumstances under which the compound is split into components of dual number.

(2) Under the rule *"īdūdeddvivacanam pragṛhyam"* (1-1-11) Pat has discussed the four ways in which the rule can be interpreted.[11]

If it is interpreted as *īdādyantam yad dvivacanāntam tat pragrhyam* i.e., that which has a dual suffix at its end and ends either in *i* or *ū* or *e* gets the designation *pragṛhya,* proh- ibition of the application of the designation in regard to instances where there is *luk* is to be made. To illustrate, when the two pairs *kumāryor agāram and vadhvor agāram* are compounded, they arrive at a stage *kumārī+agāra* and vadhū agāara which leads to the final compounded form *kumāryagāram and vadhvagāram.* Since the former member of these compounds are *kumārī and vadhū* that end in *i* and *ū* respectively and are *dvivacanānta* by virtue of the *pratyayalakṣaṇa* of the suffix *os* that has elided, they are liable to be designated as *pragṛhya* in the aforesaid interpretation of the rule. Here also Kṭ raises the doubt as to how the components in dual number can go to make the compounds *kumāryagāram and vadhvagāram* considering that the specific number in the sense of the components is not conveyed by the *vṛtti* like *samāsa.*

He clears the doubt saying that just as in the expression *tāvakīnaḥ* which comes under *taddhitavṛtti* and formed by the addition of the suffix *khañ* to the base *yuṣmad* the sense of *ekatva* is conveyed by the substitute *tāvaka* of *yuṣmad* by the rule *'tavakamamakāvekavacane'*, (4-3-3) Pat points out in the said passage that if the term *pragṛhya* relates to the part *kumārī* of the compound, the term shall procure *prakṛtibhāva* and imply the sense of duality since as otherwise the *prakṛtibhāva* cannot be explained.

Refuting Kṭ, NBh points out that in the compounds *kumāryagāram* and *vadhvagāram* the former part is never endowed with the term *'pragṛhyam'* and the interpretation of the rule in the aforesaid manner is not accepted at the end of the discussion.[12] And as such the expression *kumāryagāram* in the sense of *kumaryor agāram* is liable to be treated as erroneous since the part *kumārī* of the expression is devoid of the term *pragṛhya* which is described by Kṭ as implying the sense of duality and Pat would have to be accused of carelessness by making such an erroneous usage. As it cannot be so, it is to be accepted that, NBh suggests, the explanation given by Kṭ stands untenable. In a compound NBh points out that the sense of number is conveyed only to distinguish the sense of the former member of the compound and the sense of the component words is never conveyed with specific number. This however allows the fact that though a specific number in the sense conveyed by the component, is not conveyed by a compound, there can be the expression of the idea of more than one and as such the compound *kumāryagāram* in the sense of *kumāryor agāram* stands correct and rightly explained.

7. The idea conveyed by the word anaci in the rule "anaci ca" (8-4-87).

Kṭ upholds that *ac* is not a determining factor of the operation of *dvirvacana* enjoined by the rule *anaci ca"* (8-4-47)[13]. If the word *'anaci'* be explained as *aci na,* the rule shall mean *yaraḥ aci dve na* and so *dvirvacana* shall operate on that *yar* alone which is not followed by *ac* and thus *ac* has to be treated as one determining factor of reduplication. Kṭ therefore takes the word *anaci* to mean *hali*. The expression *anaci* is a *nañ* compound and the *nañ* according to him used in the technical sense of *paryudāsa. Anac* denotes that which is non-identical with and similar to *ac* and such a letter is *hal* i.e, consonant. Now that the rule means, *yar* gets reduplicated when followed by *hal, ac* or vowel never becomes a determining factor of the prohibition of reduplication. NBh is of opinion that *ac* need not be taken into consideration for the operation of reduplication. But he does agree to the explanation given to the word *anaci* by which it means *hal*. This is because one cannot justify the reduplication of the letter of *k* of the word *vāk* since it is not followed by *hal*. Besides, if hal were to be meant by the word *anac,* Pāṇ could have more precisely stated the rule as *'hali ca'* instead of *"anaci ca"*. Hence NBh finds it difficult to agree with Kṭ.

In the opinion of NBh the word *anac* means *ajbinna* i.e., somethings different from *ac*. The rule *"anaci ca"* means *yar* gets reduplicated when followed by something different from *ac*. In this explanation *ac* does not appear directly as a determining factor of *dvirvacana* and in instances like *vāk* the consonant *k* will get reduplicated since the absence of letters that follows *k* is something different from ac.

The fact that the status of *ac* as a determining factor of reduplication is necessary for the prohibition of *sthānivadbhāva* of the substitute *y* of *i* in the operation of reduplication in instances like *suddhyupāsyaḥ* where Pat says the rule *"acaḥ parasmin pūrvavidhau"* (1-1-57) allows *sthānivadhāva* of a substitute even when *ac*, the *sthānin* of the substitute, does not stand as a the sthānin of the operation concerned.

5. Complication involved in the absence of the word aṇ in the rule "uraṇ raparaḥ" (1-1- 51).

Pat says that if in the rule *"uraṇ raparaḥ* (1-1-51) the word *aṇ* is not mentioned, the *sūtra* may mean that any substitute that replaces *ṛ* shall become *rapara* and hence the elision taught by the rule *ḍhaki lopaḥ* (4-1-13) may become *rapara* as it has to replace the vowel *ṛ* in the base *pitṛṣvasṛ* and consequently the form *paitṛṣvaseyaḥ* is hardly obtained.[14] Therefore in the absence of the word *aṇ* in the rule, *raparatva* will have to be prohibited with reference to elision.

Kṭ examines the contingency caused by elision being *rapara*. He points out that if the elision becomes *rapara*, the resultant form will be *paitṛṣvasreyaḥ*. Since such a form is easily obtainable by the function of the rule *"iko yaṇaci"* (6-1-77) the prescription itself of elision by the rule *"ḍhaki lopaḥ"* (4-1- 33) which leads to the said form will be of no avail.[15] To avert the same, it is to be noted that the complication in the event of non-utterance of the word *aṇ* in the rule *"uraṇ raparaḥ"* (1-1-51) is that, the elision taught by the rule *"ḍhaki lopaḥ"* (4-1-133) becomes *rapara* and is contingent to replace the whole base *pitṛṣvasṛ*.

NBH refutes this remark of Kṭ. He points out that the elision, must have the status i.e., the substitute of *ṛ*, so that it can be *rapara* and hence it cannot be the substitute of the whole base *pitṛṣvasṛ* in which case it cannot be stated as the substitute exclusively of *ṛ*. Therefore *ṛ* alone is to be replaced by the elision which is *rapara* and there is the consequent barenness of the prescription of elision, since the form thus got, can as pointed out earlier, be obtained by the rule *"iko yaṇaci"* (6-1-77). That itself is the defect caused by the non-utterance of the word *aṇ* in the rule *"uraṇ raparaḥ"* (1-1- 51).

Elucidation of Vārttikas

1. The remodelling of the vārttika 'varṇānupaladbhau cānarthagateḥ as varṇānupalabdhau cātadarthagateḥ

Under the Śivasūtras *"eoṅ"* and *"aiauc"*, while discussing the question whether letters are individually possessed of sense or not, Pat suggests the vārttikas *varṇānupalabdhau cātadarthagateḥ* as an amendment to the vārttika *varṇānupalabdhau cānarthagateḥ* which answer the question in the affirmative on the basis of the fact that on the disappearance of a letter in a word, the sense is not understood.[16] To the objection that in words like *vṛkṣa,* a sense is understood even on the disappearance of the letter *ṛ* there, Pat gives the amendment *atadarthagateḥ* to the part *anarthagateḥ* in the vārttika. He then gives two different interpretations of the part *atadarthagateḥ*. *"Tasyārthaḥ* tadarthaḥ. tadarthasya gatistadarthagatiḥ. na tadarthagatiratadarthagatiḥ atadarthagater iti. Athavā so'rthastadarthastadarthasya gatiḥ tadarthagatiḥ. na tadarthagatiratadarthagatiḥ. atadarthagater iti".[16] Kṭ says that in the former interpretation i.e., *"tasya arthaḥ...."* the word *tad* refers to a letter. The amended vārttika therefore means that on the disappearance of a letter in a word, the sense conveyed by the letter is not understood. Kṭ continues that now there may arise an objection i.e., the inference being at a stage when it is not established that the letters are individually possessed of sense, an argument based on the same is baseless. It is therefore that, Kṭ opines, Pat resorts to an alternate interpretation of the word as *"so'rthastadarthaḥ...."* wherein the part *tadartha* is treated as a *karmadhāraya* compound instead of the *ṣaṣṭhītatpuruṣa* compound. The word *tad* refers to the sense which is understood from *vṛkṣa* at the time of the presence of the letter *v (saḥ = prakrto'rthaḥ).* It is quite correct to say that since that sense (which is understood at the time of presence of a letter) is not understood on the disappearance of the letter in the word, letters can be inferred to be possessed of sense individually itself.

NBh differs with Kṭ here. In his opinion the word *tad* in the former interpretation as *tasya arthasya gatiḥ* does not refer to the letter *v* in *vṛkṣa,* but to *vṛkṣa* namely, that which has the letter *v* as its component. There is no impropriety in saying that the sense namely *vṛkṣa* is not understood on the disappearance of the letter *v* in it. In the latter interpretation *"so'rthaḥ..."* the sense, understood when *v* is there in the word, is, as told by Kṭ, referred to by the word *tad.* Thus NBh says that the interpretation of *tadartha* as *ṣaṣṭhītatpuruṣa* compound is quite in harmony with the context. It is only to secure ease of effort that Pat resorts to *karmadhāraya* compound. NBh says that the further statements of Pat during the discussions, *"sakakāreṇa kaścidartho gamyate"*, favour his interpretation of the word *tad* as refering to the collection of letters namely *vṛkṣa kūpa* etc.

2. *The vārttika "samprayogo vā naṣṭāśvadagdharathavad".*

Under the rule *"sthānentaratamaḥ"* (1-1-50) Kāt points out that where *ṛ* is to be replaced by *guṇa* or *vṛddhi,* all the letters designated as *guṇa* or *vṛddhi* are contingent to replace *ṛ* since none of these substitutes designated as *guṇa* or *vṛddhi* is *antaratama* to the *sthānin,* so as to be selected as the specific substitute of *ṛ*. Kāt himself offers the solution to this doubt and then Pat gives his own explanation. He states that in instances where *guṇa* is enjoined to *ṛ, a* shall replace *ṛ* since *a* and *ṛ* are respectively *antaratma ādeśa* and *sthānin* in as much as one is devoid of *antaratma sthānin* and the other of *antaratama* substitute. Pat then proceeds to introduce the vārttika *'samprayogovā naṣṭāśvadagdharathavad'* and elaborates on it as follows :- "Or they are in close association like two men, one being *naṣṭāśva* and the other being *dagdharatha*. It is explained as follows. Your horse is dead and my chariot too is burnt and let us make use of both, we have, and associate them. Similar is the case here. You do not have a *sthānin* similar to you and I do not have an *ādeśa* similar to me and let us both be associated together".[17]

Apparently the former solution given by Pat and the ensuing vārttika cited above seem to convey the same idea. Lest the vārttika should be understood as a repetition and so as to consider these two as alternative assertions, Kṭ gives an explanation. The former statement of Pat is made on the basis of the rule *"sthānentaratamaḥ"* (1-1-50) according to which closest similarity is the deciding factor of *sthānyadeśabhāva* between the substitutes and *sthānin*. The vārttika is based on the refutation of this rule. Even if there is no rule as *"sthānentaratamaḥ"* (1-1-50) *ṛ* will get *a* as the *guṇa* substitute just as two strangers one devoid of the horse and the other of the chariot, are associated in one action.

NBh differs with Kṭ here. The basis described by Kṭ viz. the existence of the sūtra and the refutation of the sūtra, to explain the statement of Pat and Kāt, does not hold good because both of them imply one and the same deciding factor of *sthānyadeśabhāva*. The rule at its existince proclaims *āntaratamya* as the deciding factor and the rule is discarded on the same ground that even without a plain statement like *'sthānentaratamaḥ'* closest similarity shall be the deciding factor of *sthānyadeśabhava*. Thus these explanations still leaves the vārttika to be a repetition of the previous statement of Pat. NBh therefore gives a different introduction to the vārttika. The statement of Pat is based on the fact that closest similarity is the deciding factor of *sthānyadeśabhāva*. **Ṛ* gets *a* as the substitute, since both of them are similar to each other in as much as both of them have the common characteristics viz. being devoid of similar *sthānin* and *ādeśa*. The absence of similar *sthānin* and *ādeśa* is treated as a similarity of the *sthānin* and substitute. To those who do not view non- similarity as a similarity Kāt offers the solution. Just like two strangers associate in one action, *ṛ* and *a* that are entirely dissimilar are incorporated in *sthānyadeśabhāva*.

3. The vārttikas 'nirvṛttapratipattau nirvṛttiḥ' 'anarthakam ca' and 'uktam vā'.

Under the rule *"sthānentaratamaḥ"* (1-1-50) Pat discusses the question whether the rule is an independent rule by which *antaratama* substitutes are enjoined or the same is a discriminatory rule (*viśeṣapratipādaka* rule) which adds the characteristic namely *antaratamaiva* to the substitutes that are enjoined by other rules.[18] To point out an objection in the latter view according to which the rule decides correctly what is enjoined by another sūtra, the vārttika *'nirvṛttapratipattau nirvṛttiḥ'* is cited and Pat says *'nirvṛttapratipattau nirvṛttiḥ na siddhyati sarve sarvatra prāpnuvanti"*. This is followed by the question 'kim tarhyucyate, nirvṛttir na siddhyatīti, na sādhīyo nirvṛttiḥ siddhā bhavati? The answer clearly pointing out the objection is given 'na brūmo nirvṛttin na siddhyatīti, kim tarhi? iṣṭā vyavasthā na prakalpyeta, na sarve sarvatra iṣyante. A counter-question is raised now, 'idam idānīm kimartham syād' and the objector points out the consequence with the vārttika *'anarthakam ca'*, anarthakam etad syād'. Yo hi bhuktavantam brūyān mā bhuktahāḥ, iti kim tena kṛtam syād?" Answering the objection, Pat cites the vārttika *'uktam vā'* and says 'kim uktam siddham tu ṣaṣṭhyadhikāre vacanāt' iti ṣaṣṭhyadhikāre ayam yogaḥ kartavyaḥ, sthānentaratamaḥ ṣaṣṭhīnirdiṣṭasya iti'.

Kṭ says that the initial assertion *'nirvṛtta- pratipattau.... prāpnuvanti'*, pointing out the objection in the view of treating the rule as *pratipādaka*, is that since rules are ever an authority and considering that in this view the vidhisūtras enjoin substitutes which may be *antaratama* or *ananthāratama* to the *sthānin* and the rule *"sthānentaratamaḥ"* selects only the *antaratama* substitutes, both the forms wherein *antaratama* substitutes have replaced the *sthānin* and *anantaratama* substitutes have replaced the *sthānin* would have to be treated as optionally correct. The latter assertion clearly pointing out the objection, *'na brūmo....sarvatreṣyante'* is that since the viddhisūtras have enjoined substitutes, they operate in the respective forms irrespective of the fact that they are *antaratama* or not, and hence such forms are to be uniformly treated as correct and their correctness cannot be removed by the rule *"sthānentaratamaḥ"*, since forms derived by an authoritative rule does not have the *sāmānyaviśeṣabhāva* in between them so as to be totally superseded by a few of them on the basis of another rule, though it be authoritative. This results in the barrenness of the rule *"sthānentaratamaḥ"* which is pointed out in the vārttika *'anarthakam ca'*. Kṭ says that by the vārttika *'uktam vā'* and the bhāṣya passage accompanying the same we are told of the difference of treating the rule *'sthānentaratamaḥ'* from the latter view treating *sthānentaratama* as *pratipādaka*. The rule *"sthānentaratamaḥ"* unites itself with the viddhisūtras that deal with the substitutes of *sthānin* and by means of this *ekavākyatā* the vidhisūtras enjoin *antaratama* substitutes alone to replace the *sthānin*.

NBh offers a different explanation. He says that the initial assertion under the vārttika *'nirvṛttapratipattau nirvṛttiḥ', nirvṛttapratipattau nirvṛttir na siddhyati sarve sarvatra prāpnuvanti"* means that if the rule *"sthānentaratamaḥ"* be treated as deciding *antaratama* substitutes, it has to be accepted that the forms wherein *antaratama* substitutes have replaced the *sthānin* on the strength of the rule, are averted by the rule *"sthānentaratamaḥ"*, just as *luk* averts the suffixes that operates by virtue of the rules enjoining them. Hence the *vidhisūtras* cannot retain all the forms sanctioned by them. The next assertion *"na brūmo nirvṛttiḥ.....sarvatresyante"* is made by one who does not understand the said idea. He says that the forms sanctioned by the *vidhi* rules are contingent to be treated as correct uniformly. However the rule *"sthānentaratamaḥ"* becomes futile. This is conveyed by the vārttika *'anarthakam ca'*. In the vārttika *'uktam vā'* by which Pat solves the difficulty, Pat refers to the vārttika *"siddham tu ṣaṣṭhyadhikāre vacanāt"* and here NBh agrees to the interpretation given by Kṭ. However, in the interpretation of Kṭ, the significance of the word *vā* is not brought out and NBh gives the same. It means that even if there be no *ekavātkyatā* of the *vidhi* rules and the rule *sthānentaratamaḥ"* and they stand aloof the latter as a discriminatory rule, one has to accept necessarily the exclusion of forms having *anantaratama* substitutes formed by virtue of the *vidhi* rule. This is because though it is true that he, who asks one not to eat after one has eaten, accomplishes nothing, the rule *"sthānentaratamaḥ"* cannot be treated as futile on the authority of the statement of Pat under the rule *"vṛddhirādaic" "varṇenāpyanarthakena na bhavitavyam kim punar iyatā sūtreṇa"*. So in order to secure the purposefulness of the rule *sthānentaratamaḥ*, the forms with *anantaratama* substitutes are to be averted by the said rule.

4. The interpretation of the vārttika 'viṣayeṇa tu nānāliṅgakaraṇāt siddham'.

In order to meet the objection that the existence of the rule *"sthānivad ādeśo nalvidhau"* (1-1-56) paves the way for the contingency of the shooting of the *kārya* concerning a general rule to the exception by means of *sthānivadbhāva* whereby *ṇitkārya* may shoot to the suffix *ka* which is the *apavāda* of the suffix *aṇ*, Pat refers to the vārttika *'viṣayeṇa tu nānāliṅgakaraṇāt siddham'* which he has dealt with previously under the *Sivasūtra 'aiuṇ'*.[19] The suffix *ka* taught by the rule *"āto' nupasarge kaḥ"* (3-2-3) is endowed with the *anubandha k*. The word *tu* in the said vārttika means 'again' (the sense conveyed by the **indeclinable** *punaḥ*) and Kṭ says that the vārttika means **that,** since Pan uses the symbol *k* again in the suffix *ṭak* which is the *apavāda* of the suffix *ka* and which can by virtue of *sthānivadbhāva* be treated as *kit*, the *kārya* of the general rule will not shoot to the exception by virtue of *stānivadbhāva*.

NBh refutes this interpretation of Kṭ. He argues that if the purpose of the vārttika be as such, the alternate solution given subsequently by Pat cannot be explained as having any difference with this solution. The alternate suggestion given by Pat is that since Pāṇ reads *śyan, śnam, śnā, śa, śnu,* with the symbol *ś* as *anubandha* in the *apavāda* rules even when in the *utsarga* rule *"kartari śap"* (4-1-68) *śap* has the *anubandha ś* it is understood that the *kārya* of the general does not shoot to the exception. The explanation given by Kṭ of the said vārttika is identical with this statement of Pat and this contingency is not desirable. Moreover the idea given by Kṭ cannot be got literally from the words in the vārttika. Again even in the interpretation of the word *tu* as conveying the sense *'again'* the significance of the word *nānā* in the vārttika is not brought out and it remains as not related to the idea of the vārttika. In support of his refutation of the interpretation given by Kṭ, NBh adds that under the rule *'aiuṇ'* Pat has cited the cārttika *'viṣayeṇa tu punarliṅgakaraṇāt siddham'* as a remodelled version of the vārttika *'viṣayeṇa tu nānāliṅgakaraṇāt siddham'* In this remodelling, the word *punaḥ* is used whereas *tu* is retained and it shows definitely that the word *tu* is not used in the sense of the word *punaḥ*. NBh therefore says that the vārttika conveys the ideas that, since Pāṇ provides various symbols like *k, ṇ,* etc. in different places like *ka, aṇ,* etc., it is to be understood that every suffix or sound procures that operation alone caused by the *anubandha* with which it is endowed in the rule and hence no overlapping of the operations caused by *anubandha* in any way.

The Explanation of Certain Expressions

1. The expression 'sāmānyabhūtam' in the sentence "yat tarhi tad bhinneṣu abhinnam cchinneṣvacchinnam sāmānyabhūtam sa śabdaḥ'.[20]

In the above sentence Pat expresses the doubt, whether the genus cow which becomes the object of cognition when one utters *gauḥ* to be, the *śabda*. Kṭ commenting on this, takes the word *bhūta* in the expression *sāmānyabhūtam* to be conveying the sense of similarity as in the expressions like *pitṛbhūtaḥ* (meaning one who is like a father). *Sāmānya* means the general sum-total of qualities, *sattā* and the word *sāmānyabhūtam sa śabdaḥ*" is interpreted as conveying the sense, "Is *śabda* then that (i.e., the sum-total of qualities like *gotva*) which like *sattā* ever exists when the individuals are broken or destroyed. Kṭ says that here *gotva* the sum-total of qualities is compared to *sattā* the general sum-total of qualities. Bhar also has got the same opinion.[21]

NBh refutes this explanation and we cannot but agree with him. He says that the comparison between *gotva* and *sattā* i.e., between *vyāpyajāti* and *vyāpakajāti* is not admissible as they are the general and the particular. If a comparison involves between the general and the particular, there is the contingency of the expression *vṛkṣavad āmraḥ* meaning a mango tree is a like a tree. Again the word *sāmānya* can denote *gotva* as well as *sattā* since both are *sāmānya* i.e., sum-total of qualities. Therefore there is no reason in restricting the sense of the word *sāmānya*, and it does not singularly contribute anything in the context. There is also the comprousness of supplying a word like *gotva* as a particular sum-total of qualities in order to make the comparison perfect.

NBh's attack on Kṭ here is vehement. He says that the expression *pramāṇabhūtaḥ* made by Pat in the second *āhnika* has been explained by Kṭ without resorting to the sense of similarity.[22] So here too Kṭ could have more wisely adopted that kind of an interpretation. There the word *bhūta* is interpreted to convey the idea of the word *prāpta*. The word *bhūta* is derived by the addition of the suffix *kta* to the root *bhū* meaning to attain (*prāpti*). Here too *sāmānyabhūta* derived similarly can well suit the context in as much as it will mean, 'that which has attained the status of *sāmānya*' in other words, *sāmānya* itself. Again NBh says that the illustration of Kṭ's interpretation by the word *pitṛbhūta* is not sound. There the word *bhūta* does not denote the idea of the word *sadṛśa*. However the whole word means one who is like a father and this idea is got on the basis of the *nyāya* '*antyatra anyaśabdaprayogo sādṛśyaparaḥ*' (The usage of a word to denote a thing which it does usually denote, shows the similarity on the thing, of the exact thing conveyed by that sound). According to NBh it is therefore better to take the word *bhūta* in the sense of the word *svarūpa*. *Sāmānyabhūta* means *sāmānyasvarūpa* 'that which is *sāmānya* in nature'.

2. The reason for the operation and non-operation of pumvadbhāva enjoined by the rule pumvatkarmadhārayajātī-yadeśīyeṣu (6-3-42) in the forms gomatībhutā and mahadbhūtā respectively.

Under the rule "*pratyayalope pratyayalakṣaṇam* (1-1-62) while discussing the purpose to be served by the rule, Pat refers to the word *gomatībhūtā* used in the sense of *agomatī gomatī sampannā gomatībhūtā*.[23] By virtue of the rule "*kṛbhvastiyoge sampadyakartari cviḥ*" (5-4-50) the word *gomatī* when in association with the word *bhūtā*, get the suffix *cvi* which elides wholly and the two words are compounded by the rule "*kugatiprādayaḥ*" (2-2-18) and the form *gomatībhūtā* is got. Here Kṭ says that the *pumvadbhāva* taught to a feminie base by the rule "*pumvatkarmadhārayajātīyadeśiyeṣu*" (6-3-42) does not operate on the part *gomatībhūtā*. But the rule operates on the part *mahatī* of the compound *mahadbhūtā*, formed similarly and the form *mahadbhūtā* is obtained.

Kṭ tries to explain this discrepancy on the basis of the meaning conveyed by the suffix *cvi*, namely *abhūtatadbhāva*, "the change of a thing (*prakṛti*) to a nature which it does not possess previously (*vikṛti*). The compound forms *gomatībhutā* and *mahadbhūtā* mean *agomatī gomatībhūtā* and *amahatī mahatībhūtā*. Here it can be seen that *amahatī* and *agomatī* are the originals i.e., *prakṛti* and *gomatī* and *mahatī* are *vikṛti*. The word *bhūtā* denotes *bhavanakaṛthrī* or *janikartrī* and if the *prakṛti* is treated as *janikartrī*, the word *gomatī* which is *vikṛti* cannot be treated as *samānādhikaraṇa* with the word *bhūtā* and so it does not entertain the *pumvadbhāva* prescribed to a feminine base when followed by an *uttarapada* which is *samānādhikaraṇa*, by the rule "*pumvatkarmadhārayajātīyadeśīyeṣu*". In the compounded form *mahatībhūtā* the *vikṛti* namely *mahatī* is treated as *janikarthrī* and hence being *samānādhikaraṇa* with the latter part *bhūtā* of the compound it undergoes *pumvadbhāva* and the form *mahadbhūtā* is arrived at. Kṭ adds that this alternative treatment of *prakṛti* and *vikrti* as *janikartrī* in these instances is due to the fact that sounds are eternal and cannot be discarded of one's own accord.

NBh refutes this explanation totally. He points out that it is the *prakṛti* which is always the *janikarthrī* where there is *abhūtatadbhāva* i.e., in the compound and in the *vigrahavākya*. In the compound, the words *gomatī* and mahati which are *vikṛti* denote the *prakṛti* by the expressive power of *śabdas*, known as *gauṇī*. Thus *mahatī* and *gomatī* being the *prakṛti* though of course in a secondary sense, are *samānādhikaraṇa* with *bhūtā* and hence *mahatī* gets *pumvadbhāva*. But the absence of the same in the word *gomatī* of the form *gomatībhūta*, is because that it is not *bhāṣitapuṃska* (that which can be used in masculine gender without change of meaning), to which alone subject to the satisfaction of other conditions also, *pumvadbhāva* is enjoined by the said rule. In the sentence *agomatī, gomatībhūtā*, the part *gomatī* of *agomatī*, denotes the river by name *gomatī* and the sentence means a river which was not the river by name *gomatī*, becomes the river by name *gomatī*. Here the word *gomatī* denoting the river, cannot be used in masculine gender and hence is not *bhāṣitapumska*. He adduces another argument in support of his statement that in the compound the word *mahat* though *vikṛti* is *gauṇa* in as much as it is used in the sense of *prakṛti*. The absence here of lengthening of the final element of the word *mahat* enjoined by the rule *"ānmahatassamānādhikaraṇajātīyayoḥ"* (6-3-46) shows that the word *mahat* is *gauṇa* here, otherwise, it would have undergone the lengthening. NBh thus points out that absense of *pumvadbhāva* in *gomatībhūtā* is not based on the fact that *gomati* is not *sāmānadhikaraṇa* with *bhūtā*.

3. The expression 'avyapavṛktam'.

Under the Śivasūtras *"eoṅ"* and *"aiauc"* Pat makes an assertion, *"yathā tarhi tailam na vikretavyam māmsam na vikretavyam iti vyapavṛktam ca na vikrīyate, avyapavṛktam gāvaḥ sarṣapāśca vikrīyante"*, wherein occurs the expression *avyapavṛktam.*[24] The passage means that if so when it is said that oil should not be sold, they are not sold when they are separated from the whole, but the cows and mustards wherein they are not separated are sold. Kṭ takes this expression as an *avyayībhāva* compound in the sense of *arthābhāva* prescribed by the rule *"avyayam vibhaktisamīpasamardhivyṛddhyarthābhāva...."* (2-1-6). Refuting this view of Kṭ NBh says that *avyapavṛktam* is a *tatpuruṣa* compound according to which the splitting of the compound be as *na vyapavṛktam avyapavṛktam*. Quite reasonably NBh finds that one may entertain a doubt as to how the word *avyapavṛktam* in singular number can correspond to *gāvaḥ* and *sarṣapāḥ* which are plural in number and with which it seems to have semantic relation. NBh points out that the word *avyapavṛktam* relates to *tailam* and *nāmsam* which relates to *gāvaḥ* and *sarṣapaḥ* and the former group and the latter group relate to each other in accordance with the context. NBh adds that the *nipāta nañ* does not make the *avyayibhāva* compound and this is made clear by Pat under the rule *"nañ"* (2-2-6).

4. *The component compound 'daśamyuttaram' in the whole word daśamyuttarakālam.*

While dealing with the accessory benefits accrued from the study of grammar Pat quotes a sentence from *smṛti* wherein occurs the compound *daśamyuttaram* in the whole word *daśamyuttarakālam.*[25] Kṭ splits the compound as *daśamyāḥ uttaram* saying that this compound comes under the split rule *"pañcamī"* from the rule *"pañcamī bhayena"* (2-1-37). The authority cited for this compound, namely the split rule *"pañcamī"* means, *"pañcamyanta* word compounds with any *subaantas* having semantic relation with it. Then follows the other rule *"bhayena"* wherein the word *pañcamī* is got by the process of *anuvṛtti* and it has got the usual meaning ascribed to the rule. The compound *daśamyuttaram* gets the *bahuvrīhi* compound with the word *kālam* as *daśamyuttaram kālam yasmin tat daśamyuttarakālam.*

Refuting the view of Kṭ, NBh says the part *daśamyuttaram* in *daśamyuttarakālam* is compounded by the authority of the rule *"saha supā"* (2-1-4) which means that a *subanta* is compounded with another semantically related *subanta.* Generally the justification for a compound by resorting to *yogavibhāga* is not favoured by grammarians as it implies the absence of any other regular resort for justification. Such a justification is treated as *agatikagati.* This is why, it seems, NBh resorts to the rule *"saha supā"* to justify the compound and that is a regular resort.

5. The compound "paraśśatāni".

Under the rule *"nājjhalau"* (1-1- 10) Pat cites the word *paraśśatāni*. Kṭ splits the compound as *śatāt parāṇi* and says that the two words are compounded on the authority of the word *bahulam* in the rule *kartṛkaraṇe krtā bahuḷam"* (2-1-32).[26] Refuting this opinion of Kṭ NBh says the compound can well be justified by the rule *"mayūravyamsakādayaśca"* (2-1-72) or by the rule *"saha supā"* (2-1-4). Here also NBh's effort to justify a compound on the authority of a definite rule as against resorting to the *yogavibhāga* of a word which explains the context vaguely, is evident.

6. The component compound 'padādi' in the rule "sātpadādyoḥ" (8-4-111).

Under the rule *"na lumataṅgasya"* (1-1-63) while refuting the vārttika *"uttarapadatve cāpadādividhau'* Pat gives the derivation of the compound *padādi* in *sātpadādyoḥ* (8-4-111) as *padāt ādḥ padādiḥ* instead of *padasya ādiḥ*.[27] As a result of this kind of derivation the part *padādi* means the initial letter which follows the *pada* (*padāt paraḥ ādhiḥ*). Here Kṭ tries to justify the compound *padāt ādiḥ padādiḥ* by means of the *yogavibhāga* of the rule *"pañcamī bhayena"* (2-1-37) into *pañcamī* and *bhayena* and says that the split rule *pañcamī* means a word in the ablative case gets compounded with a semantically related *subanta*.

NBh finds fault with Kṭ here. He says that in the derivation of the compound *padādiḥ* as *padāt ādiḥ* the word *padāt* is not semantically related with the word *ādi* since *padāt* relates to the sense of the word *para* and so *padāt* and *ādiḥ* not being semantically related words, they must not get compounded. The compound here is therefore to be treated *sautra* that is, a peculiarity found in the rules of Pāṇ alone.

7. The word 'praśān'.

Under the rule *"kṛnmejantaḥ"* (1-1-39) Pat makes an assertion *'ācāryapravṛttir jñāpayati na pratyayalakṣaṇenāvyayasamjñā bhavati iti' yadayam praśānśabdam svarādiṣu paṭhati"*.[28] In this passage there occurs the word *praśān*. It is formed by the addition of the suffix *kvip* to the root *śam* prefixed with the *upasarga, pra*. It gets the designation *avyaya* by the rule *"svarādinipātamavyayam"* (1-1-37). Kṭ points out that the same form can be obtained by adding the suffix *kvip* to the root *śān (śāna tejane)* prefixed by *pra*. This is also prone to get the *avyayasamjñā* since in the *svarādi* list the form *praśān* is not mentioned. But this contingency does not occur, Kṭ points out, because, the usage of the root *śān* being added with the suffix *kvip* is seen nowhere in usage and so there is no question of its being designated as *avyaya*.

Refuting Kṭ, NBh says that in the *svarādi* list, the actual form read is *praśām* and not *praśān*. The *svarādi* word *praśām* becomes *praśān* by the rule *"mo no dhātoḥ"* (8-2-64) only in the usage. Thus the *svarādi* form being *praśām*, there is no question of the form *praśān* formed from the root *śān* being designated as *avyaya*. NBh supports his argument by pointing out that in the *svarādi* list, the initial one is also read as *svar* and only in the usage we get the form *svaḥ* by the function of the rule *"kharavasānayor visarjanīyaḥ"* (8-3-15). Therefore NBh concludes that even if the form *praśān* from the root *śān* with the suffix *kvip* and prefix *pra* be accepted it does not get *avyayasamjñā* since in the *svarādi* list the form included is *praśām* and it can only by from the root *śām*.

Explanation of the Passages in the Bhāṣya

1. sūtre vyākaraṇa ṣaṣṭhyartho nopapadyate - vyakaraṇasya sūtram iti kim hi tad anyad sūtrād vyākaraṇam yasyādaḥ sūtram syād?"[29]

Beginning the discussion on the meaning of the word vyākaraṇa, Pat says that if it denotes sūtra the meaning of the sixth case in the expression *vyākaraṇasya sūtram* won't suit. He asks, "Is it then that *vyakaraṇa* which is different from sūtra, so that it may be said that this sūtra is of that?" Commenting on this passage, Kṭ says that the unsuitability of the meaning of the sixth case implying difference arises since both the words sūtra and *vyākaraṇa* are used to denote the *Aṣṭ*. He then makes a remark that if the two words sūtra and *vyākaraṇa* as used in a general and particular sense respectively i.e., the word sūtra denotes aphorisms of any science and *vyākaraṇa* denotes aphorisms of the science of grammar, the expression *vyākaraṇam sūtram* just as *puruṣo manuṣyaḥ* is possible. He then adds that if the word *vyākaraṇa* denotes the *Aṣṭ* and the word sūtra is taken as denoting a part of the *Aṣṭ*, the meaning of the genitive case suffix is quite befitting in the expression *vyākaraṇasya sūtram.*

NBh says that Kṭ takes the word sūtra to denote the part of the *Aṣṭ* on the basis of assertion of Pat, *"sūtrāṇi cāpyadhīyānaḥ iṣyate vaīyākaraṇa iti"*, where the word *sūtrāṇi* refers to the parts of the *Aṣṭ* as otherwise (if it denotes the *Aṣṭ*), the plural number in *sūtrāṇi* cannot be explained. Kṭ is therefore of opinion that though Pat has stated the meaning of the sixth case suffix does not suit in the expression *vyākaraṇasya sūtram* when the word *vyākaraṇa* denotes sūtra, the same is quite suitable in the said expression if the word *vyākaraṇa* denotes the *Aṣṭ* and sūtra denotes a part of it.

NBh refutes this view of Kṭ. He says that the part of the *Aṣṭ* too can be directly designated as *vyākaraṇa*. Even indirectly at least it shall be treated as *vyākaraṇa* since it is the part of the *Aṣṭ* which is *vyākaraṇa*. Thus both the words sūtra and *vyākaraṇa* being indicative of the same sense, the meaning of the sixth case suffix implying difference between sūtra and *vyākaraṇa* is quite unsuitable. Hence the assertion in the said passage of Pat with regard to the impropriety of the meaning of the sixth case suffix in the expression *vyākaraṇasya sūtram* is justified in every respect.

2. *"anusvāra - anusvāraśca na siddhyati dviṣantapaḥ parantapaḥ mo'nusvāro hali ityanusvāro na prāpnoti"*[30]

Under the rule *"midaco'ntyāt paraḥ"* (1-1-47) Pat discusses the question whether *mit* (that possessed of *m* as an *anubandha*) is *pūrvānta, parādi or abhakta,* in relation to that to which the *mit* is enjoined. In the quoted passage, Pat points out a difficulty in the view which holds *mit* as *abhakta* i.e., neither the final or an initial element, but as standing individually in relation to that to which it is enjoined. The passage means that *m* cannot be replaced in the words *dviṣantapaḥ* and *parantapaḥ* (where *mum* i.e., *mit* is enjoined by the rule *"dviṣatparayostāpeḥ"* (3-2-39) on the strength of the rule *"mo'nusvaraḥ"* (8-3-23) which by the *anuvṛtti* of the word *hali* from the sūtra *"hali sarveṣām"* (8-3-22) prescribes *anusvāra* as a substitute of *m* when followed by a consonant and when *m* is the final element of the *pada* and in the cited instances *m* taught by the rule *"dviṣatparayostāpeḥ"* cannot be designated as the final element of *pada,* if it stands as *abhakta.*

Here Kṭ makes the remark that in the said passage the citation of the instance *dviṣantapaḥ* by Pat is only accidental and Pat does never intend to convey that there is difficulty in getting *anusvāra* in the said instance when *m* stands as *abhakta.* This is because, Kṭ says, in the word *dviṣat* the *m* comes after the vowel *a* by the rule *"midaco'ntyātparaḥ"* (1-1-47) and since it, though be *abhakta,* thus falls within the word *dviṣat* the resultant form *dviṣamt* can be treated as *dviṣat* by the maxim *tanmadhyapatitastadgrahaṇena gṛhyate.* So the *padasamjñā* with which the form *dviṣat* is endowed, relates to the form *dviṣamt* also. In this stage the final *t* elides by the rule *"samyogāntasya lopaḥ"* (8-2-23) and the remaining form *dviṣam* is treated as *pada* by the maxim *"ekadeśavikṛtam ananyavad".* Now that *m* is the final element of the *pada,* it gets itself replaced by the *anusvāra* by the rule *"mo'nusvāraḥ"* (8-3-23). The object namely substitution of *m* by *anusvāra,* even if *m* be *abhakta* is thus achieved by the maxim *"tanmadhyapatitastadgrahaṇena gṛhyate".*

NBh refutes this assertion of Kṭ. He points out that the maxim *"tanmadhyapatitastadgrahaṇena gṛhyate'* is unknown when this is explained and the citation of the instance *dviṣantapaḥ* may be on the presupposed absence of this maxim. What NBh points out, seems to be that the interpretation of a passage in the text of *Mbh* is to be made on the strength of maxims that are already referred to by Pat and not on the basis of those that are to be mentioned later on. Pat has not mentioned the said maxim anywhere before making this assertion. Hence the citation of this instance cannot be refuted as pointed out by Kṭ, on the basis of this maxim. NBh therefore supports the statement of Pat and if *mit* be held as *abhakta* there shall be difficulty in getting the substitute of *m* by *anusvarā* in the instance like *dviṣamtapaḥ.* NBh adds that the absence of the achievement of *anusvāra* is definitely due to the treatment of *mit* as *abhakta* and not to any other maxim say for example *'asiddham bahiraṅgam antaraṅge"* by which it can be said when the letter *m* is to be substituted by *anusvāra* the *bahiraṅga* rule *"samyogāntasya lopaḥ"* (8-2-23) becomes invalid and thus *t* remaining as the final element, *m* cannot be designated as the final element of the *pada.* This maxim is not responsible for the non-achievement of *anusvāra*, since according to him, the same does not function in regard to rules that fall within the scope of *tripādi*.

3. *"na hi ke pare'ṇaḥ santi"*[31]

Under the Śivasūtra *"laṇ"* Pat says that in the rule *"keṇaḥ"* (7-4-13) the letter *ṇ* in the *pratyāhāra aṇ* relates to the mute letter of the sūtra *'laṇ'* and not with that of the sūtra *'aiuṇ'*. This is because the suffix *ka* is never, in any instance, preceded by letters like *ṛ ḷ* etc. that are additionally included if the *pratyāhāra* be with *ṇ* of the rule *"laṇ"*.

Kṭ here adduces words like *alpopānatkā* and *gīṣkā* as instances of the same negated by Pat. In these, the *t* and *s* that precedes *ka* are the substitutes of *gh* and *visarga* that have replaced *h* and *r* by the rules *"naho ghaḥ"* (8-2-34) and *"kharavasānayor-visarjanīyaḥ"* (8-3-15) respectively. The rule *"pūrvatrāsiddham"* makes the substitution by *gh* and *visarga* of *h* and *r* respectively, invalid. Thus from the point of the view of the sūtra *"kéṇaḥ"* which is in *sapādasaptādhyāyī h* and *r* are the ones, in the instances cited, that preceed the suffix and they come under the letters comprehended additionally by the *pratyāhāra* formed with *ṇ* of the Śivasūtra *'laṇ'*. In the passage quoted there is the negation of such instances by Pat. In order to justify the same, Kṭ resorts to a *yogavibhāga* in the rule *"na mu ne"*, (8-2-2) which is preceded by the rule *"pūrvatrāsiddham"* (8-2- 1). The rule is split as *na and mu ne*. The former one *'na'* prohibits the invalidity enjoined by the rule *"purvatrāsiddham"*. On the strength of this prohibition of invalidity, we treat the substitution by *gh* and *visarga* of *h* and *r* as valid from the point of the view of the rule *"keṇaḥ"*. Now the letters that preceed the suffix *ka* in *alpopānatkā* and *gīṣkā* are *gh* and *visarga* and they do not come among *ṛ ḷ* etc. Hence the statement of Pat that nowhere the suffix *ka* is preceded by letters from *ṛ* upto *l* in the Śivasūtras.

NBh refutes the justification of Kṭ on the basis of *yogavibhāga*. He points out that the *yogavibhāga* suggested by Kṭ is nowhere mentioned or referred to by Pat. The justification of a statement of Pat on the basis of a principle about which he has not made even any indication does not hold good. It is better to accept the *anabhidhāna* of such forms to justify the statement of Pat. NBh points out that the subsequent passage *"nanu cāyam asti dṛṣṭānthaḥ gokā naukā* iti" shows that such words are to be treated as not in vogue. If they were accepted in usage, they could also have been included in the said passage side by side with *goka* and *naukā* because this passage cites, instances where letters like *ṛ ḷ* etc. precede the suffix *ka*, in order to refute the former statement *"na hi ke paréṇaḥ santi"*. Moreover the statement *"na hi....santi"* with the word *pare* used in plural number points out three or more letters among *ṛ ḷ* etc. additionally comprehended by the *pratyāhāra aṇ*. Hence the refutation of this statement by the passage citing the instances *alpopānatkā gīṣkā* etc. in addition to *gokā* and *naukā* would have been more effective, as the same cites instances where many letters namely *h, r, o and au* are noticed to be preceding, the suffix *ka*. Even then they are not mentioned by Pat. Hence both these passages lead one to the conclusion that such forms are treated to be not in vogue and the statement of Pat *"na hi ke pare'ṇaḥ santi"* is fully justified.

4. *"yadi tarhi ṛkāragrahaṇe ḷkāragrahaṇam sannihitam bhavati, uran raparaḥ ḷkārasya raparatvam prāpnoti ḷkārasya laparatvam vakṣyāmi"*[32].

In this bhāṣya passage under the rule *"tulyāsyaprayatnam savarṇam"* (1-1-9) NBh refutes the explanation, of the sense of the word 'vaksyāmi', given by Kṭ. The vārttika *'ṛḷvarṇayoḥ mithaḥ savarṇyam vācyam'* treats *ṛ* and *ḷ* as cognates. Hence it is argued in the cited passage that just like *ṛ*, *ḷ* also will be replaced by *ar* on the strength of the rule *"uraṇ raparaḥ"*. Pat gives the answer *"ḷkārasya laparatvam vakṣyāmi"*. Kṭ takes the word *vakṣyāmi* to mean 'I shall interpret. In the rule *"uraṇ raparaḥ"* (1-1-31) it can be interpreted that *ḷ* is enjoined to be replaced by *al*. The interpretation is as follows. In the expression *raparaḥ* the part *ra* is a *pratyāḥara* by the rule *"ādirantyena sahetā"* (1-1-71). The letter *r* in the Śivasūtra *hayavaraṭ* is used with the *anubandha a* in the sutra *"laṇ"* (The *a* in the sutra *'laṇ'* is *anunāsika* and is therefore an *it* by the rule *"upadese janunāsika it"* (1-3-2). Hence the *pratyāhāra ra* indicates *r* and *l*. Thus the expression *raparaḥ* means *raparaḥ* and *laparaḥ*. On account of *āntaratamya ṛ* derives *ar* and *ḷ* derives *al* as their substitutes.

NBh does not admit that the *a* in the sūtra *'laṇ'* is anunāsika in which case it would have been an *'it'*. If it were *anunāsika* and consequently an *'it'* Pāṇ would have mentioned the rule *"ato lrāntasya"* (7-1-3) as *'ato rāntasya'*. The non-usage of the *rapratyāhāra* in the instance cited, shows that *a* in *laṇ* is not an *it* which implies its being devoid of nasalization. Therefore NBh points out that it is not possible to arrive at a *pratyahāra* as *ra*. Hence one cannot interpret the *laparatva* of *ḷ*. The statement of Pat *ḷkārasya laparatvam vakṣyāmi* means, says NBh, 'I make a fresh statement that *ḷ* will be replaced by *al*. Thus NBh treats the *laparatva* of *ḷ*, the result of a statement made by Pat.

5. *'Nipāta iti kimartham ? cakārātra jahārātra"*[33].

At the outset of the rule *"nipāta ekājanāṅ"* (1-1-14) we get a question and answer, "what is the need for the word *nipāta*? *cakārātra jahārātra"*. According to Kṭ this question arises thus. The word *nipāta* here should exclude *pratyaya* but, since one-vowelled *nipāta* alone has meaning, since *pratyaya* cannot be used independently, since it has no meaning, since it has its existence only through the creation of grammarians and since they are not unanimous in form, *pratyaya* will never have the designation *pragṛhya* even if the wording be *'ekājanāṇ'*. Hence there is no need of the word *nipāta* to bring the exclusion of the suffixes from the range of the pragrhyasamjñā. And the answer *cakārātra* and *jahārātra* means:- If the word *nipāta* is not mentioned in the rule, *pratyaya* (suffixes) also will come within the range of the term *pragṛhya*. This is because in the instances cited there is a one-vowelled *pratyaya* namely, *a* that has got meaning by *anvayavyatireka* (inference both in affirmative agreement and logical discontinuance) in accordance with the grammar of Pāṇ. Consequently the *a* at the end of *cakāra* and *jahāra* which is not *āṅ*, will get the designation of *pragṛhya* and consequently there will be no *dīrghasandhi* between *cakāra* and *atra* and between *jahāra* and *atra*.

Refuting this interpretation of Kṭ, NBh states that it is clear from the bhāṣya under the rule *"ot"* (1-1-15) that *nipāta* here refers to even those which have no meaning. Hence it cannot be said that this rule refers to only those which are *arthavat*. The question arises since the expression *anāṅ*, by the technical sense of *paryudāsa* of the *nañ* in it, may suggest *nipāta*. The answer is that by virtue of the mention of the word *nipāta* one can say that there is no authority in taking recourse to *paryudāsa* here. The word *nipāta* excludes pratyayas but not the imitation of pratyayas which are *nipātas* by the rule *"anukaraṇam cānitiparam"* (1-4-62). Thus the answer shows that the word *nipāta* excludes pratyayas alone and not their *anukaraṇas* even though on the strength of the maxim *prakṛtivadanukaraṇam,* they can be treated as pratyayas. These *anukaraṇas* when followed by *iti* get the *nipātasamjña* by the above mentioned rule.

NBh further refutes the instances *āgaccha (a+āgaccha)* cited by kṭ along with cakarātra and jaharātra. Kṭ means that the *a* in the instance is a suffix one vowelled and having a meaning. So the absence of the word *nipāta* may cause the *samjñā* to operate on this *a* also. *A* is the vocative singular of the base *a* formed by the addition of the suffix *ḍa* to the root *at*. NBh points out that it is difficult to agree with Kṭ. The *a* in the instances cited by Kṭ deserves *pluta* and hence there shall be *prakṛtibhāva.* The *sandhikārya* can be justified only if the non-operation of *pluta* is optional. So *āgaccha* becomes *pratyudāharaṇa* only when the *pluta* is treated as not operating here.

6. *"Athavā pratisiddharthoyam ārambhaḥ o'ṣu yātam marutaḥ"*[34]

Pat declares that the sutra *"ot"* (1-1-15) is intended to give *pragṛhyasamñjā* denied to *o* by the part *anāṅ* of the rule *"nipāta ekāj amāṅ"* (1-1-74). *o* is the *ekādeśa* of the two *nipātas āṅ* and *u*. Kṭ says that *o* is deprived of the *pragṛhyasamjñjā* only if the *nañ* in *anāṅ* is accepted in the technical sense of *prasajyapratisedha.* If the sense of *nañ* is *paryudāsa, o,* on account of the very same fact that it is *anāṅ,* gets the *samjñā* by the rule *"nipāta ekāj anāṅ"* (1-1-14). Kṭ explains that the letter *o* by virtue of the rule, *ādguṇaḥ"* (6-1-87) is an *ekādesa* of the *nipātas a* and *u,* the two *sthānin,* which are *pūrva* and *para* respectively. The rule *"ādyantavadekasmin"* (1-1-20) provides the *ekādesa* with a status by which it derives the benefit enjoyed by the *pūrvasthānin* and *parasthānin* respectively known as *pūrvantavadbhāva* and *parādivadbhāva.*

The state of affairs being much, one has to clarify the meaning of the word *anāṅ* in the rule *"nipāta ekāj anāṅ".* If *nañ* is used in the sense of *prasajyapratiṣedha* the sūtra denies the *samjñā* to *āṅ*, "*āṅ pragṛhyasamjñam na*". In the sense of *paryudāsa*, the part *anāṅ* means *āṅbhinna* which is *āṅsadṛśa* as well and the rule provides the *samjñā* directly to *āṅbhinna nipāta*. It follows therefore that if we treat the *ekādeśa* as *āṅ* by *pūrvantavadbhāva*, the prohibition enjoined to *āṅ*, applies on *o*. The sūtra *'ot'* is therefore necessary to provide the same with the *samjñā*. On the otherhand, the *ekādeśa o* can be *āṅibhinna* by virtue of the *parādivadbhāva* and the sutra in the sense of *paryudāsa* as pointed out previsously, provides the *samjñā* to *o*. Therefore the rule "*ot*" need not confer the same on it.

NBh refutes Kṭ's interpretation of the passage resorting to the *prasajyapratiṣedha* and establishes that the statement of bhāṣya well applies on *o* even when the sense of *paryudāsa* is taken into consideration. He makes clear that the sūtra *ādyantavadekasmin*, either by *pūrvantavadbhāva* or *parādivadbhāva* provides the *ekādeśa* the *śāstrīyakārya* in as much as the rule, by providing the *samjñā* to *āṅbhinna* in the sense of *paryudāsa* implies the *pragṛhyatvābhāva* to *āṅ*. In the sense of *prasajya-pratiṣedha*, the rule directly enjoins the *pragṛhyatvābhāva* to *āṅ*. Therefore in order to provide the *śāstrīyakārya* viz. *pragṛhyat-vābhāva*, the rule "*ādyantavadekasmin*" (1-1-200) operates on *o* and makes it *aṅ* by *pūrvāntavadbhāva*. Here it is to be noted that though *o* is *āṅbhinna* by its own nature, the *anitva* got by the rule "*adyantavadekasmin*", makes it ineffective or removes it. Thus the *ekādeśa o* is denied of the *pragṛhyasamjñā* by the rule "*nipāta ekājanāṅ*" irrespective of the sense of *nañ* being *paryudāsa* on *prasajyapratiṣedha* and hence the statement of Pat that the rule *'ot'* provides *o* with the same need not be interpreted as based on the sense of *prasajyapratiṣedha* alone of the *nañ* in *anāñṅ* of the rule "*nipāta ekājanāṅ*".

7. "*katham punar jñāyate sa pūrvaḥ pāṭhaḥ ayam punaḥ pāṭhaḥ iti ? tāni hi pūrvāīni, imānyavarādīni imānyapi pūrvādīni*"[35].

In the rule "*pūrvaparāvaradakṣiṇottarāparādharāṇi vyavas-thāyāmasamjñāyām*" (1-1-33), the necessity for giving the complete list of *purva para* etc. in the rule is doubted by the *pūrvapakṣin* as they are being read in the *gaṇapāṭha*. Thereupon the question arises, 'how is it then understood the fact that *gaṇapāṭha* is anterior and the *pāṭha* in the said sutra is repetition? The answer is given *"tāni hi pūrvīdīni"* (They are *pūrvadīni*), *imānyavaradīni* (These are *avarādīni*). Again a doubt arises, *"imānyapi pūrvādīni"*.

Kṭ takes the answer *'tāni hi pūrvīdīni'* to mean that those (the bases mentioned in *gaṇapāṭha*) begin with *sarva (pūrva* in *pūrvādīni* denotes *sarva* since the same being uttered formerly than *pūrva* preceeds the same), and *imānyavarādīni* means these (the bases mentioned in the rule) begin with *pūrva (avara* in *avarādīni* denotes *pūrva* since the same being uttered later than *sarva* follows the same). Thus the idea of Kṭ is that the statement *sarvādīni* in the rule *"sarvādīni sarvanāmīni"* (1-1-27) itself is a proof that *gaṇapāṭha* existed earlier. Otherwise how can Pāṇini mention a list as *sarvādi*? After interpreting the answer in this manner Kṭ explains the further doubt *"imānyapi pūrvādīni"* (these too are *pūrvādīni*) as follows. Without stating a particular reason one cannot accept the fact that *gaṇapāṭha* is anterior to *sūtrpāṭha*.

NBh clearly points out the defect underlying the explanation given by Kṭ to the said passage. The statement *'tāni hi pūrvādīni'* in the sense of *'tāni hi sarvādīni"* is of course a clear proof for the anteriority of *gaṇapāṭha*. But the statement *'imānyavarādīni'* in the sense that these are *pūrvādīni* does in any way help to establish the repetition of the *sūtrapāṭha* and this part becomes superfluous. Again according to Kṭ the statement *sarvādīni* derived from the above explanation, itself, is a sound argument for the acceptance of the said fact. Hence the further explanation "that without stating a specific reason one cannot accept the said fact" does not seem to corroborate with his previous statement. All these lead one to the conclusion that the explanation of Kṭ is not agreeable.

After refuting Kṭ thus, NBh gives the meaning of the statement *"tāni hi pūrvādīni"*. It simply means those (the bases in the *gaṇapaṭha*) are anterior and these (the bases in the *sūtrapāṭha*) are posterior. In *pūrvādīni* and *avarādīni*, the word *ādi* is used in the sense of *āśraya* just as in the statement *bhiṣmādiśca suyodhananḥ* where by the word *ādi* in the said sense, we get the meaning *bhiṣmaśrayaḥ suyodhanaḥ*. *Pūrvādīni* means *pūrvakālaśrayāṇi* and *avarādīni* means *avarakālāśrayāni*. To the question how can the fact that *gaṇapāṭha* is the former one and *sūtrapāṭha* a repetition the answer is simply given as *gaṇapātha* is posterior and *sūtrapāṭha* is anterior. Hence the doubt arises "these (too) are anterior" meaning that without giving a specific reason one cannot understand that they (bases mentioned in gaṇas are *pūrvapātha* and these mentioned in *sūtra* are *punaḥ-pāṭha* and this interpretation suits well.

8. "prayojanam hrasvatram tugvidheḥ grāmaṇikulam grāmaṇikulam senānikuḷam ityatra hravatve kṛte hrasvasya piti tuk iti tuk prāpnoti. samnipātalakṣaṇo vidhiranimittam tadvighātasya iti na doṣo bhavati.

This passage occuring under the rule *"kṛnmejantaḥ"* (1-1- 39) means, "benefit is that *hrasvatva* is *(animitta)* to *tugvidhi* as in *grāmaṇikulam* When *i* in *grāmanī* and *senāmanī* is shortened in the words *grīmaṇikulam* and *senānikulam* (by the sūtra *"iko hrasvoṅyo gālavasya"* (6-3-61) *tuk* has a chance to set in by the sūtra *"hrasvasya piti kṛti tuk"* (6-1-71), but it does not do so by the dictum *'sannipātalakṣaṇo vidhiranimittam tadvighātasya"*.

In this passage Pat states that the forms *grāmaṇikulm* and *ṣenānikulam* owes their existence to the dictum *'sannipāta...."*. Otherwise there is the contingency of *tuk* after *i* in both instances. Kṭ remarks that the *sannipātaparibhāṣā* can avert *tuk* only if *tuk* comes as a part of *i* and not of *senānī* or *grāmaṇī* and on the conception that the part of the organ is not regarded as the part of the whole comprising the organ. By the arrival of *tuk* as the *āgama* of *hrasva,* the pronximity of *pūrvapada* and *uttarapada* which was responsible for *hrasva* there will be removed. Thus owing to *sannipātavirodha* in case *tuk* arrives as the part of *i,* the *paribhāṣā "sannipālalakṣano......."* can avert *tuk.*

NBh objects to this view of Kṭ. On the arrival itself of *tuk* as the organ whether of *i* or of *senānī*, the *pūrvapada* ending in *i* will be disconnected with the *uttarapada* so also the *pūrvapada* will be devoid of its designation as *ajanta*. This much itself is the *sannipātavirodha* involved in the arrival of tuk and based on this the *paribhāṣā "sannipātalaksaṇo ...." can very well avert tuk.* Hence there is no necessity of stressing the point that *tuk* must be the augment to *i* only, for averting the same by the said paribhāsā. NBh presupposes an objection that the *tuk* as a part of *i* can be treated as *i* itself on the strength of the maxim *'yadāgamās tadguṇībhutāh tadgrahaṇena gṛhyante"* and clears the same saying that the *paribhāṣa* won't operate here on account of the *jñāpaka 'ānemuk'* (7-2-82) which points out that the *paribhāṣā* does not apply universally.[36] Therefore *tuk* always makes the *pūrvapada* devoid of the connection with the designation as *ajanta.*

Moreover the conception that the part of an organ is not the part of the *avayavin* cannot be accepted. The fingers which are the parts of the hand are treated as the organ of the arm and of the body. Again the prohibition of *guṇa* to *iṭ* which is an *avayava* of the *aṅga bhavitas* and it is to the *ik* which is the *avayava* of *aṅga* that *guṇa* is enjoined. Hence *i* devoid of the status of the *avayava* of the *aṅga* will never be eligible for *guṇa*. Hence the conception referred to above cannot be accepted. Thus the explanation of *sannipātavirodha* given by Kṭ is refuted by NBh.

Misscellaneous

In addition to the expression of his difference of opinion with Kṭ and refutations of the assertions of Kṭ, NBh has occasionally pointed out that there are certain statements in *Prdp* which are contradictory to the statements of Pat and to his own statements elsewhere. Moreover his critical mind has also dared to attempt a slight criticism even on Pāṇ and Pat.[37] We are now concerned with such statements in the *Udy*. Under the rule *"aṇudit savarnasya cāpratyayaḥ"* (1-1-69), while discussing the purpose to be derived by the word *aṇ* of the rule, Pat incidentally says that only the *śabda* which is pronounced can comprehend another and the *śabda* which is comprehended, cannot comprehend another. As an illustration he points out that if one mentions *rk* only the text is understood and not its meaning. His words are *"hrasvasampratyayād iti cet tanna kim kāraṇam? uccāryamāṇaḥ śabdaḥ sampratyāyako bhavati na pratīyamānaḥ. Tadyathā ṛgityukte sampāṭhamātram gamyate nāsyā artho gamyate"*[38] NBh points out that Kṭ has made assertions which are contradictory to this statement.

Under the rule *"igyaṇaḥ samprasāraam"* (1-1- 45), Pat begins the discussion as to which the term *samprasaraṇa* relates i.e, whether to the *vākya* or to the *varṇa*. He says *"kimiyam vākyasya samprasāraṇasamjña igyaṇaḥ ityetadvākyam samprasāraṇasamjñm bhavatīti āhosvid varṇasya.........iti".*[39] Here commenting on this Kṭ says that here the word *vākya* means *vākyārtha* and the doubt is as to whether the term relates to the *vākyārtha, yaṇaḥ igbhavati*. Kṭ continues to give an alternate explanation. The doubt is as to whether the term *samprasāraṇa* relates to the *vākya* itself. Accordingly in rules like *"syaṅaḥ samprasāraṇam......"*, (6-1-13) the term *'samprasāraṇa'* shall denote the sentence *'igyaṇaḥ' which in its turn conveys the idea'yaṇaḥ ig bhavati'*.

NBh informs us that this latter explanation given by Kṭ is contradictory to the statement of Pat referred to above. It is clear that the sentence *igyaṇaḥ* is comprehended, in rules like *"ṣyaṅaḥ......"* (6-1-13), by the word *samprasāraṇa* and hence being not pronounced it cannot convey its sense. By making such a statement, Kṭ contradicts the assertion of Pat *'uccāryamāṇaḥ śabdaḥ sampratyāyako bhavati na pratīyamānaḥ"*

Again under the rule *"saṣṭhīsthāneyogā"* (1-1-49) commenting on the bhāṣya passage, *"sampratyayamātram etad bhavati nahyanuccārya śabdam liṅgam śakyamāsaṅktum"* Kṭ remarks that by virute of *svaritatvapratijñāna* a *śabda* uttered in a rule can be inferred to be included in the latter rules also, but the *liṅgāsaṅga* (attaching a symbol) is possible only to a *śabda* which is pronounced in a rule and not to that which is inferred to be included in a rule.[40] NBh brings to our attention the fact that here also Kṭ contradicts the statement of Paṭ. If a word is inferred to be included in a rule it comes out that it is not pronounced there and as such it must not convey any sense. But Kṭ says that by virtue of *svaritatvapratijñāna* a *śabda* is inferred in latter rules to convey the desired idea. Hence this statement is also contradictory to the assertion of Pat that only a *śabda* which is pronounced can comprehend another and not that which is comprehended.

NBh adds that by virute of *svaritatvapratijñāna* the reader infers a *śabda* in the latter rule and he himself by pronouncing that *śabda* derives the idea from it. This explanation of NBh is in consistance with assertion of Pat.

Under the Śivasūtra *'hayavaraḍ Pat states that if letters are treated as arthavat,* each component letter in a base shall consequently get the *prādipadikasamjñā, suppratyaya* and *padasanjñā* and so in regard to bases like *dhanam, vanam,* etc., *lopa* of the letter *n* and the like are contingent to take effect.

Kṭ here makes the remark that though in *dhanam, vanam,* etc. each letter gets *suppratyaya* as stated above it won't be heard there since the *luk* enjoined by the rule, *"supo dhātuprātipadikayoḥ"* (2-4-71) operates on it. The component letters *dh, a,* etc. and the *samudāya, dhana vana,* etc. simultaneously get the *prātipadikasamjñā* by the rule *"arthavadadhāturapra-tyayaḥ prātipadikam"* (1-2-45). The *sup* of each component letter has fallen within the *samudāyaprātipadika* and is comprised in it. This is because of the *paribhāṣā, 'tanmadhyapatitaḥ tagdgrahaṇena gṛhyate'*. Thus in this context Kṭ treats the *sup* as the *avayava* of the *samudāyaprātipadika* and admits the operation of *luk* on it by the rule *"supo dhātuprātipadikayoḥ"* (1-2-45).

NBh draws our attention to the Kṭ's statement on the opening passage of bhāṣya on the rule *"itthambhūtalaksaṇa"* (2-3-21) where he says the *tṛtīyā* (sup) that is contingent (this contingency is brought about in the absence of the addition of the word *atatstha* in the rule *"itthambhūtalakṣaṇe")* to come after the part kamaṇḍalu of the *samāsaprāsaprātipadika kamaṇḍalupāni,* is not the *avayava* of the *samāsaprātipadika kamaṇḍalupāṇi* and so it won't elide by the rule, *"supo dhātuprātipadikayoḥ"*. The *sup* is not the *avayava* of the *prātipadika* which is *samāsa,* since only after the operation of *samāsa,* the *sup* has come into being. Hence Kṭ's statement in this context *"na ca tṛtīyāyāḥ luk prāpnoti, samāsaprātipadikānavayavatvāt tasyāḥ, kṛte samase utpādanāt"* is contradictory to the statement, *"yadaiva avayavānām prātipadika-samjñā tadaiva samudāyasyāpi. Tatra tadantargatatvāt vibhakter-lukā bhavitavyam* made under the rule *'laṇ'*. In spite of the *paribhāṣā "tanmadhya..............."* he does not accept the *sup* as the *avayava* of the *samāsaprātipadika kamaṇḍalupāṇi,* which is a *samudayaprātipadika,* whereas he accepts the same in the context cited above under the sūtra *laṇ*. The contradiction is therefore clearly evident.

However as an earnest elucidator NBh tries to justify the *luk* contingent to occur in *dhana vana* and the absence of the same in *kamandalupāni* and tries to rectify the contradiction. He corroborates the *luk* of the *sup* of the *samudāyaprītipadika* excluding that in the *samāsaprītipadika* as follows. In *dhana vana,* etc. each letter gets the *prātipadikasamjñā* which is *antaraṅga* by the rule *"arthavadadhāturapratyayaḥ prātipadikam"* and consequently a *sup* comes after each letter. After that, the *prati-*

padikasamjñā, which is bought about by virtue of *kṛdantatva* enjoined by the rule "*kṛttaddhitasamāsāśca*" (1-2-46) operates on the *samudāya* which is comprised of the *sup* also and thus the *sup* after each component letter in *dhanam vanam* etc.being the *avayava* of the *samudāyaprātipadika* is liable to the operation of *luk*. However, in words like *dhinvanti* etc. each letter even on the assumption that letters are *arthavat* individually, does not get *prātipadikasamjñā* by the prohibition *adhātuḥ* and *apratyayaḥ* denoting the exclusion of *dhātu dhātvayava, pratyaya* and *pratyayāvayava*. Hence there is no contingency of *suppratyaya* after each component letter of the *dhātu* and *pratyaya* nor does the question of their *luk* arise. In *samāsa* of course the *sup* i.e., *tritiyā* in the context does not get the *luk* since after its coming we can't give the *prātipadikasamjñā* to the *samāsa* comprised of them on any basis. Thus in *dhana vana* etc. the *sup* that comes after each component letter gets the *luk*, but in *kamaṇḍalupāṇi* the *sup* i.e., *tritiyā* does not get the *luk*.

Under the rule "*pūrvaparāvaradakṣiṇottarāparādharāni rāṇivyavasthāyāmāsamjñāyām*, Pat cites the vārttika "*avarādīnām punaḥ sutrapāṭhe gahaṇānarthakyam gaṇe paṭhitatvād*" with which the discussion as to the necessity of giving the complete list of the seven words viz. *pūrva para avara* etc. in the said rule, begins. In this vārttika the seven bases beginning with *pūrva* and mentioned in the said rule, are referred to by the term *avarādi*. Since the first one in this list of seven words, is *pūrva,* there may naturally arise the doubt as to why there are referred to as *avarādi* instead of being referred to as *pūrvādi*.

Kṭ gives an answer to this doubt. He points out that the word *ādi* in the expression *avarādīnām* is in the sense of *prakāra,* i.e., similarly and so *avarādi* means those that are similar to *avara* and not those beginning with *avara*. Since, just like the word *avara, pūrva* and *para* are mentioned in the rule all these are referred to by the expression *avarādīnām*.

NBh on the other hand says that the reference to the words *pūrva para* etc. as *avarādīnām* has got a significance.[41] He says that Kāt has purposefully refered to these words, mentioned in the order of *pūrva para avara* etc. as *avarādīnām*. This is to show that in the expression *pūrvaparāvara*............ *dharāṇi* which is a *dvandva* compound, *avara* deserves *pūrvanipāta* since the same is *ajādi*, beginning with a vowel and ending in *a* and also is *laghvakṣara* possessed of vowels termed *laghu*. The rule *"ajādyadantam"* (2-2-33) and the vārttika *laghvakṣaram pūrvam* lay down that the component of a *dvandva* compound, if be *ajādi* and *adanta* or be *laghvakṣara*, deserves *pūrvanipāta*. It is clear that among the components of the *dvandva* in the said rule, *avara* being *ajādyadanta* and *laghvakṣara* deserves *pūrvanipāta* and *pūrva* and *para* are to be mentioned only after the same, whereby the seven bases ought to have been referred to as *avaradakṣinottarāparādharapūrvaparāṇi*. But Pāṇ has referred to them as *pūrva ....dharāṇi*. Hence, NBh says that Kāt is criticising Pān for his deviation from grammatical rules. Though NBh says that by the expression *avarādīnām*, Kāt is criticising Pāṇ, it is well evident that he himself is attempting a criticism on Pāṇ here.

Even though, as a rule, NBh uses the method, of anticipation of objections and consequent clarification of the same, with a view to elucidate the text of the *Mbh*, he at times adopts the method to indicate his criticism on the relevant passage which he is elucidating. For example, an instance may be noted here. In order to refute the view that word *nimitta* is to be inserted into the rule *'kṅiti ca'* (1-1-2) so that the *ik* which is the *upadhā* (penultimate), shall come under the scope of the prohibition of *guṇa*, Pat offers four solutions. One among them is the *jñapaka* for the prohibition of *guṇa*, i.e, the prescription of *kitva* to the suffix *san*, by the rule *"halantācca"* (1-2-10). His words are *"athavācāryapravṛttirjñāpayati - bhavatyupadhālakṣaṇasya pratiṣedha - iti. yadayam trasigṛdhi ghṛṣikṣipeḥ knuḥ "iko jhal, halantācca" iti knusanau kitaukaroti"*. To the question *"katham kṛtvā Jñāpakam?"* he gives the answer *"kitkaraṇe etat prayojanam - gunaḥ katham na syāditi yadi cātra guṇapratiṣedho na syāt, kitkaraṇam anarthakam syat, Paśyati tvācaryaḥ bhavatyupadhalakṣaṇasya pratiṣedha iti tataḥ knusanau kitau karoti"*. The idea is that if the penultimate *ik* is not to be prohibited *guṇa*, by the rule *"kṅiti ca"* the prescription of *kitva* to the suffix *san*, added to *halanta* roots wherein *ik* can only be the penultinate and never be the final, becomes superfluous and thereby become the *jñāpaka* for the said fact.[42]

NBh anticipates an objection to considering the *kitva* enjoined by the rule *"halantācca"* (1-2-10) as the *jñāpaka*. He points out that the rule is never superfluous in ascribing *kitva* to *san*. It is beneficial in the case of the roots *sṛj, dṛs* and *dabh*. The roots *sṛj* and *dṛs*, can by virtue of the *kitva enjoined to san*, get the prohibtion of the augment *am* by the part *'akiti'* of the rule *"sṛjidṛśorjhalyam akiti"* (6-1-58) so that the forms *didṛkṣati* and *sisṛkṣati* are obtained. So also the root *dabh* can enjoy the elision of the letter *n* (enjoined by the rule *"aniditām...."* (6-4-24) in forms like *'dhipsati'* on the basis of the *kitva* assigned to *san* by the rule *"halantācca"* (1-2-10). The *kitva* assigned to *san* by the rule *"iko jhal"* (1-2-9) can never be the *jñāpaka*, since the scope of the rule *"iko jhal"* does not comprehend the *ik* which is *upadhā* since in the instance which are to be benefitted by the rule *ik* shall always be immediately preceded by *san*. Thus NBh objects to considering *kitva* assigned to *san* by the rule *"halantācca"* as the *jñāpaka*.

Now, follows the statement of NBh to establish the *kitva* assigned to *san* as the *jñāpaka*. If, as pointed out in the above objection *sṛj dṛś* and *dabh* only were the roots to be benefitted by the *kitva* enjoined to *san*, Pāṇ could have omitted the rule *"halantācca"* which now comes after the rule *"iko jhal* (1-2-9) and have framed the other rules in the form, *"sṛjidṛśorjhalyamakitsani" iko jhal*, and *dambeḥ* which is more simple than reading them as *"sṛjidṛśorjhalyamakiti" "iko jhal"*, *"halantācca"* and *"dambhaicca*. But Pāṇ has framed a rule in the form *halantācca* whereby he assigns *kitva* to *san* which is added to all the roots ending in *hal* (consonant) and wherein *ik* can only be the penultimate (*upadhā*). This results in the *jñāpaka* that prohibition of *guṇa* by the rule *"kṅiti ca"* (1-1-5) extends to the *ik* which is the penultimate of an *aṅga*.

NBh then adds that the prescription of *kitva* to *san* and *ktvā* added to the roots *rud vid muṣ* and the prescription of *kitva* to *ktvā* added to the roots *mṛḍ mrd, gudh, kuṣ* and *klis'*, by the rules *"ruda vidamuṣagrahisvapipracchah samsca"* (1-2-8) and *"mṛḍamrdagudhakusakliśavadavasām ktvā* (1-2-7) are the *jñāpaka* for the said fact. Thus apparently it may seem that NBh reaffirms the *jñāpaka* noted by Pat and supplements him, but when we analyse the facts mentioned by him, it is quite clear that he is criticising Pat here. Whereas Pat establishes that the *kitva* enjoined to *san* is the *jñāpaka*, since it is enjoined by the rule *"halantācca"* NBh considers that it is the framing of the rule in the form of *halantācca* instead of omitting the same along with making a simple change in the wording of the rule *"sṛjidṛsor....."* (6-1-58) that becomes the *jñāpaka*. Probably NBh is hinting that Pat has not given true attention in establishing the *jñāpaka* and that is why he adds that the *kitva* enjoined to *ktvā* and *san* by the rules referred to above, is the *jñapaka* for the prohibition of *guṇa,* to the penultimate *ik* of an *aṅga,* by the rule *"kṅiti ca"* (1-1-5)

REFERENCES

1. *Mbh* p. 86
2. *Mbh* p. 168
3. *"nābhi nabham cā"* and *"parastrī paraśu cā"* are two gaṇa-sūtras which come respectively in the gaṇas headed by the words, *śarat* and *bida,* referred to in the rules *"avyayībhāve śaratprabhṛtibhyaḥ"* (5-4-107) and *anṛṣyānantarye bidādibhyoñ"* (4-1-104)
4. *Mbh* p. 136.
5. The roots *bhid* and *chid* added with the suffix *kta,* produce the forms *bhinnam* and *chinnam.*
6. *Mbh* p. 137.
7. *Mbh* p. 144 and *Prap* p. 145.
8. *Mbh* p. 146.
9. *Mbh* Vol. I, Part II, p. 35.
10. *Mbh* p. 145.

11,12. *Udy* p.. 166-167.

13. *Prdp* p. 318.
14. *Mbh* pp. 177-178. The form *paitṛṣvaseyaḥ is derivable by the addition of the taddhita suffix ḍhak to the base pitṛṣvasṛ.* Ṛ is dropped by the rule *"ḍhakilopaḥ"* (4-1-133). In the resultant form *Pitṛṣvas+ḍha i* is substituted by *vṛddhi* and *ḍha* by *eya* on the strength of the rules *"kiti ca"* (7-2-118) and *āyaneyīnīyiyaḥ phaḍhakhajhaghām pratyayādinām"* (7-1-2).
15. In the stage *pitrsvasr+dha,* elision replaces *ṛ* and *ṛ* becomes absent and since elision is *rapara, r* comes there and thus we get the form *paitrsvasreyaḥ.* The same form is also possible if *r* replaces *ṛ by the rule "iko yaṇaci"* (6-1-77).
16. *Mbh* p. 92.
17. *Mbh* p. 274.
18. *Mbh* p. 170. *"Kim punar idam nirvartakam antaratamā anena nirvartyante, āhosvid pratipadakam anyena nirvṛttānām anena pratipattiḥ"?*

19. Mbh p. 298. "apavādaprasaṅgastu sthānivatvād. apavāde tu utsargakṛtam ca prāpnoti. Karmaṇyaṇ āto 'nuipasarge kaḥ' iti kepi anitkrtam prapnoti kim kāraṇam ? sthānivatvād.
20. *Mbh* p. 11.
21. Vide *Mahābhāṣyapradīpikā*, p. 16.
22. *Prdp* p. 107.
23. *Mbh* p. 342.
24. *Mbh* p. 83.
25. *Mbh* p. 37.
26. *Prdp* p. 160.
27. *Mbh* p. 352.
28. *Mbh* p. 228.
29. *Mbh* p. 57.
30. *Mbh* p. 260.
31. *Mbh* p. 98.
32. *Mbh* p. 152.
33. *Mbh* p. 172.
34. *Mbh* p. 175.
35. *Mbh* p. 119.
36. *Supra* p. 117.
37. Vide infra pp. 206-209.
38. Mbh p. 372
39. Mbh p. 251.
40. *Prdp* p. 263.
41. *Udy* p. 218.
42. *Mbh* p. 139.

Part Three
Observations

Chapter VIII

Some Observations

In addition to the matters dealt with in the earlier chapters, we find certain observations made by the author in the course of the work. They are dealt with here classified as conceptual, phonological and interpretational.

Conceptual

In his work, aimed at commenting on the *Mbh* and the *Prdp*, NBh has referred to certain important grammatical theories and has expressed his views on them concisely whereas they are dealt with in full detail in other works of his own.

1. Sphoṭa

NBh refers to the tradition ascribing this theory to sage Sphotāyana, mentioned as an authority by Pāṇ himself and assumes that he has arranged and expounded the *sphoṭa* theory [1]. He has referred to this theory in many places in *Udy* whereas he has dealt with the same in all its detail in his other works like *Sphoṭavāda* and *Manj*.

The term *Sphoṭa* is derived from the root *sphuṭ* which means to burst and linguistically the word means that from which the meaning bursts forth i.e, shines forth [2]. In other words *sphoṭa* is *vācaka* i.e, that which expresses a meaning and is established to be an entity manifested by letters. NBh says that the justification for the existence of *sphoṭa* and its unity, is the realization in the form, 'This is one word, this is one sentence[3]. The *sphoṭa* the word or the sentence located in the minds of the speaker and the listener and taken as an integaral symbol, is revealed by the sounds produced in a fixed order. The sounds are only the manifesting agencies and have no function other than that of revealing the woru symbol. Each sound helps in manifesting this *sphoṭa* the first one vaguely, the next one more clearly and so on, until the last one, aided by the impressions of the preceding perceptions, reveals it clearly and distinctly[4]. It is one and the same *sphoṭa* that is revealed by each one of these letters. The *sphoṭa* is one and indivisible, the sounds uttered to reveal this *sphoṭa* cannot be considered as parts of the essential word or *sphoṭa,* but only as diacritical marks to reveal the identity of the whole word.

NBh enumerates eight different varieties of the *sphoṭa*[5]. The fundamental argument in all these cases is meaningfulness *(vācakatva).* The eight sub-divisions of *sphoṭa* are 1. *Varṇasphoṭa,* 2. *Padasphoṭa* 3. *Vākyasphoṭa,* 4. *Akhandapadasphoṭa,* 5. *Akhand-avākyasphoṭa,* 6. *Varṇajātisphoṭa,* 7. *Padajātisphoṭa* 8. *Vākyajāt-isphoṭa.* Of these eight, NBh says that *Vākyasphoṭa,* (ie, *vākyajātisphoṭa* is the one accepted as the most important by the grammarians[6].

2. *Ākṛtipakṣa and Vyaktipakṣa*

The speculations in regard to the sense conveyed by a word has led the grammarians to formulate views known as *Ākṛtipakṣa* and *vyaktipakṣa.* These are also called *jātipakṣa* and *dravyavda* respecetively. NBh points out that the word *akrti* denotes both the form and the genus since both distinguish their abode from another one belonging to another group or category[7]. He also points out that the form is indicative of genus. That the form, denoted by the word *ākrti,* is also regarded to be compraisedd in the meaning conveyed by a word, is pointed out by NBh by quotting the rule of Gautma namely *jatyākṛ-tivyaktayastu padārthāh. Vyakativāda* is that the word denotes the individual. Pāṇ has accepted both the views, he has formulated the rule 5*"jatyākhyāyām ekasmin bahuvacanam anyatara- syām"* (1-2-58) on the basis of *jātipakṣa* and the rule *"saruupānāmekaśeṣa eka-vibhaktau"(1-2-64) on the basis of vyaktipakṣa.* NBh points out that these two view points are accepted by grammarians wherever they facilitate the justification of the derivation of a correct word and also ref 2utes the view of Kṭ that the maxim *"sakṛd gatau vipratiṣedhe yad bādhitamtad badhitam eva"* can be accepted only on the basis of *jātipalṣa* and the maxim *'punaḥ prasangavijñanāt siddham'* on the basis of *vyaktipakṣa* alone.[8].

3. *Śakti, the Expressive Power of a Word*

The nature of *śakti* or the exact nature of the relations existing between the word and what it denotes, form the subject matter of a hot controversy between Naiyāyikas and Vaiyākaraṇas. The traditional views of Vaiyaākaraṇas is that the relation existing between a word and the object denoted by it is one of identity-cum-difference; the distinction between language and thought is real, the identity between the two being conjured up by imagination. But NBh propounds a new theory. He asserts that the relation between the word and its corresponding concept is not one of identity-cum-difference, but one of complete identity i.e, the word and that which is denoted by it are identical in essence. Thus according to him the identity between the word and the object denoted by it is called *sakti*[9]. That is why, he says, one meets with expressions such as "the disyallabic word Rama leads to annihilation of the pride of archers", in which the identity of word Rāma and the meaning i.e, the person converyed by it, is accepted[10].

However NBh anticipates an objection. It is pointed out that as the word resides in the capacity of our mouth because our speech organ produces the transient sound, and the concept or the thing resides in the objective world outside, there is no spatial association between them and things between which there is no spatial or temporal association are never identical with one another. In reply to this possible objection NBh asserts that by word is meant that word, which is mental in construction and consequently resides in our mind in the form of eternal unit.[11] This word is that principle which is referred to by the term *sphoṭa*, a name which brings into light its dual role that it is revealed by the transient sound produced by our speech organs and delivers the meaning. By meaning also, NBh says, that thing is signified which resides in the realm of our intellect and not necessarily in the empirical world outside. He points out that words, signify things that reside in the realm of our intellect. These things may not have objective existence in the outside world of our experience. When the relation of identity is declared as existing between word and its corresponding concept, what is actually meant is this, that word which is intellectual in consruction is identified with a concept which resides in the realm of intellect. Thus as both the word and the meaning reside in the realm of intellect and consequently as spatial association is capable of being predicated of the two, NBh contends, nothing stands in the way of establishment of the relation of identity between the two. He calls this establishment of identify as *adhyāsa* and this justifies the acceptance of words like *vandhyāsuta* etc. mentioned in the verse.

"eṣa vandhyāsuto yāti khapuṣpakṛtaśekharaḥ |
kuromanūrmakṣīracaye snātaḥ śaśaṛngadhanurdharaḥ ||

as meaningful.[12] So also the questionof the pronounciation of the word 'fire' leading to a feeling of burning sensation in the tongue, or the word 'honey' leading to the enjoyment of a sweet taste, does not arise because it is always asserted that the identify between a word and its corresponding concept is only a mental construction though they are always different in the outside world.

4. The Conception "Guṇasamooho Dravyam".

NBh refers to this theory while explaining Kṭ's elucidative assertion on the Bhāṣya passage in the Paspasānhika,'"*atha gaur ityatra kaśśabdaḥ*". He points out that this theory is favoured by Pat in the rule "*tasya bhāvastvatalau*" (5-1-119). Pat has also referred to this under the rules "*striyām*" (4-1-3) and "*saṁkhyāyā avayave tayap*" (5-2-42).[13] The word *guṇa* here, denotes the organs and qualities or attributes compraising *guṇa*[14] The components and qualities make the *dravya*. Hence the *samooha* of *guṇa*s is treated as *dravya*.

Kṭ points out that several concepts appear in the mind of the hearer when one utters the word *gauḥ* and the question "*atha gaur ityatra kaśśabdaḥ*" enquires the one which among these is designated by the term *śabda*[15]. Elucidating this assertion of Kṭ, MBh says that the different concepts that appear in mind when one utters *gauḥ*, are the individuality cow, her action, her qualities, genus cow, the shape of thẹ cow and also the word made up of *g*, *au* and *visarga*. Justifying the question doubting quality action etc. to be the *sabda*, NBh says that qualities action etc. can be well treated as being denoted by the word *gauḥ*. The word *gauḥ* denotes the *dravya* which is the *samudāya* or sum-total of qualities. So when the word denotes the *samudāya* it goes without saying that it denotes the *guṇas* of which the *samudāya* is made up and hence the question doubting qualities action etc. to be the *sabda*.

5. Yoga and rūḍhi and the conception 'rūḍhir yogāpahāriṇi'.

Yoga and *rūḍhi* are the expressive powers of words on the basis of which words are grouped as *yaugika* and *rūḍha*.[16] When a word retains the signification which belongs to it according to its *etymology* it is called *yaugika* or derivative and the expressive power is known as *yoga*. The meaning of such words is determined by those of its component parts and it does not signify anything more or less other than the meanings of its parts. When a word has a meaning which is not directly connected with its derivation it is called *rūḍhi*. In this case expressive power is known as *rūḍhi*. In this case the meaning is determined by the whole word independently of the part meanings. It is generally accepted, as pointed out in the statement *rūḍhiryogāpahāriṇī*, the meaning got by *rūḍhi* is more authoritative than etymological meaning. Grammarians too admit this [17] NBh points out that though it is true that *rūḍhi* versus etymology, one has to adhere to *yoga* in certain instances and he dwells on such instances.

Under the rule *"bahugaṇavatudati saṅkhyā"* (1-2-25) Pat refers to the maxim *"kṛtrimākṛtrimayoḥ kṛtrime kāryasampratyayaḥ"* and states that one resorts to *kṛtrima* on the basis of the said maxim only because of the context or a particular sense which favours the resort to *kṛtrima*. But Pat continues, when one says 'bring *gopālaka* or 'bring *kaṭajaka*' to a man who has just come and is quite unaware of the context of the conversation; he may understand from the word *gopālaka*, the person named *gopālaka* as well as the person who protects cows (with a stick in his hand). Paṭ then adds that, it is more probable that he may understand one who protects cows[18].

Here NBh points out that the word *gopālaka* denotes the person named *gopālaka* when it is treated as the *rūḍhaśadda*; the same wod conveys the sense of a person who protects cows, when it is treated as a *yaugikaśabda*. Thus he draws our attention to the fact that it is by *rūḍhi* that the idea of the person named *gopālaka* is got and it is by *yoga* that the person who protects cows is understood from the word. Even so, Pat says that most probably the man may understand from the word, the person who protects cows. This is because of the fact that though generally *rūḍhi* versus *yoga, yoga* can supersede rūḍhi, if the former is favoured by the context[19]. The man who has just come, may entertain a doubt as to what is intended to ne conveyed by the term *gopālaka,* but so long as he isnot aware of a person named *gopālaka,* he may take by the word only that person who protects cows.

Here NBh points out that the word *gopālaka* denoted the person named *gopālaka,* when it is treated as the *rūḍha sabda,* the same word conveys the sense of a person who protect cows, when it is treated as a yaugika sabda. Thus he draws our attention to the fact that it is by *rūḍhi* that the idea of the person named *gopālaka* is got and it is by *yoga* that the person who protects cows is understood from the word. Even so, Pat says that most probably the man may understand from the word, the person who protects cows. This is because of the fact that though generally *rūḍhi* versus *yoga, yoga* can supersede *rūḍhi,* if the former is favoured by the context. The man who has just come may entertain a doubt as to what is intended to be conveyed by the term *gopālaka,* but so long as he is not aware of a person named *gopālaka,* he may take by the word only that person who protects cows. Thus NBh specifies the fact that *rūḍhi* versus *yoga* only when one is aware of the sense got by *rūḍhi* and not otherwise.[20]

Under the rule *"tulyāsyaprayatnam savarṇam"* (1-1-10) Pat says the word *āsya* in the rule does not denote the idea of the mouth, but it denotes the sense, *'asye bhavam',* the word *āsya* being derived by the addition of the suffix *yat* to the base *āsya*[21]. Here NBh points out that the word *āsya* denotes the sense of the mouth by *rūḍhi* whereas it denotes the idea *āsye bhavam* by virtue of *yoga* and thus it can be seen that here *yoga* versus *rūḍhi* quite contradictory to what is said, in the statement *rūḍhir yogāpahāriṇi*[22]. This is because of the fact that if Pāṇ intended to convey the idea of the mouth, he would, never have used the word *āsya,* he could have framed the rule as *"tulyadesaprayatnam savarṇam"* in which case, the word *deśa* will refer to mouth alone. But Pāṇ has used the word *āsya* and it is the uage of the same in the said rule that favours the denotation of the sense got by *yoga.*

6. The Dyotakatva and Vācakatva of Upasargas and Nipātas.

NBh maintains that all the nipātas are dyotakas as well as *vācakas* and the criterion which determines their *dyotakatva* and *vācakatva* is *lakṣyānurodha* i.e, accordance with the correct usage. In certain instances like *sumadrāḥ* formed as *tatpuruṣa* compound which is *uttarapadārthapradhāna,* nipātas are dyotakas and in certain instances like *sumadram* wherein the compound forming the same is *avyayībhava* which is *pūrvapdārthapradhāna,* nipatas are vācakas. This view of NBh is based on the statement of Pat under the rule *"avyayam vibhaktisamīpasamṛddhi ..."* (2-1-6), in answering to the question why *avyayībhavasamāsa* does not occur in instances like *sumadrāḥ suputraḥ* etc.[23] There it has been made clear that in *sumadrāḥ the sense of samṛddhi* is conveyed by the *uttarapada* itself viz. *madrāḥ* and the *nipāta, su* is only *dyotaka* of that sense. *Avyayībhāva* is enjoined only when the nipatas are the *vācaka* of the particular senses mentioned in the rule *"avyayam vibhaktisamipasamṛddhi ...."* (2-1-6) Thus NBh holds *"nipatānām dyotakatvam vacakatvam ca. Lakṣyānurodhād vyavastheti bhavaḥ.*

With regard to the upasargas, NBh holds that they are always dyotakas. It is clear from the statements of Pat and NBh under the rule *"gatirgatau"* (8-1-70) that a root first becomes united with a particular sense and then it gets the suffix namely *tin* or *Kṛt* denoting the different kārakas and then to indicate the sense in which the root is used the *upasargaśabda* which is the *dyotaka* of that particular sense is added to it[24]. It is on the basis of the *dyotakatva* of *nipātas,* that usages like *anubhūyate sukham, sakṣātkriyate guruḥ,* etc. wherein, the suffix is in the sense of *karman,* are obtained. If upasargas were vācakas, the root *bhū* which is *akarmaka* cannot take after it the suffix which is in the sense of *karman*[25].

7. Conception of the Four Phases of Speech

Pat refers to the Ṛg Vedic hymn *"catvāri vākparimitāni padāni .... etc.* while enumerating the benefits accrued from the study of Vyākaraṇa[26]. NBh while commenting on the words of Pat on the said hymn, speaks about the four phases of speech *(vāk)*[27]. He points out that the transition of the eternal *sphoṭa* or *sabdabrahman* from the highest level to the form of the spoken or audible word or sound at the lowest level is described as occuring in four stages technically known as *parā, paśyantī, madhyamā* and *vaikharī, Parā* is too subtle to be comprehended. *Pasyanti* also is too subtle to be comprehended except by the yogins. *Madhyamā* stage may be comprehended through practice like *japa* while the *vaikharī* is what is uttered by vocal organs, and is capable of being head by ordinary people[28]. *Parā* is the eternal *sabdabrahman.* This also is referred to as *nāda.* The phases of speech are also referred as *trayī*, says NBh[29]. Both *Parā* and *Pasyantī* are classed as *sūkṣmasphoṭa* (subtle). *Madhyamā* is referred to as *āntara sphoṭa* (internal). *Vaikharī* is manifested as *bāhya* (external) *sphoṭa* by vocal organs and is capable of being heard by others.

8. Yadṛcchaśabdas

Yadṛcchāsabdas form one group among the four categories of standard sounds spoken by Pat under the Śivasūtra *"ṛḷk"*. Based on the *pravṛttinimitta* or connotation of words which are categorized as universal *(sāmānya* or *jāti)*, quality *(guna)*, action *(kriyā)* and the substance *(dravya)* there are four divisions of sounds namely *jātisabda, guṇasabda, kriyāsabda* and *samjñāsabda.* The fourth category, *samjñāsabda* or proper names are sounds liked *evadatta, ditha,* etc. The essential difference between the proper names and the three other categoreis is that while the usage of the latter is conditioned by the objectivity of one of these three attributes, namely universal, quality, and action, there is no conditioning factor, the absence or the presence of which can prevent or promote the uisage of what are known as proper names. It is because of this that the proper names have been significantly styled as yadṛcchāsabdas (words coined at random or words of casual utterance). Hence NBh remarks

- *evañca svecchayā ekasyām vyaktau saṅketyamānaḥ śabdo yadṛcchāsabda ityuktam*[30].

NBh also points out that the imitatory sounds (anukaraṇasabdas) are treated as jātisabdas by Kṭ. This is because the imitatory sounds indicate sounds which are anukāryas and in which universal or *jāti* is always present. The *anukārya śabda* possessed of the universal is indicated by the *anukaraṇaśbda* and this is the basis of Kṭ's assertion. But, NBh says that certain other scholars consider anukaraṇasabdas as yadṛcchāsabdas since these imitatory sounds are used according to the will of the speaker to denote a particular sound[31].

NBh brings home to our mind that though there is thus a fourth variety of sounds known as yadṛcchaśabdas, only those which are used by śiṣṭas (the learned men) and are in keeping with grammatical rules are accepted as yadṛcchāśabdas or proper names and not all of them as such. That is why Pat refutes the enunciation, of the letter ḷ in the Śivasūtras, which is meant for bringing *ackārya* i.e, vowel operation in regard to yadṛcchāśabdas. By this, NBh says, Pat means that sounds like *ḷtaka* being not used by śiṣṭas need not be accepted[32].

9. The Conceptions "Udbhūtāvayavabhedaḥ Samudāyaḥ" and 'Avayavavayavaḥ Samudāyāayavaḥ'.

Dealing with the *samudāya* and *avayava*, NBh elucidates in *Udy* the two conceptions, *'udbhūtavayavabhedaḥ samudāyaḥ'* and *avayavāvayavaḥ samudāyavayavaḥ*. In the *Mbh* under the rule *"uraṇ raparaḥ"* (1-1-51), the *pūrvapakṣin* argues that the *raparatva* enjoined to the *aṇ* also which substitutes *ṛ* and another letter and is called *ekādeśa*. Pat points out that there is no necessity of the extension of *raparatva* to the *ekadeśa aṇ* also since the *aṇ* which replaces the *samudāya* constituted of *ṛ* and another letter can well be treated as the substitute of the part of that *samudāya*, i.e, *ṛ*. He illustrates the same saying that when it is said *"māṣa"* shall not be eaten the substance which is mixed with *māṣa* also is not consumed[33]. Kṛ says that *ekādeśa* is enjoined in the place of the two sthānins, the *pūrva* and the *para* by the rule *"ekaḥ pūrvaparayoḥ"* (6-1-84) which denotes *udbhūtāvayavabhedaḥ samudāyaḥ*.

NBh elucidates the conception *'udbhūtāvayabhedaḥ samudāyaḥ'*. In the rule *"ekaḥ pūrvaparaypḥ"* (6-1-84) the *samūdaya* is mentioned as identical with the avayavas. The *samudāya* constituted of the *pūrva* and *para sthānin* is denoted by *pūrvaparayoḥ* which is an expression by the *itaretarayogadvandva* compound in dual number. Otherwise, if the *samudāya* was not treated as identical with the avayavas, the expression ought to be *pūrvaparasya* which is formed as a *samaharadvandva* compound. This treatement of the *samudāya* as identical with the avayavas is what is known as *udbhūtavayavabhedaḥ samudāyaḥ*. Therefore the *ekādeśa aṇ* replacing the *pūrva* and *parasthānin* i.e, *ṛ* and another letter, can well be treated as the substitute of *ṛ* also.

With regard to the conception *"avayavāvayavaḥ samudāyāvayavaḥ"* which means the part of an organ of a *samudāya* is the part of the *samudāya* itself, NBh says that the treatment of the part of an organ as the part of the *samudaya* can be accepted only when the organ along with that part can be pointed out as possessed of the *dharma* which was there on the organ of the *samudāya*[34]. This is just like considering fingers as the part of the body, since the hand which is the organ of the body can be treated as the organ of the body when the hand is possessed of fingers. Similarly in grammar also when an augment is enjoined to the *arthavatśabda* i.e, the *vikaraṇa* suffix *tās(i)*, the augment too can be treated as the *avayava* of the *aṅga* of the suffix *ḍa* in the instance *bhū+itas+(ḍ)a* of the verb *bhavitā*. This is because the suffix *tās* which is *arthavat* and part of the *aṅga*, can be treated as an *arthavat* part of the *aṅga* when the same *(tās)* is combined with the augment *iṭ* i.e, when it becomes *itās*. Therefore *i* too is being treated as *avayava* of the *aṅga* and that is why Pāṇ frames the rule *"dīdhīvevītām"* (1-1-6) wherein the augument is prohibited of the *gunaṛddhī* which replaces the *ik* which is *aṅgāvayava*. NBh continues saying that under the rule *"alontyasya"* (1-1-52), Pat says that the genitive case which is in the sense of *sthāne* alone is the basis for the function of the rule *"alontyasya"* (1-1-52).

If all the genitive cases, irrespective of their meaning is subjected to the rule *"alontyasya"* there is the contingency of all augments i.e, *tit*, *kit* and *mit*, to be the *avayava* of the final letter[35]. *'arthavata āgamastadguṇībhutaḥ tadgrahaṇena gṛhyate'* cannot function. NBh adds that at such a contingency of the augment, occuring as the part of the final letter, cannot be treated as the *avayava* of the whole *samudāya*. This is because the *dharma* on the final letter cannot be said to be existing on the same when it is combined with the augment. That is why NBh says, Pat points out that if the rule *"alontyasya"* (1-1-52) function on all genitive cases it will cause an undersirable contingency.

Phonological

Certain phonological observations are made by NBh while commenting on the *Mbh* and *Prdp* under the rule *"tulyāsyaprayatnam savarṇam"* (1-1-9). They mainly relate to *sthāna* and *prayatna*.

1. *The Nose as the Place of Articulation (sthāna)*

Indian grammarians classify sounds mainly from two points of view, viz. 1. the place of articulation and 2. the mode or process of articulation. The place of articulation is known as *sthāna*. However an important terminological distinction underlying a large number of the ancient descriptions is that of *sthāna* and *karaṇa* (literally meaning place and organ) which generally speaking denote the passive and active organs of articulation. The terms closely correspond to the point of articulation and articulator[36]

To apply the system of specifications of *sthāna* to the feature of nasality leads to confusion, the nose being stated by some treatises to be the articulator and by others the point of articulation. NBh maintains that nose is the *sthāna* i.e, place or point of articulation. His opinion in regard to the question of considering the nose as the *sthāna* within the buccal vavity or external to it, as also the question of considering the nose as the *sthāna* for all the nasal sounds, is noteworthy.

Kṭ maintains that the *nāsikā* is not a *sthāna* outside the buccal cavity. He considers nose as the line connected with the inner skin which lies spread within the buccal cavity and by the striking of the breath stream there, a nasal sound is produced[37]. NBh maintains that in regard to the production of sounds, nose is considered to be a *sthāna* outside the buccal cavity. The rule *"mukhanāsikāvacanonunāsikaḥ"* (1-1-8) itself proves the same.

Pat gives the splitting of the part *mukhanāsikā* in the word *mukhanāsikāvacanaḥ*, as *mukham ca nāsikā ca* and also as *mukhadvitiyā nāsikā*. NBh points out that if the nose is treated as a *sthāna* within the buccal cavity, Pat could never have split the word as pointed out above, since such a derivation does not suit to a compound formed of two sounds denoting the part *(avayava)* and the whole *(avayavin)*. In compounds like *sahasto (devadattaḥ)* the *purvapada saha* is used in the sense of the word *vidyamānaḥ*. This is because *devadatta* being the *avayavin* and *hasta* being the *avayava*, the derivation of the word *sahastaḥ* with *saha* in the usual sense of *sahita* is not correct and hence is split *saha* (vidyamānaḥ) hasto yasya saḥ.

Moreover under the rule *"mukhanāsikāvacanonunāsikaḥ"* Pat says *"mukhavacanonunāsika itīyatyucyamāne kacaṭatapānāmeva prasajyaeta"* meaning if the wording of the rule be in the form *mukhavacano'nunāsikaḥ*, the term shall extend only to the sound *k, c, ṭ, t* and *p* which are *mukhavacana*[38]. NBh points out that if nose is treated as a *sthāna* within the buccal cavity yama sounds and consonant nasals like *ṅ, ñ, ṇ, n* and *m* can also be described as *mukhavacana* and so the word *eva* used by Pat in the cited passage, with the intention of excluding *yama* and consonant nasal sounds, would be of no avail.

He adds that the *prāsādavāsinyāya* resorted to by Pat to refute the part *mukha* in the rule *"mukhanāsikāvacano'nunāsikaḥ"* also implies the fact that nose is never considered as a *sthāna* within the buccal cavity. On the strength of the *prāsādavāsinyāya* Pat refutes the part *mukha* in the expression *mukhanāsikāvacanaḥ* since even in the wording *nāsikāvacanaḥ* the term shall extend to those sounds that are purely *nāsikāvacana* and also to those sounds which are *mukhanāsikāvacanaḥ*. This implies that the *nose* is not the *sthāna* within the buccal cavity, and if it were so, Pat could not say that even in the wording *nāsikāvacana*, the term shall extend to those that are *mukhanāsikāvacana*.

In the opinion of Kṭ who maintains that nose is the *sthāna* within the buccal cavity, NBh reminds us that the part *mukha* in mukhanāsikāvacanaḥ is to be taken as denoting the sense, *mukhāvayava* by which, on the basis of *brāhmaṇavasiṣṭhanyāya*, all the organs, within the buccal cavity, except the nose is to be comprehended and the word *eva* in the cited passage is to be understood in the sense of the *nipata, api*.

In regard to treating the nose as the *sthāna,* he points out that in regard to the vowel sounds, nose is never a *sthāna* for them, since the distinction of breath stream as any vowel sound is made by means of the respective *sthāna* namkely *kaṇṭha tālu,* etc. and the nose gives only a colouring i.e, *raga* to the vowels. But with regard to the consonants *ṅ, ñ, ṇ, n* and *m* nose is also the *sthāna* for them since they cannot be produced by one alone, i.e, not merely by *kaṇṭha tālu* etc. or not merely by the nose[39]

2. Yāvatsthānasāmya (idendity of the place (s) of articulation) a Deciding Factor of Cognateness

The rule *"tulyāsyaprayatnam savarṇam"* (1-1-9) points out identity of place of articulation within the buccal cavity as the deciding factor of homogeneity *(sāvarṇya)* between sounds. In this regard NBh furnishes an additional information that in order to secure cognetness of two sounds one has to ascertain whether the sounds in question have identity with regard to the place(s) of articulation[40]. For instance the sound *v* which has *danta* as *sthāna* is never a cognate of the sound *l* which has the same *sthāna* because *v* is produced jointly by the two places of articulation namely *danta* and *oṣṭha* and *v* and *l* thus lack *yāvatsthānasāmya,* identiy of all the places of articulation. NBh states that this fact has been indicated by Pāṇ by the expression *tadvān* in the rule *"tadvānāsāmupadhānō mantra ..." (4-4-125). If l* and *v* were regarded as cognates the rule *"torli"* (8-4-60) enjoining *parasavarṇa* on the precedance of *l,* ought to have operated here since, *v* is also to be comprehended by the letter *l* mentioned in the rule as *'li'* and the absence of the same points out that *v* is never a cognate of *l* which shows that *yāvatsthānasāmya* is the deciding factor of cognateness. He adds that it is with this idea in his mind that Pat refutes the assertion of cognateness between the sounds *ai* and *au.* The contingency is brought about by the fact that these *ai* and *au* have identity of the process of articulation. Pointing out that they have no identity of place of articulation in as much as one i.e, *ai* has the *sthāna (s)kaṇṭha* and *tālu* and the other i.e, *au* has the sthāna (s) namely *kaṇṭha* and *oṣṭha* Pat states *"naitau tulyasthānau".* Here it is to be remembered that *ai* and *au* have one identical place of articulation, i.e, *kaṇṭha.* Even then the negation of the identity of place of articulation by Pat shows that identity of all the places of articulation, is the deciding factor of cognateness says NBh.

3. Prayatna, the Process of Articulation.

The basic articulatory processes named *prayatna* are divided into two main types, *ābhyantara,* internal and *bāhya,* external. The first type comprises processes occuring within the buccal cavity (intra-buccal). The sūtra *"tulyāsyaprayatnam savarṇam"* (1-1-9) which lays down conditions for determining the homogeneity *(sāvarṇya)* between two sounds, speaks of identity of the articulatory processes within the buccal cavity. These intra- buccal processes namely *spṛṣṭa, īṣatspṛṣṭa vivṛta saṃvṛta* are therefore the primary efferts in the determination of *sāvarṇya.* Their function is mainly articulatory and NBh points out why they are called *ābhyantara* and are named *spṛṣṭa,* etc.*"āsyāntargatatattatsthāneṣu jihvāgrādīnām varṇābhivyaktijanakasparśadūrā vasthānasamipāvasthānarūpābhyantarakāryyakāriprayatnaviśeṣa etaiḥ padairucyante. teṣām cāsyavṛttitvam āsyāntargatatattatsthāneṣu vāyusamyogajanakatveneti bodhyam.*[41]

The other class of efforts whose function is mainly acoustic gives to each sound in the alphabet its distinctiveness. These are called *bāhya* or external in that they occur outside the buccal cavity mostly in the larynx, the term *ābhyantara* and *bāhya* being used with reference to the mouth within and without. NBh making this clear says "tatra ye tattasthānābhighātakā yatnāste āsyantargatatattatkāryakāritvād āsye prayatmā' 4ityucyante' ābhyantarāḥ iti prārambhaḥ iti ca. galavivaravikāsadikarāścāsyabahirbhūtadeśe kāryakaratvād bāhyā iti.[42] Bāhyaprayatnas are secondary in the sense that although for deciding sāvarṇya they are not necessary, they are taken into consideration when the ābhyantarapraytnas by themselves are unable to serve the purpose of determining the nearest equivalent *(āntaratamyaparīkaṣā).*

Interpretational

In the course of the work NBh incidentally gives his views in regard to the interpretation of certain rules and makes mention of certain nyayas or maxims in order to interpret the *Mbh* and the *Prdp.*

He also resorts to the technical device knows as *anabhidhāna* to justify or contradict the forms which in spite of any kind of interpretation, fall outside the scope of the grammatical rules. Observations of NBh in this regard are now dealt with.

1. The Nipāta, ca, in the Rule "Karmaṇi ca" (2-2-14)

NBh points out that the *nipāta, ca* in this rule is to be interpreted in the sense of the *nipāta iti*.[43] The rule which prohibits *ṣaṣṭhīsamāsa* means that the word ending in the genitive case which is sanctioned by a rule possessed of the word *'karmaṇi'* does not get compounded with other semantically related words. By taking the *nipāta,ca* of the rule to be in the sense of *iti*, the rule arrives at the sense *karmaṇi iti sabdamuccārya vihitā ṣaṣṭhī na samasyate'* and hence the above said idea is got. The prohibition of *samāsa* enjoined by this rule relates to instances where the genitive is sanctioned by the rule *"ubhayaprāptau karmaṇi"* (2-3-66) and not to instances where the genitive case is sanctioned by the rule *"kartṛkarmaṇoḥ kṛti"* (2-3-65). If the *nipāta ca* is not taken in the sense of *iti*, the rule may mean that words ending in genitive case which is in the sense of *karman* does not get compounded. As a result, it may not be easy to get the compound *sabdhānusasanam* wherein the genitive case in *sabdānām* is enjoined in the sense of *karman* by the rule *"kartṛkarmaṇoḥ kṛti"* (2-3-65). But the compound is got since as pointed out above the prohibition relates to the genitive case sanctioned by the rule *"ubhayaprāptau karmaṇti"* 2-3-66) which alone is possessed of the word *karmaṇi*.

2. The Anuvṛtti of the Nipāta ca in the Rule "Samjnāyām", (2-1-44).

Under the rule *"īdūtau ca saptamyarthe"* (1-1-19) Pat refers to the compounds *vāpyasvaḥ* and *nadyātiḥ* and gives the *vigraha* as *vāpyām aśvaḥ* and *nadyām ātiḥ* in the sentence *"athavā pūrvapadasya mābhūdityevamarthaṃ arthagrahaṇam. vāpyām asvaḥ vāpyaśvaḥ, nadyām ātiḥ nadyātiḥ"*[44] The compound *vāpyaśvaḥ* and the like is formed by the rule *"samjnāyām"* (2-1-44(which means words ending in locative case get compounded with other semantically related *subanta* forms to denote a proper name. As the rule *samjnāyām"* enjoins the formation of the compound only when the compounded word is a proper name, it comes out that the *samāsa* enjoined by the rule is a *nityasamāsa* which is defined *asvapadavigraha;* since the componets used without composition are in the form of a sentence and cannot be a proper name. Hence a doubt is quite relevant here as to the propriety of using the components of the compound, without composition as *vāpyām asvaḥ*. NBh clears this doubt says that it is to be admitted that the compound enjoined by the rule is similar to the *nityasamāsa* since the componets used without composition i.e, *vāpayạm asvaḥ* is not a proper name. But as there is the *anuvṛtti* of the word *vā* from the rule *"pāremadhya ṣaṣṭhyā vā"* (2-1-18) to the rule *"samjnāyām"* (2-1-44) the components of the compound can however be used without composition. Hence Pat gives the *vigrahavākya, vāpym aśvaḥ and nadyām ātiḥ*. NBh adds that one thing to be borne in mind is that the compound abtained by this rule, *"vāpyaśvaḥ"* and the like are rūḍhisabdas and the meaning of the componets in no way is conveyed by the compound expression. The *vigrahavākya* i.e, *vāpyām aśvaḥ* is given only to point out the derivation of the compound.. The word *rathantara* which is the name of a particular hymn, is given the *vigrahavākya, rathena tarati* and it is quite obvious that this sense of the compounds does not relate in any way to the *ṛk* (hymn) which is named *rathantara.* Therefore, such samāsas illustrate *jahatsvārthā vṛttiḥ* whereby a word denotes a particular sense neglecting the sense conveyed by the components. He concludes saying that that is why, learned men say *"jahatsvārthā tu tatravia yatra rūḍhir virodhinī"* which means that the particular expressive power of words. known as *jahatsvārthā vṛttiḥ* is accepted with regard to those words wherein the sense got by *rūḍhi* contradicts the sense delivered by the componets. In *jahatsvārthā vṛttiḥ* the components become devoid of their individual meaning and the word as a whole denotes quite a different idea.

3. The idea behind the rule enjoining Luk

Under the rule *"kṅiti ça"* (1-1-5) in the passage *'naitāni santi prayojanāni iha tāvad hato hataḥ iti prasaktasyābhinirvṛttasya pratiṣedhena nivṛttiḥ śakyā kartum atra ca dhātūpadesāvasthāyāmevākāraḥ"* Pat refutes the assertion of the *pūrvapakṣin* that the insertion of the word *nimitta* in the rule *"kṅiti ca "* (1-1-5) brings the benefit of retaining of the vowel *a* in the forms *hataḥ hathaḥ* etc. where *a* having the designation *guṇa* is contingent to be removed by the rule *kṅiti ca* if read without the insertion of the word *nimitta*[45] What Pat means is that the rule *"kṅiti ca"*, which prohibits *guṇa* and *vṛddhi* cannot remove the *a* in *hataḥ* and *hathaḥ*. This is because a rule involving *pratiṣedha* can prohibit anything only at a stage when it is contingent to operate and has not yet functioned. Hence Pat points out that the rule cannot avert the *a* in said instance since they are already there and are not at a stage of being contigent to operate.

Here Kt makes the remarks that though the rule *"adiprabhṛtibhyaḥ śapaḥ"* (2-4-72) enjoins the elision which results in the prohibition of *śap* at a stage when it has functioned, yet the same is accepted since there is no other go. In the formation of the form *hataḥ*, the root *han* takes *laṭ* after it and is substituted by the *parasmaipada* termination tas after it. The rule *"kartari sap"* (3-1-68) provides the suffix *sap* to the root and we reach a state *han+(s)a(p)+tas*. Now the *a* of *sap* is removed by the rule *"adiprabhṛtibhyaḥ sapaḥ"* (2-4-72) and it is in regard to this instance that Kṭ makes the above remark.

NBh here brings out the idea behind the rule enjoining *luk* and thus explains the apparent exception pointed by Kṭ to the statement of Pat. He points out that the rule which enjoins *luk* to the suffix *sap* informs us that there is no necessity of the addition of the suffix *sap* to the roots and the like. Hence it can be stated that when the suffix *śap*, by virtue of the rule *"kartari sap"* (3-1-68) is contingent to operate at the stage *han+tas*, and has not yet taken effect, the rule *"adiprabhṛtibhyaḥ sapaḥ"* (2-4-72) prohibits the same. The prohibition is quite normal here since it is made in regard to a suffix which is only contigent to operate and has not yet taken effect.

Nyayās

To achieve the purpose of the elucidation of the *Mbh* and the *Prdp* NBh makes the application of suitable nyayās. He has made use of a number of nyayās and they are *cchatrinyāya bhraṣṭṭāvasaranyāya, rājapurapravesanyāya, gobalīvardanyāya, tuṣyatudurjannanyāya vicītaraṅganyāya, kadambamukuḷanyāya, kṛtvācintānyāya etc., and nyāyas in the form of tadabhinnābhinnasya tadabhinnatvam, bahūnāmanugraho nyāyyaḥ, āgantunām ante niveśah, vṛscikabhiyā palāyamanasya āsiviṣamukhe vinipātaḥ, prakṣalanaddhi paṅkasya dūradasparśanam varam*, etc.[46] A few nyāyas among these are now dealt with.

1. *Chatrinyāya*

While examing the necessity of the word *ikaḥ* in the rule *"iko guṇavṛddhī"* (1-1-3), the objector points out three resources which help in preventing *akāra*, consonants and dipthongs from being substituted by *guṇa* in spite of the absence of the word *ikaḥ* in the rule. Among those three, one is the *upadeśasāmarthya* of the dipthongs and the other two are jnāpakas, viz, the *ḍiktaraṇa* and *kitkaraṇa* of a suffixes enjoined by the rules*"āto'nupasarge kaḥ"* (3-2-3) and *"saptamyām janerḍaḥ"* (3-2-97). In the statement of *siddhantyekadesin "naitani santi jñāpakāni"* all these three are referred to as Jnāpakas[47] The plural in *jñāpakāni* cannot correspond to these three as one of them i.e, the *upadeśasāmarthyya* is only a grammatical tecchnique and not a *jñāpaka*. This inaccuracy is elucidated by NBh by the mere mention of the fact that this statement is in accordance with *cchatrinyāya*. this *nyāya* derives its origin from the statement *cchatriṇo yānti* to designate a grroup of people among whom some alone have umbrellas. It means that all those who pass by belong to one and the same mercandile group. So also as the *upadeśasāmarthya* as well as the two jnāpakas bring forth the one and same benefit of pointing out the non-essentiality of the word *ikaḥ* in the rule *ikoguṇavṛddhī"* (1-1-3) all these three are designated as jnāpakas in the statement *"naitani santi jñāpakāni"*.

2. *Bhraṣṭāvasaranyaya:*

Under the rule *"iko guṇavṛddhī"* (1-1-3) there is a question "is there another place where the general rule does not operate when there is an exception". The answer is given that "asti ityāha sujāte aśvasūnrte adhvaryo odribhiḥ sutam śukram te anyat iti. pūrvarūepe pratiṣiddhe ayādayopi na bhavanti.[48] In the instance like *sujāte aśvasūnṛte* when a dipthong is followed by the vowel, *pūrvarūpa* the *apavāda* of the rule *"ecoyavāyāvaḥ"* (6-1-78) is prohibited by the rule *"nāntaḥ pādamayapare"* (6-1-115) and there the rule *"ecoyavāyāvaḥ"* too does not operate. Here NBh says *"bhraṣṭāvasaranyāyeneti bhāvaḥ"*. The *nyāya* is *"yasyavasaro bhrastaḥ tanna"* or *"bhrastāvasaro na pravartate"* according to which something does not take place when the occasion for the taking place of it, has once gone by. NBh means that in the said instance first of all the rule *"ecoyavāyāvaḥ"* is contingent to operate but this contingentcy is warded off by its *apavāda* rule, *"enaḥ padāntād ati"* (6-1-109) which teachers *pūrvarūpa*. Thus the chance of operation being once warded off, the rule, *"ecoyavāyāvaḥ"* (6-1-18) does nto operate and this non-operation is in accordance with what is known as *bhraṣṭāvasaranyāya*. It may be noted here that this statement is pointed out to be the assertion of *siddhyāntyekadesin* and therefore NBh point out that *nyāya* is not resorted to in the science of grammar.[49]

3. *Rājapurapraveśanyāya*

Under the rule *"na padānta...."* (1-1-58) refuting the argument that a separate statement i.e, *"svaradīrghayalopeṣu lopādeśo na sthānivat"* is to be made with regard to the said rule, Pat says that the desired idea intented to be conveyed by making a fresh statement can already be got by connecting semantically the words *lōpa, ādeśa, vidhi,svara, dirgha* and *yalopa* among which the word *ādeśa* is got by *anuvṛtti* and others are mentioned in the rule itself. The fact that these are not mentioned in the rule in the order by which this semantical relation is derived, does never obstruct the desired judgemental cognition in anyway.[50] He then decisively asserts that the required judgemental cognitiion is possible even though there be lack of contiguity *(anupūrvya)* with reference to the words denoting concepts that are intended to be semantically related, provided there be the element of syntactical expectancy *(yogyatā)*. As an example he refers to the apparently enigmatic group of words saying - *"anānupūrvyeṇāpi sanniviṣṭānām yatheṣṭam abhisambadho bhavati tadyathā - anaḍvāham* (the bull) *udahāri* (carrying water) *yā* (who) *tvam* (thou) *harasi* (carriest) *kumbham* (the pitcher) *bhagini* (oh sister) *sācīnam* (crookedly) *abhidhāvantam* running) *adrākṣīḥ* (hast see). Here the intended relational idea i.e, 'O thou sister who carriest upon thy head a pitch of water, hast thou seen a bull running crokkedly ? - is cognised even though the terms are used haphazardly without any heed to the element of contiguity *(ānupūrvya)* that their interdependence demands. Commenting on this passage Kṭ refers to the parellel dictum *pāṭhakramād arthakramo baatiyān'*. In further elucidating this NBh cites the maxim known as *rājapurapraveśanyāya* i.e, the similie of the manner of entering a royal city.[51] Just as a mob, when it is about to enter royal city through a narrow gate-way must arrange itself into a regular file in an orderly fashion, so two concepts even though expressed by words jumbled up together without any heed as to their syntactical contiguity, of necessity relate themselves with one another according to their inherrent expectancy before they can form into a self-relational judgement.[52]

Anabhidhana

Anabhidhāna is a technical device adopted by the Sanskrit grammarians to account for the absence of certain undersired forms which are otherwise contingent by the grammatical rulers and contradict certain uniformly accepted and established theories or form an obstruction to drawing certain conclusions. NBh has freely made use of this device while interpreting the passages of the *Mbh*, establishing certain jnāpakas and justifying the assertions of Kṭ[53]

We may notice the same below.

1. The locative forms yayī papī etc.

Under the rule *"īdūtau ca saptamyarthe"* (1-1-18) Pat discusses the purpose served by the word *artha*. It is pointed out that even in the absence of the word *artha* the Vedic locative forms like *gaurī* wherein the locative suffix has dropped obtain the designation. He says *"evam tarhi āhāyam", īdūtau saptamīti. Na cāsti saptamī īdūtau, tatra vacanād bhaviṣyati"*.[54] The passage means that on the authority of the rule with the wording *"īdūtau saptammī"* which provide the designation to a locative forms ending in *ī* or *ū* is available nowhere, the designation shall extend to forms like *gaurī* and *tanū* where the locative suffix has been dropped .

Here a doubt may arise. There are locative forms ending in *ī* or *ū* for example *yayī* and *papī*. These two are derived by the addition of the suffix *ṅī* to bases *yayī* and *papī* which are endowed with *nadīsanjñā*. In the resultant forms *yayī+ī* and *papī+ī* the locative suffix does not get elided but *pūrvasavarṇadīrgha* replaces *ī+ī* on the strength of the rule "*supām sulukpūrvasavṇā.....*" (7-1-39) and we arrive at the forms *yayī* and *papī* which are locative forms ending in *ī*. So the doubt as to how can the form *gaurī* wherein the locative suffix has dropped, get the designation? Thus it is clear that these forms contradict the assertion of Pat "*na cāsti spatamī īdūtau tatra vacanād bhaviṣyati*".

To avert the discrepency, scholars like Narāyaṇa assumes that what Pat meant by the statement "*tatra vacanād bhaviṣyati*" is that even by framing rules in the manner i.e., "*īdūt saptamī*", "*adasaḥ*" and "*ecca advivacanam*" instead of "*īdūded dvivacanam pragṛhyam*", "*adasco māt*" and "*īdūtau ca saptamyarthe*", all the desired forms can be provided with *pragṛhya samjñā*[55] Hence the reading of the rule as *īdūtau saptamī* as separate from *īdūdeddvicanam pragṛhyam*, which involves great effort , it can be understood that the designation defined by the rule "*īdūtau saptammī*", devoid of the word *artha* extends to gaurī, etc. where the locative suffix has been got elided.

Here NBh points out that Pat has stated that there are no locative forms ending in *ī* or *ū* and the existence of forms *yayī* and *papī* contradict this assertion. Hence it is better to accept the *anabhidhāna* of these forms. Hence there is no discrepency in the statement that in the absence of the locative forms ending in *ī*, the term extends to *gaurī* wherein the locative suffix has elided and that is what Pat implies by this statement.

Yaṅluganta forms

NBh holds that forms derived by the elision of the suffix *yaṅ* do not exist in spoken language. The basis of his assumption is the assertion of Pat, "*athavā chāndasametad dṛṣṭānuvidhiḥ chandasi bhavati*".[56] In order to refute the view that the insertion of the word *nimitta* is necessary in the rule, "*kṅiti ca*" to arrive at the form '*roravīti*', Pat makes this assertion. The form *roravīti* is vedic and hence there need not be the fear that the rule, "*kṅiti ca*" (1-1-5) in the absence of the word .*nimitta* may prohibit the *guṇa*. NBh says that this means that in the rule, "*yaṅoci ca*" (2-4-74) by virtue of the word *ca* possessed of in it there is the *anuvṛtti* of the words *bahulaṁ* and *chandasi* and hence the rule enjoin the elision of *yaṅ* in vedic usages only. He then refers to the assertion of Pat under the rule *"huśnuvoḥ sārvadhātuke"* (6-4-57). There it has been said that the mention of the word *huśnuvoḥ* indicates there are forms derived from the elision of the suffix *yaṅ* added to roots ending in *u*.

NBh remarks that on the basis of the assertion, that there can rarely be the forms derived by the elision of *yaṅ* added to roots ending in *u* and followed by a *kṅit* suffix beginning with a vowel, but it can in no way be the authority for acceptance of such forms throughout in the spoken language. Moreover he points that the said assertion is that of *ekadeśin*[57]

References

1. Vide *Sphoṭavāda* p.102.
"vaiyākaraṇanāgeśaḥ sphoṭāyanarṣermatam
pariṣkṛtyoktavāmstena prīyatām jagadiśvaraḥ"
Aṣṭ "avaṅ sphoṭāyanasya" (6-1-123).
2. Vide *Sphoṭavāda*, p.5. *'sphuṭati prakāsate'rtho'smāditi sphoṭaḥ.*
3. Vide *Udy* p. 13. *"idam ekam padam, ekam vākyam iti pratyayaḥ sphotasatve tadaikya ca pramāṇam.*
4. Vide *Udy* p. 13. "mama tu yathā nānājakadravyā hitanānāvarṇoparāgaḥ krameṇa, tāthā ekasminneva tasminnuccāraṇakrameṇa kramavāneva tattadvarṇasvarūpānurāgaḥ sa ca sthiraḥ tasya ca manasā grahaṇam iti na doṣaḥ
and
Vākyapadīya
"nādairāhitabījāyām antyena dhvaninā saha /
āvṛttiparikāyām buddhau śabdo' vadhāryate // (1-85)
5. Vide *Sphoṭavāda*, p.1.
6. Vide *Udy* p. 46. "anye vaiyākaraṇāh. apare-ta eva mukhyāḥ" on *Prdp* "anye varṇavyatiriktam padasphoṭam icchanti, vākyasphoṭam apare saṅgirante".
7. Vide *Udy* p. 16. "ākrtiḥ jātiḥ samsthānam ca. ākriyate vyavacchidyate svāśrayo nayā iti vyutpatteriti bhāvaḥ".
8. *Mbh* Vol. I, Part II *(Udy)* p. 206.
9. Vide *Udy* p.7. *"śabdārthayostādātmyameva śaktiḥ"* and *Par. Lagh Manj* pp. 26-27. "tasmāt padapadārthayoḥ sambadhāntaram eva saktiḥ vācyavācacakabhāvāparaparyāyā tadgrāhakanca itaretarādhyāsarūpam tādātmyam".
10. *Udy* p. 8.

11. Vide *Par.Lagh.Manj* p.24 - vastuto baudha evārthaḥ sakyaḥ padam api sphoṭātmakam prasiddham tayostādātmyam.
12. Vide *Par.Lagh. Manj* pp. 13 & 14.
13. Vide *Mbh Vol. III, p. 299. "dravye ca bhavataḥ kaḥ sampratyayaḥ? guṇasamudāyo dravyam and p. 563 - "kam pratyavayavo guṇaḥ ? samudāyam prati".*
14. Vide *Chaya* p. 9 "atra guṇasabdenāvayavā dharmāsca" and "ayutasiddhāvayavaviseṣānugataḥ samooho dravyam iti patanjaliriti patanjalibhāsyoktasiddhāntapakṣa ityarthḥ".
15. Vide Prdp p. 8. *"atheti gauḥ iti vijñāne pratibhāsamāneṣu vastuṣu kaḥ saabdaḥ ityarthaḥ".*
16. Words are usually divided into four classes according to the different ways in which their meaning is determined, *yaugika rūḍha, yogarūḍha* and *yaugikarūḍha.* Corresponding to these the expressive powers are called *yoga, rūḍhi yogarūḍhi* and yaugikarūḍhi. Vide K. Kunjunnii Rajah, *Indian theories of meaning,* pp. 59-69.
17. Vide *Par Sekh.* Paribhāṣā No. 101 - *"avayavaprasiddheḥ samudāyaprаprasiddhirabalīyasī".*
18. Vide *MBh* p. 194.
19. Vide *Udy* p. 194.
20. *Udy* p. 195.
21. Vide *MBh.* p. 154 and Pāṇ's rule śarīravayavācca.
22. *Udy.* p. 155.
23. *Mbh* Vol. II, p. 390.
24. *Mbh* Vol. III, pp. 346 & 347.
25. Bhṭṭojidīkṣita maintains that the nipātas are also, just like the upasargas, dyotakas. His argument is that there is no propriety in accepting the *vācakatva* of nipātas when with regard to upasargas which also come under *nipātas,* one accepts the *dyotakatva.* He is even ready to admit the fact tht both the nipātas and upasargas are vācakas. But he is quite against the view of accepting a difference between the two i.e, nipatas as vācakas and upasargas as dynotakas. Vide *Śabdakaustubha,* p.2.
26. *Mbh* p. 34.
27. *Udy* p. 35.
28. Vide *Par Lagh Manj* p. 60
29. Vide *Vāk* (1-43)
"pasyantyā madhyamāyā[1sca vaikharyāscedamadbhutam /
anekatīrthabhedāyāstrayyā vcah param padam //
30. *Udy* p. 72
31. *Mbh* p. 73.

32. "evam, yadṛcchāsabdān aṅgīkṛtya sāstrānvitānām kvacicchiṣṭaprayukktānāmeva yatra kutracit samjnātvena viniyogo nānyeṣām ityvevam ḷtakaḷphidadīnām sāstrāviṣayatvābhavānna tadartha lkāropadesa ityuktam." *Udy* p.. 74)
33. *Mbh* p. 278.
34. Vide *Udy* p. 285.
35. *Mbh* p. 285.
36. Vide W.S. Allen, *Phoneties in Ancient India*, Oxford University Press, London, (Reprint) 1961 p. 18.
37. Vide *Prdp* p. 153. "nāsikāpi na bāhyā varṇotpattinimittam kim tarhi ? āsyāntascarama vitatam asti paṇavacarmavat, tatsambaddhā rekhā nāsikā tasyām āyvabhighātād varṇotpattiḥ.
38. *Mbh* p. 151.
39. Vide *Udy* p. 154. "tatra yadyapi akārādīnam guṇamātr janikā nāsikā svarūpasya kaṇṭhādibhirevābhi-vyaktisiddheḥ; tathāpi ṇādīnām svarūpasya na kevalatālvādinā nāpi ṅādīnām svarūpasya na kevalatālvādinā nāpi kevala nāsikaayābhivyaktiriti vinigamanāvirahād ubhayāvacchinnāvāyusamyogasyaiva tajjanakatvatteṣṣām nāsikāpi sthānam" and Vide W.S. Allen, *Phonetics in Ancient India*, Oxford University Press, London (Reprint) 1961, p. 40.
40. *Udy* p. 156
41. *Udy* p. 154.
42. *Udy* p. 155.
43. *Udy* p.3.
44. *Mbh* p. 180.
45. *Mbh* p. 137.
46. *MBh* pp.. 8, 21, 31, 57, 61, 70, 78, 116, 118, 127, 239 & 325.
47. *Mbh* p. 116.
48. *Mbh* p. 127.
49. *Supra* p. 48.
50. *Mbh* p. 324.
51. *Udy* p. 325
52. Vide Bishnugupta Bhattacarya, *A Study In Language And Meaning*, Calcutta, 1962, p. 156.
53. *Supra* pp. 27, 60, 117 & 206
54. *Mbh* p. 179
55. *Mbh* with the commentary *Tattvāloka*, p. 236.
56. *Mbh* p. 139.
57. *Udy* p. 139.

Chapter IX

Conclusion

The avowed aim of NBh in writing the *Udy* was to provide an original commentary which will be neither too elaborate nor too short, intelligible to the average student and thought-provoking to the advanced scholar. In the introductory verses to *Udy*, NBh has expressed this perspective clearly.[1] The *Udy* has got the special feature that it happens to be a commentary on two works which are inter-related namely the *Prdp* as well as the *Mbh*[2]. This factor has rendered the effort of the author more laudable. The *Udy* is the product of a master mind dealing with the work of two great personalities, one the most celebrated authority in the science of grammar and the other an illustrious and distinguished writer in the same field. The *Udy* reveals NBh as an earnest elucidator and able critic.

As an elucidator NBh has attempted sincerely to enlighten us by clearly expounding the ideas of the text of the *Mbh* and the *Prdp*. He has full confidence that he is well qualified for it. He has gone through the text of the *Mbh* several times[3]. In the beginning of *Lagh.Sab.Sekh* he refers to himself as:-

"pātañjale mahābhāṣye kṛtabhūriparisramaḥ" Hence he has become an adept in interpreting the ideas of the text of the *Mbh* and *Prdp* as stated by himself, *'nāgesabhāṣitārthavicakṣaṇaḥ'* in the introductory verses to *Udy*. This fact can well be acknowledged and that is why the *Udy* is considered to be a commentary of high value.

The method of interpretation adopted by NBh is noteworthy. His commentary is lucid and intelligible. To interpret and elucidate the idea of a passage in the *Mbh* or *Prdp*, NBh uses what may be called the method of introduction. By this process the line to be interpreted is given the proper back-ground where in the purpose is made clear. For example at the outset of his gloss Kṭ says "bhāṣyakāro vivaraṇakāratvād vyākaraṇasya sākṣāt prayojanamāha, atha sabdānusāsanam iti". Here in order to clear the doubt as to why Pāṇ and Kāt have not stated this, NBh gives an introduction to the word *bhāṣyakāraḥ* used by Kṭ 'yadyapi pāṇininā brāhmaṇena niṣkāraṇaḥ ityādisruteḥ sandhyopasanādaviva pratyavāyaparihārārthitayaivottamādhikāripravṛttisambhavāt prayojanam noktam, vārttikakṛtātapi sāstrapūrvake prayoge dharmaḥ ityanena madhyamādhikariṇaḥ paramaprayojanam darsitam, bhagavāṃstu vivaraṇakāratvād mandādhikariṇām pravṛtteḥ prarocakaprayojanapratipattipravaṇatvād vyavahiteṣu svargāpūrvādiṣvanasvāsāt sākṣāt prayojanam sabdavyutpattilakṣaṇam vadatītyāha bhāṣyakāra iti".[4]

Another principle followed to interpret the text is the method of anticipation of objections and the removal of the same with clear statements. To explain an idea in a passage he gives suitable questions and thus gives the proper background for the sentence or word to be interpreted. He gives the meaning of words, *anvaya* of sentences processed of clumsy construction and points out the contextual meaning of words like *tad, anya* etc. He uses the word *manyate* to point out that the idea mentioned as such is not actually correct[5]. He uses the ending *iti abhimānaḥ* to point out the basis of the view which is not perfectly correct[6]. To refute the view of others, he cites them first and stating the reason for their refuatation concludes *'etena parāstam'*[7].

In interpreting a passage under a particular *sūtra* NBh refers to the statements of Pat under other *sūtras* far removed from it, and often from other adhyāyas of the Aṣṭ a feature which bears testimony to his thoroughness with the entire *Mbh* and the depth of his grasp. Any passage in the bhāṣya is readily available in his memory and he points out correctly the passages in the bhāṣya where relevant discussions are seen. Hence the reader is never at a loss to gather the ideas and clear for himself apparent contradictions.[8]

He elucidates the ideas of Kṭ even in cases where he has got difference of opinion with him and where he refutes his assertions. This shows the clear understanding of the views of the opponent which is the basic requisite for establishing one's own particular point of view. Moreover this enables the reader in understanding the distinct standpoints of Kṭ and NBh and also the subtle differnece underlying their statements in explaining a passage. For instance Kṭ says that even without *sthānaṣaṣṭhīnirdesa,* there can be *sthānyādesabhāva* between two sabdas mentioned in a rule. It is NBh who explains this statement of Kṭ whereby Kṭ's aim of avoiding *sthānyādeśabhāva* in the rule *"vṛddhirādaic"* (1-1-1) is achieved. It is noteworthy here that he does not favour the explanation of Kṭ. Even then as a true commentator he has brought out the idea of Kṭ in his own characteristic way[9].

In many instances he dwells at length on *Prdp* in order to justify Kṭ and says that it is not without a basis that Kṭ has made the observations. For instance it is the explanation given by NBh that justifies Kṭs usage, *"kṣudham pratihantum śakyam"* in spite of his own statement "pradhānakriyānirupit-aśaktyabhidhāne guṇakriyaśaktiranabhihitā api abhihitavad prakāśate"[9(a)] Wherever Kṭ says, *"vyākhyānānantaramatra kliṣṭatvānnoktam,* NBh gives the *vyākhyānāntara* implied by Kṭ and points out the *kleśa* involved in it.[10]

The word *"yathāmati"* in the introductory verse, "bhāṣyapradīpavyākhyānam kurveham tu yathāmati" shows that in the *Udy* we get a critical study of the *Mbh* and the *Prdp* and it is in this respect that we find a contrast between Kṭ and NBh. What Kṭ says is that :-

"mahābhāṣyārṇavāvārapārīṇam, vovṛtiplavam /
yathāgamam vidhāsyeham .... //

Here the word *yathāgaman* is interpreted by NBh as *sampradāyam anatilaṅghya* meaning 'not tresspassing the acknowledged tradition'. This gives the background on which Kṭ has woven the network of his gloss. Kṭ does not go against what has been said by Bhar while commenting on the *Mbh.* That is why he says in his introduction.

"tathāpi haribaddhena sāreṇa granthasetunā
kramamāṇaḥ śanaiḥ pāram tasya praptāsmi paṅguvat".

NBh points out that by comparing the *Mbh* to an ocean and himself to a crippled man intent on crossing over the same, Kṭ is making himself free from charges of introducing anything purely of his own. Probably NBh implies that there is lack of originality ity in Kṭ's gloss and this is quite clearly discernable in his statement,

"bhāṣyapradīpavyākhyānam kurveham tu yathāmati"

As a critic NBh has examined the whole of the *Mbh* and the *Prdp*. He does not follow anyone blindly and so finds many an instance to criticize Kṭ. It can be seen that his criticisms are logical and based on sound reasoning. When he expresses his difference of opinion with Kṭ; we feel inclined to accept his logic. When we consider the fact that the *Mbh* is a book consisting of statements in the form of dialogues, it can be said that the view held by NBh in regard to interpreting the passage *'kim punaḥ .... vyākaraṇam ...... paṭhanti'* is more correct[11]. NBh always tried to explain every passage in the *Mbh* in consistence with what we find in it earlier and later. Hence his standpoint becomes more acceptable in cases where NBh and Kṭ differ in their interpretation. The sharp intelligence of NBh is discernable when the explains the word *dvayoḥ* in the passage *'na hi dvayorākṣara ..... asti'*[12]. He gives weight to the usage of siṣṭas. His point of argumentation is clear and correct. The view which he favours shows that he is objective in his criticism. With clear and precise arguments he refutes the assertions of Kṭ and points out instances where unnecessary objections are raised by him. He vehemently attacks him in certain instances and establishes his own point of view. Such is the force of his criticism that one feels it quite convincing.

He also points out that the contradictory statements occuring in *Prdp*. He is not fettered by blind veneration to any authority. Hence he has the courage to attempt a slight criticism even on Pāṇ and Pat. He thus supports what has been stated by Kāt and prefers it to what is stated by Pāṇ.[13] It seems that he follows the dictum *'doṣā vācyā gurorapi'*.

In *Udy* we thus get an elucidation of the *Mbh* and *Prdp* as well as a critical examination of the same. There is lucidity of expression even in serious discussions. The author has great reverence for Pat and he refers to him as *bhagavān*[14].

An attempt is made by some scholars to point out defects in the *Udy* particularly in comparison with the commentary *Uddyotana* of Annambhaṭṭa. The following statement may be noted in this connection. "It is however unanimously accepted by scholars that Nāgeśa's commentary is of no mean merit in respect of explaining the inner ideas of the *Mahābhāṣya*. But it is defective in that is keeps quiet in several places where words or expressions need to be explained for the sake of the ordinary and slow-witted students, while Annambhaṭṭa explains them. For instance Annambhaṭṭa explains at great length even the name of the first āhnika called the Paspaśāhnika. (vide page 66 lines 32 ro 35 and page 67 lines 2 to 5) The main aim of Annambhaṭṭa appears to be to elucidate simplify and illustrate the meaning of the *Mahābhāṣya* and *Pradīpa* so that the student seldom entertains any doubt as regards the meaning of the particular text.

Further it would seem not all the special points and difficulties of the Mahābhāṣya have been explained by Nāgeśa. We are obliged to accord special honour to Annambhaṭṭa for well revealing in certain places the idea underlying some portions of the Mahābhāṣya, which were not even touched upon by Nāgesa"[15].

Here it is to be borne in mind that the aim of NBh in writing the *Udy* was never to provide a commentary which is simply explanatory but to make it also critical. Though he meant it to be intelligible to average students also, he has not descended to meet the needs of the slow- witted students. So the above criticism need not be taken seriously.

Criticism of NBh's interpretation is also met with. Rudradharajhā Śarma says that in interpreting the passage *'kimidam sthāneyogeti sthāne yogo'syāḥ seyam sthāneyogā saptamyalopo nipātanād trtiyāyā vā etvam. sthānena yogo' syāḥ seyam sthāne yogeti'*, NBh does not adhere to what is stated in the bhāṣya and the *Prdp* on it. Here in the expression *sthāneyoga,* the part *sthāne* is explained. Kṭ says that it is by the *nipātana* as *sthāne* in *sthāneyogā* that the said expression with the substitution by *e* is obtained. NBh says that the instrumental suffix after the base *sthāna* in the compound split as *sthānena yogaḥ yasyāḥ sā,* gets elided by the rule *"supo dhātup-rātipadikayoḥ"* (2-4-71) and on the strength of the *nipātana, e* is substituted for the final *a* of *sthāna* whereby the expression *sthāneyogā* is got. Rudradharajhā Śarma says that on the very strength of the *nipātana* the instrumental suffix after *sthāna* does not got elided and is substituted by *e* and the rule *"ato guṇe"* (6-1-97) enjoining *pararūpa* operates on the final *a* of *sthāna* and *e* the substitute of the suffix. There is no doubt that *vṛddhi* will replace *a+e* because the rule *"ato guṇe"* (6-1-97) supersedes it.

Thus Rudradharajhā Śarma claims that he has explained the expression *sthāneyogā* on the *nipātana* mentioned in *Prdp* whereas NBh resorts to the *luk* of the suffix and resorts to the *nipātana* only partially for getting the form[16].

When we consider the magnitude and magnificance of what NBh has given us, in his *Udy* as a result of the penetration of his keen intellect into the whole of the *Mbh* and the *Prdp*, criticisms like the above, levelled against his work are insignificant and may be ignored. It can be thus quite justifiably stated that *Udy* is of indispensable and inestimable help for the correct understanding of the full significance of what the *Mbh* and *Prdp* presents to us.

References

1. Supra p. 17.
2. *Supra* p. 18.
3. Vide Yudhiṣṭhira Mīmāmsaka, *Saṃskṛta Vyākaraṇa Śāstrkā Itihās*, Vol. I, p. 392.
4. *Udy* pp. 3 & 4.
5. *Udy* pp. 164 & 256.
6. *Udy* pp. 116, 163, 253 & 261.
7. *Udy* p. 15.
8. *Udy* pp. 104, 111 & 261.
9. *Udy* p. 108.

9a. *Udy* p. 51.

10. *Supra* p. 101 & *Mbh* p. 170.
11. *Supra* p. 140.
12. *Supra* p. 141-142.
13. *Supra* pp. 206-209.
14. *Udy* pp. 4 & 263.
15. Vide the introduction by T. Chandrasekharan to the *Mbh* with the commentaries *Prdp* and *Uddyotana*, Vol. I pp. X & XI. The explanation given by Annambhaṭṭa to the word *paspaśa* is:-
    śāstrasyārambhako granthaḥ upodghāta itīritaḥ /
    sa eva grantha sandarbhaḥ paspasaḥ kathito budhaiḥ //
16. Op. cit. p. 366.

BIBLIOGRAPHY

I. Original Works in Sanskrit:

Aṣṭādhyāyī of Pāṇini — Venkateswar Steam Press, Bombay, Samvat, 1966.

Aṣṭādhyāyīsūtrapāṭha — of Panini, edited with vārttikas and gaṇas by S. Chandrasekhara Sastrigal, Trichirapoly, 1912.

Kāsikāvivaraṇapañcikā — (*Nyāsa*) of Jinendrabuddhi, edited by Suresh Chandra chakravarti, Varendra Research Society, Rajshahi, in 3 Vols. Vol. I 1913-16, Vol. II 1919, and Vol. III 1925.

Nirukta of Yāska — with the Sanskrit commentary of Devaśarma Sāstri and Hindi commentary of Bhagīratha Śāstri, Published by Meharcandra Laksmandas, First edition Delhi, 1963.

Paramalaghumañjūṣā — of Nāgeśabhaṭṭa (1) with the com mentary *jyotsnā*, edited by Kālikāprasadasukla Baroda Sanskrit Mahāvidyalaya, M.S. University of Baroda, Baroda, 1961.

edited by Akhaladeva Śarma, Chowkhamba Sanskrit Series, Varanasi, 1974.

Paribhāṣenduśekhara — of Nāgesabhaṭṭa, (1) edited by K.V. Abhyankar, Part I, Poona, 1962.

with the commentary *Gadā* of Vaidyanātha Pāyaguṇḍe, edited by Harinārāyaṇa Apte, *Anandasramasamskṛtagranthāvali* No. 72 Punyākhyapattanam, 1913.

Prauḍhamanoramā of Bhaṭṭojidiksita, edited by Pandit Sadashiva Sharma Shastri, Chowkhamba Sanskrit Series, Benares, 1934.

Bṛhacchabdenduśekhara of Nāgesabhaṭṭa, edited by Sītārāma Śāstri Saraswathibhavana granthamālā, No. 87, 3 Vols. Benares, 1960.

Mahābhāṣya of Patanjali, with the commentaries, *Pradīpa* of Kaiyaṭa, *Uddyota* of Nāgesabhaṭṭa and *Chāyā* of Vaidy anātha Pāyaguṇḍe, Motilal Banarsidas, Delhi, 3 Vols. 1967.

edited by B.S. Joshi, Nirnayasagar Press, Bombay, 1942.

with the commentaries *Pradīpa* of Kaiyata and *Uddyotana* of *Annombhaṭṭa* Part I edited by P.P. Subrahmania Śāstry and A. Sankaran, Madras Govt. Oriental Manuscripts Library, 1948 Part II edited by Chandrasekharan, T Madras Govt. Oriental Manu scripts Library, 1952.

Mahābhāṣya of Patanjali, with the commentaries *Pradāpa* of Kaiyaṭa, *Uddyota* of Nāgesabhaṭṭa and *Tatvāloka* of Rudrdhrajhā Śarma, Chowkhamba Sanskrit Series, Benares, 1954.

(first three āhnikās), edited by Cīrudeva [sāstri, Motilal Banarsidas, Benares, Sa I mvat, 2019.

with English Translation and Notes edited by K.V. Abhyankar & Jayadev Mohanlal Shukla, Fasciculus-1, Poona, 1969.

MahābhāṣyaṭīKā of Bharthṛhari, edited by V. Swaminathan, Beneras Hindu University, Benares, 1965.

Mahabhaṣyapradīpikā of Bharthṛhari, edited by K.V. Abhyankar and V.P. Limaye, Bhandarkar Oriental Research Institute, Poona, 1970.

Mahābhāṣyapradīpoddyota of Nāgesabhaṭṭa, edited by Bahuvallabha Śāstri, 3 vols. Calcutta, 1909.

Laghusabdendusekhara of Nāgeśabhaṭṭa, edited by Guruprasād Sāstri, Bhargava Pustakalaya, Benares, 1936.

Vākyapadīyam of Bharthṛhari, Benares Sanskrit Series, Nos. 11, 19, 24 and 95, 1887.

Vaiyākaraṇasiddhīntalaghumañjūṣa of Nāgesabhaṭṭa, (1) edited by Mādhava Śāstri Bhandari, Chowkhamba Sanskrit Series, Fasciculus I to XV, '926.

edited by Sabhāpati Śarma Upadhyāya Chowkhamba Sanskrit Series, Varanasi, 1963.

Siddhāntakaumudī of Bhaṭṭojidikṣita (1) with the commentary Bālamanoramā of Vāsudeva Danīkṣit, Kashi Sanskrit Series 136.

with the commentary *Tattvabodhinī* of Jñānendrasarasvati, edited by Śivadatta, Venkateswar Steam Press, Bombay, 1959.

Śabdakaustubha of Bhaṭṭojiodīksita, Chowkhamba Sanskrit Series, Benares, Part I, 1933, Part II, 1929.

II. Modern Works

a) English

Abhyankar, K.V. *A Dictionary of Sanskrit Grammar,* Gaekward Oriental Series, 134, 1961.

Agrawala, V.S. *India as known to Pāṇini,* Second edition, Benares, 1963.

Allen, W.S. *Phonetics in Ancient India,* London Oriental Series No. 1, 1961.

Aufrecht. *Catalogus catalagorum,* Second edition, 1962.

Belvalkar, S.K. *Systems of Sanskrit Grammar*, Poona, 1916.

Bhattacharya, Bishnupada. *A Study in Language and Meaning*, Calcutta, 1962.

Burrow, T. *The Sanskrit Language*, London, 1955.

Chatterji, Kshitis Chandra *Technical Terms and Technique of Sanskrit Grammar*, Part I, Calcutta, 1948.

Faddegon, Barend. *Studies in Pāṇini's Grammar* (Reprint), Amsterdam, 1963.

Gode, P.K. *Studies in Indian Literary History*, Poona, Vol. III, 1961.

Goldstuckes, T. *Pāṇini, his place in Sanskrit Literature*, (Reprint) Chowkhamba Sanskrit Studies Vol. 48, 1945.

Iyer S. Venkitasubramonia. *Nārāyaṇabhaṭṭa's Prakriyasarvasva A Critical Study*, Kerala University Dept. Publication No. 1, Trivandrum, 1972.

Iyer K.A. subramania. *The Vākyapadīya of Bharthṛhari* Deccan Collage, Post-graduate and Research Institute, Chapter III Part I, Poona, 1971.

Kane, P.V. *History of Dhrmasāstra*, Vol. I, Poona, 1930.

Kielhorn, F. *Kātyayana and Pataānli*. Their relation to each other and to Pāini. Indological Book House Bans Phalak, Varanasi, India, 1963.

Paribhāsenduśekhara of Nāgōjibhaṭṭa (English Translation) Bhandarkar Oriental Research Institute, Second Edition, Part II, Poona, 1960.

Krishnamacariar, M. *History of Classical Sanskrit Literature*, Motilal Banarsidas, Third Edition, Delhi, 1974.

Limaye, V.P. *Critical Studies on the Mahābhāṣya* Vishveshvaranand Vedic Research Institute, hoshiarpur, 1974.

Misra, Vidya Nivas. *The Descriptive Technique of Pāṇini* Mounton & Co., The Hague, Paris, 1966.

Radhakrishnan, S and others; *Dr. S.K. Belvalkar Felicitation Volume*, Motilal Banarsidas, Delhi-6, 1957.

Raja K. Kunjunni *Indian Theories of Meanings*, Madras, 1963.

Sarma, K. Madhavakrishna. *Pāṇini Katyayana and Patañjali* Shri Lal Bahadur Shastry Rashriya Sanskrit Vidyapeeth, Delhi, 1968.

Sastri, P.S. Subramanya. *Lectures on Patañjali's Mahābhāṣya*, Annamalainagar Vol. I, 1947, Vol. II, 1951 and Vol. III, 1955.

Staal, J.F. *A Reader on Sanskrit Grammarians*, Cambridge, Marsachuseth and London, England, 1972.

Sen, Sunitkumar. *Pāṇini ca*, Calcutta, 1970.

Varma, Siddheswar. *Critical Studies in the Phonetic observations of Sanskrit Grammarians*, (Reprint) Delhi, 1961.

The Etymologies of Yaska, Visveswaranand Indological Series No. 5, Hoshiarpur, 1953.

Whitney, W.D. *Sanskrit Grammar*, 4th edition Boston, 1913.

b) Sankrit

Miśra, Radhesya *Vyākaraṇa Śāstradṛṣṭyā jātisvarūpavimarśaḥ, Srisivasankaṭaharanadarsasamskrtamahavidyalaya*, Uttarpradesh, Saṃvat 2027.

Pāṇdeya Rāmājña. *Vyākaraṇadarsanabhūmikā* The Superintent Printing and Stationary, Allahabad, U.P.

Śāstri, Peri Sūryanarayana. *Nāgesabhāvaprakāsaḥ*, Govt. Sanskrit College, Vizianagaram, A.P. 1970

c) Hindi

Bhattacarya, Ramasankar. *Pāṇinīya Vyākaraṇ Kā Anusīlam*, Indological Book House, Varanasi, 1966.

Yuddhisthira Mīmāmsaka. *Samskrt vyākaraṇa sāstr kā Itihās,* Bharatiya Pracya Vidya Pratisthan, Ajmere, Part I, Second Edition, Samvat 2020, Part II Samvat 2019/

Misra Remakanta. *Vyakaraṇa Śāāstr kā Samksipta Itihās* Chowkhamba Vidya Bhavan, Varanasi-1, 1966.

Śāstri, Kapila Dev. *Samskṛt Vyākaran mem Ganapath kī paramparā aur Pāṇini,* Bhartiya Vidya Pratisthan, Ajmere, Sam 2010.

Varma, Satyakama. *Samskrit Vyākaraṇ Kā udbhav our vikās,* Motilal Banarsidas, Delhi, 1972.

III Journals and Articles:

Abhyankar, K.V. 'Euphonic Combination of *R and *L with *R and L *Indian Linguistics,* Vol. 26, 1966.

Chatternee, Kshitis Chandra. 'How Pāṇini has been misunderstood' *Indian Linguistics,* Vol. 17, 1957.

Iyer, K.A. Subramania. 'The Point of View of the Vayā}karaṇas' *The Journal of Oriental Research,* Vol. XVIII Part II, 1951.

Iyer, S. Venkitasubramonia. 'The difference between Bhattoji Dīkṣita and Nārayaṇa Bhatta with regard to certain phonetic observations' *Vishveshvaranand Indolo- gical Journal,* Vol. VIII, 1970.

Kielhorn, F. 'Some devices of Indian Grammarians' *Indian Antiquary,* Vol. XV, 1886.

'Noteson the Mahābhāṣya' *Indian Antiquary,* Vol. XVI, 1887

Notes on the Mahābhāṣya' *Indian Antiquary,* Vol. V. 1876.

Pandit, M.D. Pānini - A study in Non-compounded word structures' *Vishveshvaranand Indological Journal,* Vol. I, No. I, March, 1963.

Sastri, Kapil Dev. 'Significance of the word 'Prakāra' in the sutras of the Aṣṭdhyāyī' *Vishveshvaranand Indological Journal*, Vol. I, No. I, March, 1963.

Varma, Siddheswar. 'Scientific and technical presentation of Patañjali as refelected in the Mahābhāṣya' *Vishveshvaranand Indological Journal* Vol. I, No.1, March, 1963.

INDEX